A TREATISE OF Morall Philosophie

Wherein Is Contained the Worthy Sayings of Philosophers, Emperours, Kings, and Orators: Their Lives and Answers.

(1547)

BY

WILLIAM BALDWIN

ENLARGED BY

THOMAS PALFREYMAN

A FACSIMILE REPRODUCTION
OF THE EDITION OF 1620
WITH AN INTRODUCTION
BY

ROBERT HOOD BOWERS

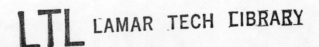

GAINESVILLE, FLORIDA
SCHOLARS' FACSIMILES & REPRINTS
1967

Scholars' Facsimiles & Reprints
1605 N. W. 14th Avenue
Gainesville, Florida 32601, U.S.A.
Harry R. Warfel, General Editor

Reproduced from a Copy in
and with the permission of
The British Museum

L. C. Catalog Card Number: 67-10126

Manufactured in the U.S.A.

INTRODUCTION

I

William Baldwin's *A Treatise of Morall Philosophie* (1547), essentially a collection of moral sentences, was an Elizabethan best seller that went through 23 editions (*STC* Nos. 1253-69; Bishop[2], Nos. 1257.1, 1259.1, 1265.1, 1267.1; Wing B-547). He was evidently a shrewd judge of the book market as he enacted his ink-smudged role as editor, and possibly as compositor (?), since he also fathered *A Myrroure for Magistrates* (1555?) which went through 14 editions. Obviously the various editions of the Bible held first place, with some 283 editions. Thereafter Baldwin's closest competitors appear to have been the lugubrious soteriologists Arthur Dent, *The Plaine mans Pathway to Heauen* (1601) with 16 editions, and Thomas Becon, *The Sycke Mans Salve* (1568) with 15 editions; some entertainers of sophisticated London: John Lyly, *Euphues* (1578), 13 editions, *Euphues and his England* (1580), 12 editions, and William Shakespeare, *Venus and Adonis* (1593), 11 editions. The subtitle of John Spencer's *Things Old and New* (1658) sufficiently describes the class of books to which Baldwin's *Treatise* belongs: *A Storehouse of Similies, Sentences, Allegories, Apopthegms, Adagies, Apologues, Divine, Morall, Political, etc., with their seuerall applications.* Also, in his preface, Spencer wards off the charge of plagiarism, by citing the favorite Renaissance figure: "Is Bees hony the worse, for being extracted from flowers?"

But possibly we credit Baldwin with too much shrewdness: the 16th century book market, both in England and on the Continent, had an omnivorous appetite for assemblages of proverbs and commonplaces. Erasmus, a shrewder man than Baldwin, had sensed this trend by the penultimate year of the previous century; he produced in 1500 in Paris his first compilation of 818 entries, which he later augmented to 3260 entries in the magnificent Venice folio of 1508 entitled *Erasmi Roterdami Adagiorum Chiliades Tres* (the British Museum catalogue lists some 68 variant editions). And everybody borrowed from Erasmus, notably J. Sartorius of Amsterdam (d. 1566), who used a similar title for his compilation (I have only seen the 1670 edition) of 3177 entries. Of course, Erasmus quoted and borrowed too (see the Chicago dissertation of Theodore C. Appelt, 1942); and he did not differentiate sharply between classical sentences and folk sayings (see Harold E. Pagliaro in *PMLA* for March, 1964). At any rate this concern with commonplaces, with ethics—or private morals—and with politics —or public morals—was so conspicuous in Elizabethan writing that Roy Battenhouse in his study of Marlowe's *Tamburlaine* (1941) was moved to argue that moral philosophy was the dominant intellectual concern of the Elizabethan age (p. 21). Such a view might have offended the sober theologians of Emmanuel College, Cambridge, who could point to the enormous production of theological tomes from Tyndale or Jewel or Hooker through the great Puritan writers, Bradshaw, Perkins, or Sibbes. And we must remember that belles lettres, being concerned with what happens rather than with what happened, must always be ultimately proverbial in substance. Yet the problem is almost insoluble: Miss Edith Klotz in her subject analysis of English imprints for every tenth year from 1480 to 1640 (*Huntington Library Quarterly,* I [1938], 418 ff.), was forced to employ a category of both religion *and* philosophy since the two subjects could not be separated in any meaningful way.

In theory one can distinguish between ethics and

theology; in practice such metaphysical considerations as predestination or free-will impinge on problems of human responsibility, blur nice distinctions, and impose the persistent debate between justice and mercy. Also we may recall that St. Augustine urged his fellows to despoil the Egyptians and appropriate pagan ethics as long as they did not contradict Christian dogma; and that liberal medieval thinkers opted for the salvation of righteous heathens such as Trajan. Plato and Aristotle can readily be considered Fathers of the Church because of the absorption of many of their tenets; Seneca was always deemed an authority on morals; and a work such as William Fulbecke's *Christian Ethics* (1587) blends inextricably classical and Christian cultural values. Miss Klotz's findings demonstrate a steady rise in imprints of this character, from 10 in 1480, to 251 by 1640, with a startling production of 126 in 1550. These figures partly account for the popularity of Baldwin's book since they indicate the public taste; but they tell us nothing about books imported from abroad, and there is good reason to suspect that foreign books were far more numerous than English books in Elizabethan England. Yet our knowledge on this point shall probably never be precise, despite the admirable work of Sears Jayne, H. M. Adams, and Thomas James' 1605 catalogue of the Bodleian, simply because a national library with a union catalogue was nonexistent—The British Museum was not founded until 1753. And no such catalogue could tell us what books might be in private hands.

II

Nothing significant is known about Baldwin. On decidedly tenuous evidence Anthony à Wood once claimed him as an Oxford scholar (*Athenae Oxonienses,* [2nd ed., 1721], I.146). In his effort to claim as Oxford alumni as many distinguished English authors and clergymen who flourished between 1500 and 1695 as possible under the eulogistic denomination "Athenian," Wood passed over the obvious possibility that more than one

Tudor Englishman might have borne the somewhat prosaic name of William Baldwin. Nor was anything of real biographical significance garnered by Miss Eveline Feasey in 1925 (*Modern Language Review,* XX, 417 ff.). But such matters are of little moment since any clever printing house apprentice like Benjamin Franklin could have put together in his spare time a trade book which is largely a compilation from older books that proves Chaucer's observation that "out of olde bokes, in good feyth, cometh al this newe science that men lere." In an age that knew nothing of copyright laws, plagiarism did not constitute mortal sin; and the ubiquitous renaissance dogma of literary imitation, of intellectual intussusception, sanctioned the appropriation of admired quotations from "authorities"—the Renaissance, being an age of authority, venerated authority in all walks of life—ranging from St. Paul and Seneca to Erasmus and Melanchthon. Many of Baldwin's pilferings have been traced by Starnes in *Texas Studies in English,* XIII (1933), 5 ff.; and by Bühler in *Speculum,* XXIII (1948), 76 ff.

Nor is anything significant known about Thomas Palfreyman who augmented and revised the 1557 edition of Baldwin's *Treatise,* and whose name is attached to subsequent editions. Sidney Lee's *DNB* article states that Palfreyman, who died in 1589, was a gentleman of the Chapel Royal. Evidently hoping to emulate the success of Baldwin's *Treatise,* he produced in 1578 *The Treatise of Heauenly Philosophie* (*STC* 19138), a collection of "pithie sentences" from the Bible and the Fathers; but this work survives in but one edition. There were many similar books: e.g., Nicolaus Hanapius, *Ensamples of Virtue & Vice gathered oute of Holy Scripture* (1561).

III

The title of the Baldwin-Palfreyman book is misleading since it contains no systematic analysis of ethics such as we find in Abelard's *Ethica seu Scito Teipsum,* but in the 16th century such a title was sometimes used to designate a collection of moral apothegms (e.g.,

Thomas Crewe, *The Nosegay of Morall Philosophie* (1580), or a collection of admonitory essays (e.g., Haly Heron, *A New Discourse of Morall Philosophie* (1579). The book in the present sixth edition is segmented into 12 chapters (the early editions had four), as the table of contents below on pp. 190-192 indicates. Chapters 3 through 11 offer precepts of worldly wisdom, of prudence, with the exception of chapter 9 which is concerned with the efficacy of faith and prayer in times of distress, prefaced (p. 140) with a definition of man's conscience as "true knowledge of Gods holy law, through the light of grace," which proves again that it is impossible to distinguish between secular ethics and religious doctrine in Renaissance moralizing.

In a very real sense the Baldwin-Palfreyman *Treatise* is a medieval book, that is to say, it continues medieval cultural and literary traditions. The first chapters contain thumb-nail biographies and bits of doxography of famous "philosophers" such as Galen, Ovid, and Seneca. This section therefore follows the style of the *Lives of the Philosophers* of Diogenes Laertius ,who regarded philosophy as mainly ethics, and similar works by Eunapius and Philostratus, all of which were known during the Renaissance and could have served as models. Yet as early as 1260 (?) John Waleys (or Johannes Gallensis), a Franciscan lector at Oxford, compiled his *Compendiloquium* (Venice, 1496), a similar work (see Antoine Charma, *Étude sur le Compendiloquium de vita, moribus et dictis illustrium philosophorum de Jean de Galles,* Paris, 1866). Later, Walter Burley, one of the illuminations of Merton prior to the grim visitation of the Black Death in 1348, made a free adaptation of Diogenes; Caxton's first publication on English soil, *The Dicts and Sayings of the Philosophers* (1477), drew on a similar but different ultimate source, the *Liber Philosophorum Moralium Antiquorum* of Abu'l Mubeschschir ben Fatik, an Arab writer resident of Damascus (c 1053). The first ambitious history of philosophy in England that attempts analysis of metaphysical and physical problems as well as ethical

ones, that of Thomas Stanley (1655), draws heavily on Diogenes, as did the first comprehensive work on the Continent, Johann Jakob Brücker, *Historia Critica Philosophiae* (1742-44). The reputation of Diogenes before the bar of scholars seems still undecided: Zevort, who translated him into French in 1847, spoke of him as an "epigrammatiste sans esprit, érudit sans profondeur" (p.iv); Praechter, in Ueberweg's magisterial *Grundriss der Geschichte der Philosophie,* lauds his work as "das Hauptwerk über antike Philosophiegeschichte" (p. 22). A competent dissertation on Diogenes by Richard Hope (1930) propounds qualified evaluations. Yet the technique of compiling thumb-nail biographies along with attributed sayings had been part of the long tradition of hagiographical memorialization in the West, so that we should not credit this technique solely to Diogenes. It is illustrated in such popular Renaissance works as Pedro Ribdeneira, *Illustrium Scriptorum Religionis Societatis Jesu Catalogus* (Lyon, 1609), or Robert Bellarmine, *De Scriptoribus Ecclesiasticis* (Leiden, 1612). The first comprehensive survey of medieval philosophy, that by Adam Tribbechovius, employs a different style, that of discussing dogma rather than personalities, since, as its title indicates, it is animated by a Lutheran bias: *De Doctoribus Scholasticis et corrupta per eos divinarum humanarum rerum scientia* (Giessen, 1665).

Although the Baldwin-Palfreyman Treatise is written in prose, it does employ versified moral introductions as chapter headings, and hence partakes of another medieval tradition. This tradition may be observed in Old English writing, as in the "Instructions for Christians" preserved in Cambridge University Library MS Ii.1.33 (printed in *Anglia* LXXXII, 1964), down to the *Proverbial Philosophy* of Martin Tupper (1838), who next to Sir Walter Scott was one of Queen Victoria's favorite poets. Middle English verse offers many exemplars of didactic poetry which the Germans call "Lehrdichtung" or "Spruchpoesie," such as George Ashby's *Dicta Philosophorum* (*EETS ES* No. 76), or Peter Idley's *Instructions*

to his Son (ed. Charlotte D'Evelyn, 1935), to say nothing of the manifold versions of the mnemonic Cato's *Distichs,* which countless medieval children were forced to memorize after they had mastered their Psalters. The anonymous *Liber Proverbiorum* in Harley MS 7578, which is still unprinted, illustrates both the verse format and the fanciful attribution of sentences to names of note such as Plato or Hermes, another medieval habit which is adopted in Baldwin's work. The Fathers are so exploited in the anonymous macaronic verses in Cambridge University Library MS Ll.4.14, and in the Vernon MS *Proverbs of Prophets, Poets & Saints,* a trilingual work (*EETS OS* No. 117).

The twelfth and last chapter of the Baldwin-Palfreyman *Treatise* contains a collection of similitudes, a delight to Renaissance rhetoricians. Sibling to Renaissance commonplace manuals from equally honored sacred and profane writers, the similitude collections served youngsters wrestling with Ciceronian invention, preachers seeking pat parables, poets seeking images to metamorphose according to the fashionable doctrine of *imitatio,* polemic writers seeking authoritative, because ancient or persuasive, writ to smite their irenic antagonists. Neglecting European exemplars, a few such English collections may be cited: Anthonie Fletcher, *Certaine Very Proper & Most Profitable Similies* (1595): Francis Meres, *Palladis Tamia,* (1598); Nicholas Ling, *Politeuphuia* (1598); Robert Cawdrey, *A Treasurie or Storehouse of Similies* (1600); John Bodenham, *Belvedere* (1600). The prototype among incunabula of this class was Iohannes de Sancto Gemiano, *Summa de Exemplis ac Similitudinibus* (Hain, Nos. 7542-47), who drew on medieval compilers such as Alanus de Insulis; and, as usual, Erasmus tapped the market with his *Parabolae sive Similiae* (1514).

IV

In his *Middle Class Culture in Elizabethan England* (1935), Louis B. Wright sees Baldwin's *Treatise* as one

of the many short-cuts to self-improvement for the rising middle class (it always seems to be rising) whose thirst for culture has always sustained the publishing industry. From this point of view it bears comparison with one of the great best sellers of modern America, Will Durant's *Story of Philosophy,* which presumably imparted culture in ten easy lessons. Perhaps it was also popular at Oxford and Cambridge, the academic life of which has been surveyed in Craig R. Thompson, *Universities in Tudor England* (1959). Elizabethan arts students and their European counterparts did not study biological ecology or nuclear physics; from grammar school through the universities they were subjected to a narrow curriculum, to a constant and intensive drill in the old trivium of grammar, rhetoric and logic, which was designed to lead to proficiency in disputation on topics such as those supplied in Lucas Trelcatius, *Scholastica et methodica locorum cummunium institutio* (Oxford, 1606). This drilling largely accounts for their facility in language—which meant primarily facility in Latin—and perhaps for their enviable social poise. We may recall that Henry Adams observed that the only real education offered by the Harvard of his day was that of social poise. One of the treasures of the Bodleian, the Latin exercise book of Edward VI (MS Autog. e. 2), shows the young prince's boyish hand copying out the worn Ciceronian sentence: Sapientia est scientia rerum divinarum et humanarum causarum; one of the treasures of The British Museum, a Saon edition of 1514 of Nannus Mirabellius, *Polyanthea,* a huge collection of proverbs and commonplaces, contains the boyish marginalia of Henry VIII. So the vast Renaissance printing of rhetorics, commonplaces, and proverbs like Polydore Vergil, *Proverbium Libellus* (1506, etc.) or Joannes Stobaeus, *Sententiae* (1559, etc.) is understandable. The recent scholarship of Walter J. Ong, S. J., Sister Miriam Joseph, C.S.C., William T. Costello, S.J., and Joan M. Lechner, O.S.U., has contributed significantly to our understanding of Renaissance rhetoric. Morris P. Tilley's dictionary of Elizabethan proverbs

(1950) is standard; and Charles G. Smith, *Shakespeare's Proverb Lore* (1963) is very useful.

V

I am obligated to the kind offices of The American Philosophical Society for a grant which enabled me to read in England during the summer vacation of 1964, and subsequently to draft this introduction. Since the various editions of *A Treatise* were continually revised and augmented, the copy text for the present reprint is the Folger Shakespeare Library copy (*STC* 1267) of the 6th edition of 1620 (?), mainly because of its fulness of content. Dr. Louis B. Wright, Folger's Director, has kindly granted permission to make this reproduction. However, a few substitutions from the British Museum copy (press mark 1080.c.34) have been inserted when a page was unsatisfactory because of poor inking or tight binding. The letter press used—the black letter popular in the middle of the sixteenth century—was probably used to give the 6th edition an appearance similar to the early editions. The bare reprint of the British Museum copy of the 1555 edition of *A Treatise* which appeared in Edward Arber's *A Christian Library,* III (London, 1907), has long vanished from the dingy bookstalls off Charing Cross Road.

ROBERT HOOD BOWERS

University of Florida
June 22, 1965

A
TREATISE
OF
Morrall Philosophie:

WHEREIN IS CONTAINED the worthy ſayings of Philoſophers Emperours, Kings, and Orators: their liues and anſwers: of what linage they came: *and of what Country they were: Whoſe* worthy Sentences, notable Precepts, Counſels, and Parables, doe *hereafter follow.*

First gathered and ſet forth by *William Bauldwin*, and now the ſixt time ſince inlarged by *Thomas Palſreyman*, GENTLEMAN.

PROVERBS 2.
If wiſedome enter into thine heart, and thy ſoule delight in knowledge, then ſhall counſell preſerue thee, and understanding ſhall keepe thee.

LONDON:
Printed by *Thomas Snodham*.

TO THE RIGHT Honourable Lord, *Henry Haſtings*, Earle of Huntington, *Thomas Palfreyman* wiſheth increaſe of grace, honour, and proſperitie.

Although I haue beene already ſufficiently perſwaded that your Honour, *euen from the Cradle, hath beene trained vp in the path-way of vertue, and (according to the profeſſion of a godly and true Chriſtian) hath receiued inſtructions, as well in the ſacred Scriptures, as alſo otherwiſe in prophane learning: the knowledge of both which, with age, hath ſo largely growne, that you neede not my helpe and furtherance for the keeping of thoſe things the better in memory which you haue with ſuch diligence read: yet hauing an eye to your ſtate, vpon whoſe ſhoulders, in time, ſome charge of this Common-wealth is like to leane, as commonly it happeneth to all Noble men, but moſt worthily indeede to thoſe whom God hath endued with the gift of vnderſtanding and knowledge. I thought it not vnfit to preſent vnto your Lordſhip, this little Booke, entituled,* A Treatiſe of Morrall Philoſophie, *very expedient to all eſtates, but moſt neceſſary, as* Ariſtotle *ſaith in his* Ethnicks, *to thoſe that by vertue of knowledge ſhall haue*

the gouernance of a Common-wealth, which ought not onely to haue good wils to doe well, but also exactly to know and search out with diligence a ready way and meane whereby they may at all times, as with a dearely beloued familiar (either in heart or in hand) receiue such aduertisements and godly counsailes, as shall neuer seeme to swerue from such intentions as be grounded in an honest and godly will: that thereby not onely the true order and high estate of Princes, of Nobility of Honour, of Iustice, and such other like vertues may effectually be knowne: but also of such be rightly vnderstood, put in vse and practised, by their due and peculiar offices, to the common comfort and commodity of their Country, purchasing to themselues the fauour and blessing of God, and gathering together the incomparable treasures of a faithfull and true heart, euen prayer and praise, or paine and losse of life, if neede shall so require.

Of which things forasmuch as this my labour doth intreat, and you of a godly disposition thereunto inclined, and like also hereafter to put in practise. I thought it good to Dedicate this my poore trauaile vnto your Honour, that it might the rather creepe forth vnder the safe conduct of your goodnesse vnto the hands of others, that likewise are bent to seeke forth and follow such godly counsailes and witty sayings as are in this present Treatise contained, to the increase of vertues and furtherance of all such good and liuely motions as shall at all times redound to the glory and praise of God, and to the necessary reliefe, ioy, and comfort of the Common-wealth.

Your Honours in all dutie,

Thomas Palfreyman.

TO THE READER.

FOraſmuch (moſt gentle and vertuous Reader) as it fortuned me of late (being in the Country) to be in company with my very friend, and finding in his hand a booke, wherewith he was paſſing the time, (entituled *A Treatiſe of Morrall Philoſophie*) which becauſe I had not before ſeene, I deſired to haue it to reade. And when I had partly read, not onely of the Philoſophers liues and anſweres, but alſo of their good Precepts, godly Counſailes, and wiſe Sayings, I was much in loue therewith, and moſt heartily deſired it of my friend, till ſuch time as I had throughly read it. That done, I called to remembrance the like worthy and notable ſentences and good counſailes, that I had often read in diuers and ſundry other works. And to the intent by placing them together, I might the better keepe them in memory, and effectually beſtow ſome ſmall part of my time in ſuch kinde of exerciſe as ſhould bee to the glory of God (who is the author of all goodneſſe, and furtherer of all good workes: and for the auoiding of that peſtilent and moſt infectious canker, *Idleneſſe*, whereby is ingendred, as we commonly ſee by experience, ſuch infection as ſhortly deſtroyeth both ſoule & body) I tooke in hand this ſmall enterpriſe, which by Gods grace I haue finiſhed. And after I had once again examined the ſaid Booke, and truely noting the effect of euery Chapter, wherefore they were written, whether they were

of themselues perfectly one matter, or one mingled with another, I found not onely in the one, but also in the other, such singular pleasure and earnest prouocation of often reading, that as a man euen in the middest of a pleasant and faire garden, enuironed with banks, beautifully set and garnished with all kindes of most delicate and dainty sweet flowers, and at liberty as him liked to take or refuse: so there I found plenty and great store of such louely pleasures as I listed to embrace: I did then confer one sentence with another, throughout the whole Booke: and as I vnderstood the matter, I placed it in the right Chapter: As if the Chapter did chiefly speake of God, of the Soule, or of the World, and so forth; such precepts, parables, and semblables as I found, were displaced and set abroad among sentences of diuers and sundry matters (and also those other necessary sayings, that I had gathered together out of other Authors) I rightly placed, not onely in Chapters, but also the sentences agreeable one to another, as a man would familiarly tell a tale.

I haue also drawne into summaries the effect of euery Chapter, and where I had at the beginning of my first worke (namely this Treatise) omitted and left out certaine Chapters (set forth by Mr. *Bauldwin*, the first author thereof,) which did shew how Philosophie began: of the three parts of Philosophie: who were the Inuenters thereof, and the manner of teaching the same, as also the Philosophers liues and answeres, notwithstanding their excellency and goodnesse, as I alwaies worthily haue and will giue them their due commendation and praise, in consideration of their necessary, honest, and godly kinde of doctrine, so pithily and learnedly set forth as before mentioned: for I had selected and chosen out a great

number

number of good counſailes, witty and godly ſayings of the Philoſophers, learned men, and noble Princes, like vnto the others (with their precepts alſo and witty ſayings) by him before gathered & put forth, doubting much that if I ſhould haue ioyned the ſaid number of ſentences to the whole ſumme of this Treatiſe, it ſhould not onely, as appeared to me, haue ſeemed ouermuch to be inlarged, but alſo the more vnhandſome of the reader to be carried. Yet notwithſtanding, ſince both the fourth and fift edition of this worke from my hand, although at thoſe times not a little inlarged, with moſt familiar ſentences, very notable and excellent, accordingly in their right places beſtowed, with the addition alſo of certaine omitted Chapters at the beginning of the Booke, with the putting-to likewiſe, although but briefly, the liues of certaine other Philoſophers, Emperours, Kings, and Orators, not mentioned before in his Treatiſe, their names, of what linage they came, and their ſentences alſo following in their places, but alſo now againe the ſeauenth time, ſeeing the eſtimation of the work, and the great pleaſure that all men haue worthily therein, for the variety of ſuch delightfull matters, as in it is contained, tending to diuers purpoſes, neither yet any let or incumbrance, being eaſie to be carried, I haue the ſeauenth time, as the breuity of time would permit, endeauoured my ſelfe gladly, as I might, to ſatisfie the godly Readers minds, not onely with the like collected ſentences as before, conueniently and duely placed throughout the Book: but alſo certaine other whole Chapters of ſundry and effectual cauſes, both touching vertue and vice, as alſo of the ſtate of mankind, of mans conſcience, and ſuch like, to the number of ſeauen or eight, orderly ſet amongſt other Chapters, as the effect of their cauſe duly requireth, beſeeching thee (*moſt* gentle & friendly

Reader) that although among these my simple doings thou shalt finde me too grose, rude, and vnlearned, barren and void of all such liuely graces and good gifts as indeede should rightly be full fraughted in the braine and vnderstanding of him that should take any such worke in hand, to the contentation and well pleasing of most men, & specially of the learned reader (whose eyes are wide open quickly to espie out such faults as are indeed worthy of reprehension,) I shall therefore most heartily desire thee, fauourably to beare with me, and with thy good contented minde, friendly to accept the ground of my earnest good will, where I haue (as before written) but little altered, and as appeareth more slenderly finished the said Treatise: which is if it be any thing at all, worthy but of small commendation, in comparison of the witty and learned handling of the other.

Vnto the author whereof (Mr. *Bauldwin*) I yet still (as before) gladly and most heartily refer the whole commendation and praise, considering that by him, and through his godly diligence, I had first occasion to write, whereon I haue (I trust without offence to God) honestly spent my time, if time herein well spent be good, and worthy the acceptation of God, although for so small a cause and little sparke of vertue. I haue here good occasion to commend vnto thy remembrance, with most humble desire, that not vnkindly, or as an vnable friend or enemie to vertue, thou contemne what God alloweth: vnto whom, and vpon whose diuine will should onely depend all our wils, our whole obedience and faithfull seruice, euery man according to the gift of God and his vocation: by whom, in consideration of his ineffable goodnesse and loue towards vs (who onely weigheth and gladly accepteth the good intents of the heart) wee are either

of

of vs encouraged without feare boldly to present and returne vnto him such liuely fruits of his grace (whatsoeuer they be) more or lesse, as hee hath mercifully grafted in vs, being the author and onely giuer of all good things, our onely patrone, our straight way, and onely marke of very felicity: from whose order and most holy will whosoeuer in any thing writeth one inch or naile breadth, he goeth beside the right path, and wandreth out of the way.

I haue therefore good hope, that there is no Christian, or one that indeed hath professed the good rule of Christ, (except he be an hipocrite or a dissembler) specially hauing the blessed benefit of God, the gift of vnderstanding and knowledge, by vertue whereof his mind should alwaies seeme in such wise to be so strongly fenced and armed with wholesome precepts, honest opinions, and godly intentions, throughout all his conuersation and working, that will at any time, or for any thing, and specially for a good thing, maligne or spite his friend or brother: and instead of friendship to purchase him enmitie, or to make of his friends his foes, though he should loose thereby (if the case so neere touch him) a great part of his owne praise and glory. For if in all our good intents we doe reuerently examine the dignity, state, or condition of our calling, straightly entering into iudgement, rather of our owne iust causes, profession and duety (either to the supplanting of vice, or erection of vertue) then rashly to stumble at other mens matters, to what end in effect I pray you, should all our diligence and study bee, during our liues, that haue professed Christ, but ioyfully to winne and allure, according to our knowledge, by our continuall trauaile, by our counsailing and faithfull working if it were possible, all men to a Christian and godly life? should

should it once appeare through our sufferance, that any poysoned euill should possesse and infect our hearts to the contrary, that through either negligence or wilfulnesse in deceiuing our selues we will loyter, delay, and dally with the time, with our duties, and with the gifts of Gods grace.

Should not the remembrance of our selues, what we are, & what we haue bin, be in vs continually quick and liuely? What haue we, that we haue not receiued? or to whose glory should all such gifts as wee haue receiued be imployed? Is there any thing in vs at all, touching properly our own nature, wherein we should reioyce or seeke to be magnified, either with the gifts of grace to purchase worldly exaltation, and not rather giue vnto God his due honour, and be out of all doubt, that whatsoeuer we doe, or howsoeuer we examine or iudge of our selues, the truth of God endureth, his iudgements are true, and according to his truth our doings (by him) shall bee tryed, and most straightly iudged? We enter not into iudgement one with another: I iudge no man, neither let any man iudge of mee, but rather pray for mee, and I will most heartily pray for all men, that God of his infinite mercy and goodnesse will vouchsafe to giue vnto vs his vnworthy seruants, the spirit of humblenesse and feare, and graciously to illuminate our eyes, that we may see euery good and perfect gift to be giuen vs of him from aboue, to be receiued & vsed with thanksgiuing, and that in his diuine presence it may alwaies and in all things appeare, that our profession and rule hath nothing to doe with the cursed spirit of enuy and strife, scornefulnesse or disdaine, & the like works of iniquity: for where such lothsome companions beare rule and are guides, there truely the wisedome & grace of God hath no place, but the wandring

spirit

ſpirit of vnſtable, and all manner of euill works, whereby is ingendred forgetfulneſſe and an vnthankfull life to God, as experience oftentimes and in diuers things hath approued.

And this is further greatly to bee lamented, that where the godly intent and diligent trauaile of diuers men, according to the gift and grace of God, hath beene imploied & ſet forth to the furtherance of vertue, knowledge, and piety, either touching themſelues or for others commodity, if it hath chanced to come to the ouer looking and handling of ſome curious or ſcornefull perſon, finding it vnpicked, empty, barren of eloquence, void of profound learning, excellency, dainty or fine perfection (although in ſome godly matters ſuch exact diligence and niceneſſe needeth not, ſo that the cauſe of God to his glory be chiefly and ſimply pretended and conſidered,) it hath ſeemed vnto them ſo loathſome, groſe, and vnſauory, ſo far contrary and diſagreeing vnto their delicate and dainty diet, that not onely they themſelues euil brooking and reiecting it, as vicious, vaine, or fooliſh, but alſo contentiouſly and by their buſie inforcement hath kindled in others the like hatred and contempt of ſuch godly purpoſes, to the great diſcouragement of faithfull and willing hearts, happily with good deſires inflamed to ſeeke the praiſe of God, and to traine by their godly endeuour vnto their fellowſhip, ſome at the leaſt to tread in the path-way to honeſty, which leadeth vnto moſt certaine and euerlaſting felicity, the iuſt reward of God, moſt gracious and bleſſed, prepared for euer vnto all the faithfull laborers and workmen in his iuſt cauſe.

This I haue noted, not as though I with the like occaſion ſhould be any thing offended, or feeling my ſelfe pricked, ſhould ſwell or ſtomacke againſt any man,

man, no truely, but only because the remembrance of such things (not a little lamented of many) came into my minde, which I haue something touched, I trust in such wise, that I haue not iustly kindled offence against any man. But if there be any (as in manner before rehearsed) that contrary to the vertue of their good gifts and calling, (through the Diuels sleightie inuasion and forgetfulnesse of the charitie of God) maliciously will depraue, spurne, defile or spot these my simple doings, or proudly extoll the glory of their owne excellency, through dispraise or spite of this that I haue thus rudely wrought: notwithstanding (I say) such ingratitude and vncharitable attempts, without minding of other reuengement, I doubt not but in the end God who is mercifull, gentle in reforming, and alwaies ready to further his good workes in them already begun, to the increase of his glory, will send them a more sure and perfect guide, will giue them grace to be more thankefull, and better to vse his benefits, remembring thereby the goodnesse and perfect will of God, that as there are diuers gifts, and diuers manners of operations in men, so there is but one spirit, and one God that giueth and worketh all in all.

And the gifts of the spirit of God are giuen to euery man to no other vse but to edifie withall, louingly to helpe one another, to comfort & incourage one another, and euery man to reioyce at anothers well doing: for loue suffereth and is curteous, it enuyeth not, it swelleth not, it seeketh not his owne, but reioyceth in all godlinesse and truth; yea, it suffereth and endureth all things, to the onely glory and praise of God, who truely doth know, that when I tooke this Treatise in hand, I minded nothing lesse then therein to be curious, to enter into comparison with any man, or pretending herein any iust imperfection, arrogantly to

reforme

reforme other mens doings, or yet to seeke thereby any preferment, praise, or glory, but onely for mine owne commoditie & pleasure. At the first, with small trauaile and little study I speedily passed it through, which notwithstanding, after I had thus simply ended, being seene, read, and throughly examined of others, who also noted the order of the alteration, what worthy sentences of diuers matters I had gathered & put in their due places, to the edifying of the Reader, to the increasing of Vertue and ciuill honesty, what incomparable delight, godly solace, and comfort of mind there would be found, considering the variety of good sayings and godly counsailes, and how profitable they should be to all estates and degrees of men: they did not a little encourage me, but most earnestly desired me in such wise to finish it, that it might be put forth to the vse and commodity of all men: and that my diligence herein (although it be but little) should not lye hid onely for mine owne purpose or priuate delight, but that I should with good will, as a common friend or seruant generally to all men, seeke their profit, and at all times doe them pleasure. Whose gentle requests I haue most heartily fulfilled, wishing that it were in no lesse good order set forth, then the excellency and goodnesse of the matter requireth.

But I yet beseech thee gentle Reader, fauourably to take in good part this my simple doing, and rather imbrace this little Booke for the worthinesse of the good counsailes and witty sayings therein contained, then to refuse or neglect it, because it is neither finely nor wittily handled, and at the least haue this alwaies in remembrance, that a good thing through the vertue and excellency of it selfe, doth at all times and in all places (with small setting forth) sufficiently appeare to be of all good men worthily imbraced. And

although

although(good Reader)that Philosophie, and the sayings of the Gentiles are not to be compared with the diuine and most holy Scriptures, yet are they not vtterly to be reiected and set at nought: for wee be (if we will seeme to credit the mindes of holy Doctors,) exhorted to the reading thereof, as appeareth plainly by the example of S. *Augustine* in his Booke, *De doctrina Christiana. Cap.xl.* when he writeth of Philosophers, and chiefly of *Plato* his sect, declaring that if they haue spoken ought that is true & appertinent to our faith,we ought not onely to beleeue it,but also to challenge and retaine it,euen as our owne from other men,who are indeed no right owners thereof.So that it shall be lawfull to credit, not onely that which is contained in the sacred Bible (which is the very perfect and true word of God,and the touchstone whereby all truth is tryed) but also all other good doctrines and sayings agreeable to the same,whether they be of Christians, Gentiles, or of Philosophers (as they are here called,)or of what nation or name soeuer they be vnder the Sunne.

And to conclude (louing Reader) I most humbly beseech almighty God, that he of his most deere and tender mercy wil vouchsafe abundantly to bestow vpon vs (his chosen children) the gifts of his grace,that like as we haue possessed his rule, and haue put vpon vs the badge and outward signe of Christianity, and haue made (as we vse to say at the Font-stone)a great and solemne vow, vnfainedly to follow, as holy and liuely members,his blessed word, and most holy commandements,and vtterly to renounce the cursed enimies of his immaculate and vndefiled Church(namely the diuell, the world, and the flesh,) and also being of our selues but earthly, sloathfull, and sluggish, and altogether vnapt to the exercise of any goodnes,so to

inspire

inſpire vs with the grace of his holy ſpirit, and to kindle in vs ſuch a zeale and feruent towardneſſe to the remembring and fulfilling of this holy profeſſion and chargeable vow, and to vnderſtand and deepely conſider of the ſacrament, what diuerſity there is between the fleſh and the ſpirit: what mortification of fleſhly luſts, burning of ſin, and what riſing againe into newneſſe of life is ſpiritually repreſented: and ſo like new borne children and perfect Chriſtians in our conuerſation to ſhew our ſelues, that generally and before all thoſe, whom wee call Gentiles or Heathen (whoſe godly ſayings, and good counſailes hereafter follow) our liues and Chriſtian conuerſation may ſo cleare ly ſhine vnto them, that the rayes and bright ſhining beames of our godly examples, kindled in vs, and comming from the euerlaſting light of all worlds, euen Ieſus Chriſt our head (who mightily poureth the light of his grace into his members, and with power vttereth ſtrength, according to the meaſure and quantity of faith) may ſo comfortably appeare vnto them, and among them, that ſo many as are called, and be lambs of his ſmall flock (diſperſed here and there throughout the whole world, and choſen to ſaluation before the foundation of the world, and are only hid to himſelfe) may be I ſay, by our vnſpotted liues and daily prayer, the ſooner trained vnto the feeling of Gods vnſpeakeable mercy, in the bloud and death of Ieſus Chriſt, his Sonne and our Sauiour: and that they may euen from their very hearts, confeſſe (they with vs, and we with them) the true Catholike faith, and ſo to trade our ſelues the one with the other in holineſſe and righteouſneſſe all the dayes of our liues, to the glory of God the Father. *Amen.*

Thomas Palfreyman.

A TREATISE OF Morrall Philoſophie.

THE FIRST BOOKE.

Of the beginning of Philoſophie.

Cap. I.

Some perhaps (ſeeing wee intend to ſpeake of a kinde of Philoſophy) will moue this queſtion, more curious then neceſſary: where, and how Philoſophy began? and who were the inuenters thereof? and in what nation? Of which, ſith there is ſo great diuerſitie among Writers, ſome attributing it to one, and ſome to another: as the Thracians to Orpheus, the Grecians to Linus, the Libians to Atlas, the Phenecians to Occchus, the Perſians to their Magos, the Aſſyrians to their Chaldees, the Indians to their Gimnoſophiſtes, of which Budas was chiefe, the Italians to Pithagoras, and the French-men to their Druides: bringing each one of them probable reaſons to confirme herein their opinions: It ſhall be hard for a man of our time (in which many writings are loſt, or at leaſt hid) fully herein to ſatiſfie their queſtion. Neuertheleſſe for as much as God himſelfe (as witneſſeth our moſt holy Scriptures) is the Author and

beginning of wisdome, yea wisedome it selfe, which is called of the Philosophers, Sophie: therefore I suppose that God, who alwayes loued most the Hebrewes, taught it them first. If ye aske to whom: I thinke (as also testifieth Iosephus) to his Seruants, Noe and Abraham, who after in their times taught it both to the Caldeans and to the Egyptians.

The Sonnes of Seth were also studious in Astronomie, which is a part of Philosophy, as appeareth by the pillars, wherein after Noes flood (which they by their Grand-father Adam had knowledge of) this Science was found by them engrauen: and after the Flood, was by Noe and his Children, taught to other Nations. Of which I grant, that he, which euery Countrey calleth the first finder, hath béene in the same Countrey, better then the rest: as among the Egyptians, Mercurious, Tresmegistus, or Hermes: whose workes both diuine, and Philosophicall, excéede farre all other that thereof haue entreated. Neuerthelesse, the Grecians (who haue béene alwayes desirous of glory) challenge to themselues the Inuention hereof: and haue therein taken great paines, naming it first Sophia, and such as therein were skilled, Sophistes or Wisards, which so continued vnto Pithagoras time, who being much wiser then many other before him, considering that there was no wisedome but of G O D, and that God himselfe was alone wise, called himselfe a Philosopher, that is, a louer of wisedome; and his Science, Philosophy. There were besides these Sophistes, another kinde called Sapientes, or Sages, as was Thales, Solon, Periander, Cleobulus, Chilon, Bias, and Pittachus: and thus there were in all

all three Sects, that is to say, Wisards, who were called Sophistes: and Sages, who were called Sapientes: and louers of wisedome, who were called Philosophers: all whose Science was Philosophie, as wee may call it, naturall Wisedome: of which the kinde called Tonica, began in Anaximander, and ended in Theophrastus. And the other kinde called Italica, began in Pithagoras, and ended in the Epicure.

Of the three parts of Philosophie. Cap. II.

Philosophie is sorted into three parts, Physicke, Ethnicke, and Dialecticke. The office of Physicke is, to discerne and iudge of the world, and of such things as are therein. It is the part of Ethnicke, to treate of life and manners: and it is the dutie of Dialecticke, that is, Logicke, to make reasons to proue and improue both Phisicke and Ethnicke, which is Morall Philosophie.

Now as for Phisicke, although it altogether be not from our purpose, because it conserueth the body in health, without which Morall wisedome auailleth little; yet because it is more then wee may accomplish, it shall be omitted: and such as therein haue delight, may read Galen, Hippocrates, Aristotle, and such other.

Logicke also, because our matter is so plaine that experience daily proueth it, shall not greatly néed for our purpose, who desire rather to be plaine and well vnderstood, then eyther with Logicke or Rethoricke to dispute, and garnish our matter. But Morall Philosophy, which is the knowledge of precepts and all honest manners, which reason acknowledgeth to belong and appertaine to mans

nature (as the things by which we differ from beasts) and also is necessary for the onely gouernance of mans life, shall be here spoken of: not reasoned to the tryall, but simply and rudely declared; yet so that such as therin delight, although not fully satisfied, shall not be vtterly deceiued of their purpose.

Of the beginning of Morrall Philosophie. Cap. III.

Necessitie (as I iudge, and that not without cause) was the first finding out of Morrall Philosophie: and Experience, which is a trusty teacher, was first maister thereof, and taught such as gaue diligence, to marke and consider things, to teach and instruct others therein. And because Socrates in a manner despising the other two kindes of Philosophie, added this as a third, and taught it more then any of the rest, therefore (because men must be the beginners of mens matters) I assent with Laertius, to call him the first beginner thereof.

For although then among the Athenians the Sages, as Thales & Solon, both spake and wrote of like matter before him, yet because hée so earnestly embraced, and equally placed it with the other twaine, he deserueth well the glory of the first beginner thereof: and although hée wrote it not in bookes (for which, as he thought, hee had a lawfull excuse, or rather a good cause) yet his disciple Plato hath written such things of his teaching as few so fully wrote of before: which was as it is euident, many yéeres before Iesus the sonne of Syrach, whose work we (for the puritie of the doctrine

therein

therein contained) reuerence and honor, which as he himselfe cals it, is a booke of Morrall wisedome, though full of diuinitie, as are also many of Platoes workes, as witnesseth Saint Augustine: and therefore because Socrates was before Iesus Syrach, I refer the inuention, I should say the beginning thereof vnto him. As for Salomons workes, they are more diuine then morrall, and therfore I rather worship in him the diuinitie, then ascribe the beginning of morral Philosophie: wishing all men, and exhorting them both to learne and to follow those so diuine and holy counsailes, vttered by him in his booke of Prouerbs.

Of the kindes of teaching Morrall Philosophie. Cap. IIII.

All that haue written of Morral Philosophy, haue for the most part taught it, either by Precepts, Counsailes and Lawes, or else by Prouerbes and Semblables: for which cause it may be well diuided into three kindes: of which, the first is, by Counsels, Lawes and Precepts, of which Licurgus, Solon, Isocrates, Cato, and other more haue written much, counselling and admonishing men to vertue by precepts, and by their lawes fraying them from vice.

The second kind of teaching is by Prouerbs and Adages: which kinde of Philosophie most commonly is vsed: in which they shew the contraries of things, preferring alwaies the best: declaring thereby both the profits of vertue, and the inconueniences of vices, that we considering both, may imbrace the good, and eschew the euill.

The third kinde is by Parables, Examples, and

Semblances. Wherin by easie and familiar truth, hard things, and more out of use are declared, that by the one the other may be better perceyued and borne in minde: Our Sauiour Christ himselfe, when hee taught the grosse Jewes any diuine thing, most commonly he vsed parables, Semblables, and Examples, which (though differing in somwhat) draw all to one end, and therefore are of one kinde. The which kinde, Æsop most of al vsed, bringing vnreasonable things, to teach and instruct men in graue and waighty matters.

Of Liues and Answeres.

Of Aristotle. Cap. V.

ARistotle the son of Nicomache a Stargerite, was well beloued of Amintas King of Macedon, both for his learning, and also for his wisedome. He was Platoes disciple, and passed farre all the rest of his fellowes. He had a small voyce, small legs, and small eyes: hee would goe richly apparelled with rings and chaines, minionly rounded and shauen. Hee had a sonne called Nicomache, by a Leman. He was so well learned, that Philip King of Macedonia sent for him to teach his sonne Alexander, who because he reproued him so much, put him to death. But Apollodorus saith that he came to Athens againe, and kept Schoole there, and dyed when he was threescore and three yeeres old. He was an excellent good Physitian, and wrote thereof many good workes. Hee vsed to wash himselfe in a basen of hot Oyle, and to carry a bladder full of hot Oyle at his stomacke: he

hée vsed also when he slept, to hold a ball of brasse in his hand, with a panne vnder his bed side, that when it fell it might wake him. Being asked what vantage a man might get by lying, he answered: to be vnbeléeued when he telleth truth. Many times when he inueyed against the Athenians, he would say, that they had found out both fruits and lawes, but knew how to vse neither of them. He would say that the rootes of liberall Sciences were bitter, but the fruits were swéet: it was told him that one railed on him; to which he answered, when I am away let him beate me too. Being asked how much the learned differed from the ignorant: he answered; as much as the quicke differ from the dead. He would say that learning in prosperity was a garnishing, and in aduersity a refuge.

To one that boasted that he was a Citizen of a noble City, he said: boast not of that, but sée that thou be worthy to be of such a noble City. Being asked what was friendship, he said, one Soule dwelling in many bodies. Being asked what he got by Philosophy: he said, I can doe that vnbidden, which some can scarce doe compelled by the Law. Being rayled on to his face, and not regarding, and the rayler asking him whether he had touched him or no, he said: good Lord, I minded thée not yet. Being reproued because he gaue wages to one that was scarce honest, he said: I giue it to the man, and not to his manners. This, and such like, he spake and wrote in many good Bookes, of which we haue (though not the one halfe) yet so much as in our age is thought sufficient for one man to haue knowne and written: out of which, his most pithy Prouerbs for our purpose, shall be added in place most conuenient.

Of Anacharsis. Cap. IX.

ANacharsis the Scithian, was the Sonne of Gnurus, brother to Caduidus, King of Scithia, but his mother was a Grecian: by reason whereof he was learned in both the languages, and wrote much both of the Scithians, and Grecians Lawes, and also of warre and martiall affaires. Socrates saith, that he was at Athens in the xlvii. Olympiade, vnder the Prince Eucrates. And Hirmippus saith, that he went to Solons house, and when he was at the gate, desired one of the house to tell Solon that Anacharsis was without, who desired greatly, if he might, to be his guest, and haue his acquaintance. When the seruant had told Solon his message, hee sent him word againe, that he made guests of his owne Countrey folkes: which when Anacharsis heard, hee went in boldly, and said: Now I am in my Countrey. And when Solon saw his wit and wisedome, he admitted him not onely for a guest, but also for a principall friend. He had this one witty saying, worthy to be noted. The Vine bringeth forth three grapes. The first of pleasure, the second of drunkennesse, and the third of sorrow. Being asked what should cause a man most to be sober: he said, to behold, see, and remember the filthy beastlinesse of drunkards.

Being on a time in a ship, after that hee knew it was but foure inches thicke, hee said that they were nigh death that sayled. Being asked what Ship was most sure: that (quoth he) that commeth safe to the hauen. When he was demanded, whether there were moe dead then aliue, he asked,

in

in which side he should count Marriners. Being vpbraided of a man of Athens, because he was a Scithian: indeede (quoth he) my Country is a reproach to me, but thou art a reproach to thy Country. To one that asked him if a wise man might marry a wife, he said, what thinkest thou that I am? and when the other assumed that hee was a wise man: well (quoth he) I haue married a wife. When he was reproued of fearefulnesse, hee said that his fearefulnesse caused him to abstaine from sinne. To a woman that said he was foule and ill-fauoured, he said, thou art so foule and filthy a mirrour, that my beauty cannot be seene in thee. When it was asked him why wise men would aske counsell, he answered, for feare of mingling their wills and their wits.

To a Painter that was become a Physition, he said, the faults that thou madest before in thy workes, might soone be espyed, but them that thou makest now, are hidden vnder the earth: for dead mens diseases are buried with them. Being asked what was both good and euill to man, hee answered, the tongue. Hee would say, that the market was a place appointed for men to deceiue in, and to apply themselues to auarice. To a young man that was his guest, which slandered him, he said: well young man, if while thou art young thou canst not suffer wine, when thou art olde, thou must be content with water. He was the first (as some thinke) that inuented the Anker. He was long time with Solon, and thence returned into his owne Country, and there intending to change their lawes, and to haue established the Grecians lawes, he was slaine of his brother with a shaft as he rode on hunting, and when hee felt his deaths wound,

wound, he said: I haue béene preserued in Grecia by wisedome and learning, but at home, and in my Countrey, I perish through enuy: some write that hée was slaine while hee was sacrificing after the manner of the Grecians. The rest of his sayings shall be spoken of in their places.

Of Antisthenes. Cap. VII.

ANtisthenes the Sonne of Nintithenes, was borne at Athens, and was disciple to Gorgias the Oratour, of whom he learned to pleade: and from him he went to Socrates, of whom he learned wisedome and Morall Philosophie. To a young man that would be his Scholler, which asked what hee néeded to his learning, he answered: a new Booke, and a new Wit. When it was told him that Plato spake euill of him, hée said: it is kingly to be euill spoken of when a man doth well. Hée would say that it was better for a man in his necessitie to fall among Rauens, then among flatterers: for Rauens will eate none but dead folkes, but flatterers will eate men being aliue. He would say, that Cities must néedes decay, where good men are not knowne from bad. Being praised of euill men, he said: I feare mée that I haue done some euill. He would say, it was a great ouer-sight (séeing they purged their Wheate from Darnell, and their warres of cowardly Souldiers) that they purged not their Common-wealth of enuious people.

Being asked of a man, what was best to learne, hée said: to vnlearne the euill that thou hast learned. Hée alwayes held Plato to be proud, disdainefull,

disdainefull, and high minded: insomuch that when he met him at a Triumph where there were many goodly and couragious neyghing horses, he said: Plato, thou wouldest haue made a goodly Horse. Hee wrote many good Bookes, and spake many worthy and witty sentences, which shall bee spoken of hereafter: Hee dyed of a disease when hee was very olde. It is said, that when he was sicke, Diogenes came to visite him, hauing a blade by his side: and when he said, who shall rid mee from my disease? Diogenes shewing him his sword, said, this same shall. To whom Antisthenes said, I spake of my griefe, not of my life. There were more of this name, but he lyeth buried at Athens.

Of Anaxagoras. Cap. VIII.

ANaxagoras was an exceeding well learned man, and came of a good stocke: His Fathers name was Eubulus. Hee was very wittie in Philosophie, and wrote much thereof. Hee was of a noble courage, and very liberall. For why? hee gaue away all his Patrimonie: and when his Friends reproued him therefore, and said that hee tooke no care of his goods: what neede I (quoth he) sith you take care therefore? At last, hee went from them, and gaue his minde altogether to the studie of Philosophie, regarding neither the Common-weale, nor his owne profit, insomuch, that when one asked him if hee regarded not his Countrey? he answered, yea, the chiefest thing I care for is my countrey? pointing with his finger toward Heauen. Hee was in Xerxes time,

time, and began to treat of Philosophie at Athens, (as saith Valerius) when hee was but twenty yeere old, and tarried there twenty yeeres. He said that the Sunne was made of burning yron, and that there were mountaines and vallies in the Moone. Some say that he told before of a stone that fell from heauen into the floud Egis. To one that asked if the mountaines of Lampsacum should euer be part of the sea: yes (quoth he) if the time faile not. Being asked for what entent hee was borne, he said, to behold the Heauen, the Sunne, and Moone. To a man that was very pensiue and heauie, because he should die in a strange country, he said, be of good cheere friend, for the way that goeth downe to hell is euery where. Silenus writeth, that in Prince Dimilus time, there fell a stone from heauen, and that Anaxagoras there-through held opinion that heauen was made of stone, and that but for the great compasse of the building, it would sodainely fall. Sotion saith, that he was accused for these and such like matters, and lost much of his goods therefore, and was banished: but others write that Tucidides accused him of treason, and being absent, was therefore condemned, at which time also his children died. And when it was told him how he was condemned, and his children dead: as touching his condemnation he said, Nature hath giuen like sentence both of my condemners and me. And as touching the children, hee said: I know that I begot mortal creatures. Neuerthelesse, afterward hee was saued by Pericles, and departed from Athens vnto Lampsacum: and being two and forty yeeres old dyed there. Being asked of the citie if hee would haue any thing done for him, hee willed that in the same Moneth in

which hée dyed, the children of the towne should yéerely play, and that they should kéepe that custome for euer. Which granted, they buryed him honourably, and set vp a goodly Epitaph vpon his Tombe. His witty sayings shall be spoken of in their places.

Of Archelaus. Cap. VI.

ARchelaus the Son of Seuthus (as saith Appollodorus) was a good Philosopher, and very studious in Platoes workes, hee was first an hearer of Antilochus a Mathematicke, and afterward of Theophrastus. He was a very witty fellow, and of a prompt spirit, and graue in communication, and much exercised in writing, and gaue his minde to Poetry. He delighted so much in Homer, that euery night before he slept, hée would reade somewhat in him. He learned Geometrie of Hipponicus, and was thereto so dull, and yet so well learned in the craft, that he would say, that Geometry fell into his mouth as he gaped. Hearing men singing ilfauordly, méeters that he made, he kicked them on the side, saying, Yée breake mine, and I will breake yours. Being called to a sicke man, perceiuing that he was sicke for thought and lacke of riches, he conueyed vnder his pillow a bag full of money, which he finding was so ioyfull that hée recouered straight-wayes. When hee was bid to solute a riddle at a banquet, he said, that the chiefest point of wisedome was to know to what purpose each time was méetest. To him that asked him why many schollers of euery sect became Epicures, but none of the Epicures became of other sects: hee said, because that Cocks were made of men,

men, but neuer men of Cocks: or, as some say, Capons be made of Cocks, but neuer Cocks of Capons. Béeing reproued because hée challenged not a yong man whom he had right to, hée excused him elegantly, saying: it is not possible to draw soft Chéese with an hooke. Being asked what man was most in trouble, thought and care, he said: he that desireth most to be at quiet and rest. Being asked whether it were better to marry a faire woman or foule, hée answered: if thou marry a foule one, thou shalt haue griefe with her: but if thou take a faire one, she will make thée a Cuckold. He called old age, the hauen of all tribulations. Hée said it was a great euill, not to be able to suffer euill. To an enuious man that was very sorrowfull, he said: I know not well, whether euill hath chanced to thée, or good to another: signifying thereby that enuious men are as sorrowfull for others prosperitie, as for their owne aduersitie. As hée sayled among théeues, by chance they met with a ship of true folkes, which the théeues espying: said, we may chance to die if we be knowne, and so may I (quoth he) if we be not knowne. These and such like answeres he gaue, and dyed at Athens, when he was eightie yeares old. His witty Prouerbes shall be spoken of hereafter.

Of Aristippus. Cap. X.

ARistippus (as saith Æschines) came to Athens to heare Seneca, whose excellent wisedome was spoken of euery where. But when Socrates was dead, he flattered Dionisius, and became a Courtier. Hée was a merry-witted fellow, and could fashion himselfe méete for all times and places,

places, insomuch that Diogenes called him the Kings hound. When he on a time had espyed Diogenes gathering of hearbs, for to make pottage, he said, if thou Diogenes couldest flatter Dionise, thou shouldst not need to gather worts. To whom Diogenes said: if thou also couldest be content to gather and eate worts, thou shouldest not neede to flatter Dionise. When one made boast that hee had learned much: hee said, thy learning consisteth not in the greatnesse, but in the goodnesse. To one that made great brags of his swimming, hee said: art thou not ashamed to boast of that that every Dolphin can doe? Being reproued because he hired a Rhetoritian to plead his cause: he said; when I make a banquet, I vse to hire a Cooke. When his Seruant that iourneyed with him, was tired with waight of money which he carried, hee said, that which is too heauy, cast out, and carry what thou canst. Bion saith, that as he sayled, perceiuing he was in a Pirates ship, he tooke his mony and counted it, and then (as against his will) let it fall out of his hand into the sea, and mourned for it outwardly, but said inwardly to himselfe, it is better that this be lost of me, then I be lost for this. Dionisius commanded that all his seruants should dance in purple roabs, which Plato would not doe, saying, I will not put on a womans garment: but Aristippus did, and when he began to dance, he said, in drunken feates the sober offend not. It chanced that he sued to Dionisius for a friend of his, and being denied, he fell downe before his feete, and when he was reproued thereof, he said: I am not in the fault, but Dionisius, who hath eares at his feete. This and many like answeres he gaue, which who so desireth to read, may looke in the Apothegmes of Erasmus,

Erasmus, where he shall find enough: which because it apperteineth not greatly to our purpose, we will omit, and entreat of his good Precepts and Prouerbs, in the places thereto appointed.

Of Agesilaus. Cap. XI.

AGgesilaus (surnamed the great) was the sixt king of the Lacedemonians. He was a Noble Prince, of excellent vertue, euen from his childe-hoode, as in truth, iustice, temperance, noble courage, liberality and continency. Wherefore he was so much honoured, and prospered so well, that he subdued to the Lacedemonians innumerable Cities and Countries in Asia & Greece, of whose wisedome and prowesse, remaineth yet many remembrances. And returning on a certaine time from Egypt, by a sodaine tempest, being driuen vpon the coast of Libia, dyed, when hee was fourescore and foure yeeres of age.

Of Alexander Seuerus. XII.

ALexander Seuerus, sometime Emperour of Rome, was a Syrian, borne in the City of Artene, his fathers name was Varius, who was lineally descended from the noble house of Mettellus, a Roman, called Mettellus the vertuous: his mothers name was Mammea: hee raigned thirteene yeeres: he was vertuous, wise, gentle, liberall, sincere, and to no man hurtfull. Hee was of visage faire and well proportioned, in body large, and goodly of personage, and therewith was strong and able to sustaine paines, as hee that knew his owne strength, and in the preseruing thereof

hee

hée was not found negligent. Therewith he was amiable, and towards euery man gentle and easie to be spoken to. By the diligence of his good parents hée was euer from his infancie brought vp in the studie of good Letters, and all manner of honest learning, as well martiall, as ciuill: hee reuerenced learned men greatly, and did nothing in the common-wealth without the assistance of wise and learned Councellors. He was at the last wickedly slaine, and his mother Mammea, by one Mariminus, whom he of a Muletter had aduanced to high dignities.

Of Alexander the great. Cap. XIII.

ALexander (surnamed the great) was the son of Philip King of Macedone. In his youth hee was instructed by Aristotle in learning: hée was fortunate in all his desires. He was of a valiant and stout courage: for being but twentie yéeres of age, hée vndertooke the enterprise to conquer all the whole world, by a certaine Army of men, prepared by his father Philip, which was of two and twentie thousand Foote-men, and foure thousand and fiue hundred Horse-men, hauing no Captaine vnder the age of thréescore yéeres. And so enterprised with most valiant courage, and did set vpon the whole world, and had alway the victory of his enemies. He raigned twelue yéeres: and returning homeward from the wars, (in the middest of his glory) at the Citie of Babylon hée ended his life.

Of Ambrose. Cap. XIIII.

AMbrose was a Romane borne, of a very ancient and noble house, and was sometime Consull of Rome. Hee was a man of great fame, and of such holinesse, such gentlenesse, and such excellent wisdome, that not onely in his life time, but also after his death, hee was had in great honour throughout all the world.

Of Augustus Cæsar. Cap. XV.

AVgustus was the second Emperour of Rome, who as soone as he heard of the death of his Uncle Iulius, he hasted from Appolonia to Rome to possesse his inheritance, & to reuenge the death of Cæsar. He raigned sixe and fiftie yeares, and ended his life at Nola, & was buried at Rome, in the field of Martius: whose death the Senate (for his vertue, wisedome, and worthinesse) did so lament, that they said that they would eyther he had not beene borne, or else being borne, he had not dyed.

Of Bias Priennius. XVI.

BIas Priennius (as saith Diogenes) was borne in Priena. His fathers name was Tucramius. Satirus called him the first of the seauen Sages, and many gesse that he was very rich. Phanodicus writeth, that he redeemed many wenches of Messena, which were captiues, and brought them vp as his owne Daughters, and afterward giuing them dowries, sent them home againe to their

country

countrey unto their friends. Not long after certaine fishers found a golden tresse or Triuet, on which was written, Sapienti, that is, Giue this to a wise man: which when the fore-named wenches Fathers heard of, they said, Bias was a wise man, and sent it him: but when he saw it, he said, Apollo was a wise man, and so he sent it to him. We find that when his countrey Priena was besieged by Aliattes, he fed two mules for the nonce, insomuch that they were exceeding fat, and droue them forth into their enemies tents: which when Aliattes saw, hee was amazed, thinking by the fatnesse of them that they had great plenty of all things, and therefore minding to raise his siege, he sent a messenger into the City to search the truth: and when Bias perceiued the Kings intent, he made many great heapes of sand to be couered with wheate, and shewed them to the messenger: which when the King heard, thinking that they had great plenty of victuals, hee made peace with them, and commanded Bias to come unto him, to which Bias answered, I command the King to eate Onions, and to wéepe. He wrote about two thousand verses. Being asked what was hard, hee said, to take in good worth aduersity after prosperity. On a time hee sayled among wicked men, and when the Ship was sore shaken with a great tempest, and those wicked men called upon God: Peace (quoth he) lest hee sée you sayling from hence. To a wicked man that asked him what was goodnesse, hée gaue no answere, and when hée asked why hee answered him not, he said, because thou enquirest of that which pertaineth not to thée. Hée would say, that he had rather be Judge among his enemies, then among his friends; for of his enemies hee should

 make

make one his friend, but amongst his friends hée should make one his foe. Being asked in what déede a man reioyced most, he answered, when hée gained. He was a good Orator, and when he was very olde, as hée pleaded a cause for one of his friends, after he had done his Oration, being weary and faint with speaking, hée rested his head in his Nephewes lap, which was his Daughters sonne, and when his aduersaries beganne afresh, and had finished, and the Iudges had giuen their sentence on his side whose part Bias tooke, as soone as the iudgement was ended, hée was found dead in his Nephewes bosome, who buryed him worthily, and the Citizens of Priena, dedicated a Chappell to him, which is called Tewtontum. He would say alway the greater part are euill. The rest of his sayings shall be spoken of in their places.

Of Chilo, the Lacedemonian. Cap. XVII.

CHilo, the sonne of Damagetus, was borne in Lacedemonia: he wrote many verses, and held an opinion, that man, by reason, might comprehend the fore-knowledge of things to come, by the might and power of his manhood. There were in his time (as saith Sosicrates and Pamphillia) diuers Officers, of which one was most noble, as the Officers called Ephorie, which were Kings fellowes. Wherefore his Brother being angry because he would not take that Office, sith he himselfe had béene in it before: O brother (quoth he) I can suffer wrong, and so canst not thou. This man, as Herodotus writeth in his first Booke of his Histories, séeing on a time Hippocrates

sacrifice

sacrifice, and vessels in Olympo to burne without helpe of fire, counselled him either to liue chaste, or if he were married, to put away his wife, and slay his children. Some say, that when Æsop (which was in his time) asked him what Iupiter did, hee answered, he meeketh the mighty, and exalteth the lowly. Being demanded wherein the learned differed from the ignorant, he answered in their good hope. To him that asked what was hard, he said, to keepe close secret counsell, to keepe a man from idlenesse, and to suffer wrong. He liued so well, that when hee was olde, he said, that hee neuer in his life, to his knowledge, had done any euill, saue that on a time when hee should haue beene Iudge among his friends, and would doe nothing contrary to the Law, he perswaded one to appeale from him to some other Iudge, that thereby hee might both keepe the law and also his friend. The Greekes reioyced in him much, because he prophesied of Githera, an Iland of Laconia: for when hee had well viewed both the nature and situation thereof; would to God (quoth he) that either this Iland had neuer beene, or else that it had beene drowned as soone as it was seene, (a worthy and Prophetly saying,) for Demararus flying from Lacedemonia, counselled Xerxes to keepe a Nauie of ships in that Iland: and surely if he had listned thereto, he should haue got great riches by Grecia: But afterward Niceas (after he had warred at Peleponesis) ouer-came the place, and made it a refuge for the men of Athens, and afflicted sore the Lacedemonians. Hee was briefe in communication, insomuch that briefe speaking was of his name called Chilonia. He was about the one and fifty Olimpiade: in which time Æsopus the

Orator was in his flower, which was in the yeere from the Worlds creation 1024. He dyed at Pisa, saith Hirmippus, while he kissed his sonne that was crowned in Olimpia, being overcome both with ioy, and also with age. The rest of his sayings shall be spoken of in their places.

Of Cicero. Cap. XVIII.

MArcus Tullius Cicero was sometime Consull of Rome, whose diuine eloquence, abundant learning, sharpenesse of wit, dexteritie in Art, and most ardent loue toward the Common-wealth of his Countrey, cannot be sufficiently expressed by any mortall mans tongue or pen. His ancestors were named Ciccrones, because that Tullius Appius a noble King of Volsts, and one of the progenie, had on his nose a marke like a Chiche, which is a kinde of pulse, called Cicer.

Of Crates Thebanus. Cap. XIX.

THe Thebane Crates, Abscondus son, was one of Diogenes Schollers: for, as Antisthenes saith, when he saw Sporculaphus in a certaine Tragedy, holding a hand-basket, he fell straight to the Sect of the Cinikes, and became Diogenes Scholler, and being a noble man, he solde away his inheritance, and the money which he made thereof (which was aboue two hundred talents of our money) hee diuided among the Citizens: and continued so constantly in his Philosophy, that Philemon saith thus of him, in a Comedie.

Estate crassum vestiebat pallium,
Sed hieme pannum, vt temporans esset.

Which

Which may thus be Englished:

In Summer time he thicke himselfe did couer,
But thinne in Winter, that he might be sober.

Diocles saith, that Diogenes perswaded him to forsake all his goods, and to cast his money into the sea. And when diuers of his kindred came to him, endeuouring to disswade and with-draw him from his purpose, hee beat them away with his staffe, and would not bée perswaded. Demetrius Magnesius saith, that hee deliuered a stocke of money to a friend of his, vpon this condition, that if it should happen his children to be fooles, hee should deliuer it vnto them, but if they became learned and Philosophers, then to distribute it to the common people: because (said hee) Philosophers neede nothing. Hee despised so much all vainnesse of apparrell, that (as Zeno saith) he sowed a shéepes skin vpon his cloake, to make it more vncomely: so little he regarded dainty fare, that when Demetrius Phalerius sent him bread and wine, hée chid with him, saying. Would God the fountaines would also yeeld wine: whereby it appeareth that he dranke water. Hee brideled so much his other affections, specially anger, that when Nichodrome, a Minstrell, had strucke him on the face, hee ware a paper on his fore-head ouer the wound, wherein he wrote, This did Nichodrome. Hee would for the nonce raile and scold with harlots, to inure himselfe to suffer all reproches. He was so euill fauoured, and filthy withall, that whensoeuer hee exercised himselfe, hee was scorned at; wherefore holding vp his hands, hée vsed to say to himselfe, hope well Crates, for thine eyes sake, and for the rest of thy body, for thou shalt by and by see these Scorners taken with

some disease, and shalt heare them say, that thou art happy, blaming themselues for their owne folly. When King Alexander asked him whether hee would haue him restore and reedifie Thebes, his natiue countrey: what needeth that (quoth hee) for peraduenture another Alexander shall plucke it downe againe? for my countrey, saith hee (which is pouerty and dispising of glory) needes no reparation, but it is so well & strongly built, that fortune can haue no power against it: for I am a Citizen of the spite that men beare to Diogenes, which needes feare no treason. This Citie he describeth properly in these verses:

Translated out of Greeke:

Est quędam medio constructa Vrbs Mantica fastu,
Pulchra quidem est, pinguis, circum flua rebus egena,
Quam nullus Parasitus adsit: stolidusue penetrat.
Deditus aut quisquam damnosis ganeo scortis:
Allia sed pane, ficus profertq; lupinos,
Non pro gloriosa capiunt, aut sordidus arma.

Which verses may be thus Englished:

There is a certaine Citie faire,
Staffe-waleton by name;
Which stands built in the very midst
Of pride, most high of fame.
Goodly it is, fertile and fat,
And flowing round about:
Yet of most dainty things it is
Both bare and poore no doubt.
To it there comes no Parasite,
No such fond glosing wight:
No such as harmefull harlots haunts,
And liues in lewd delight.

Garlike

Garlike it hath, and houshold bread,
And such plaine simple cheare:
With wholesome fruits, and such like things,
That are not bought too deare.
The folke therein liue all at peace,
To warre they list not fare:
For glory vaine, nor yet for mucke,
That breedes nought else but care.

He was maruellous hot and sharpe in reproouing of vices, and thereby got him this by-name Durexanites, as wee may say, Master Controller. For hee would goe into euery mans house, and plainly disproue whatsoeuer he disliked. He prescribed this dietary or daily wages following, to shew how preposterously all things were regarded: Giue thy Cooke ten pound, thy Physitian a groat, thy Flatterer ten talents, thy Counseller smoke, thy harlot one talent, thy Philosopher a dandiprat. To one that asked him what remedie was to quench loue, he made this answere; Hunger swageth Loue, and so also doth time, but if thou be not able to vse any of these, take an halter. He would say, men ought to studie Philosophy so long, till they perceiued Captaines of Armies to be Asse-driuers. He liued so long, that hee was crooked with very age, and then seeing himselfe draw neere his end, he looked on himselfe, and said:

Vadis nunc optime curue,
Vadis ad Orci ædes, longa gibbosa senecta.

That is:

Now goest thou hence good crooked wight,
To dwell with *Pluto* aye:
With bunched backe; yea, crookt with age,
Groueling thou goest thy way.

Of

Of Diogenes. Cap. XX.

Diogenes, as saith Diocles, was born in a towne called Tinope, his father was called Icecius Mensar, who being imprisoned for counterfeiting their coyne, Diogenes which was of counsell with him, fled, and came to Athens, where he met with Antisthenes, who unwilling to receiue him (because he neuer would teach any) he ouercame with his intreatie. And when his master on a time tooke up a staffe to beat him, hee put under his head, saying; strike, for thy staffe is not able to driue me away, so long as thou canst teach me ought. He liued simply as one that was out of his country, & comforted himselfe much with beholding the little Mouse, which neyther desired the Chamber, nor feared the darke, nor was desirous more of one meat then of another: whose nature (as nigh as hee could) he followed. He ware a double cloake, wherein he wrapped him when he slept, and made him a bag, to put therein his meat, & used one place for all purposes, both to eat, to sleepe, and to talke in. When he was diseased, he went with a staffe, which afterward hee carryed with him alwayes, not onely in the citie, but also in all other places. Hee wrote to one to make him a Cell, which because he tarried long for, he took a barrell or tun, & made that his house. When he had any graue matter, hee would call the people to heare him, which when they regarded not, hee would sing pleasantly, to which when many resorted, he would say, to heare foolishnesse yee run apace, but to heare any waightie matter, yee scarce put forth your foot. He wondred at Grammarians, who could shew other folkes

folkes lewdnesse, and neglected their owne. Hee reproued Musitians, because they tooke great care that their instruments should agree, and their owne manners agreed not. He rebuked the Mathematickes, which beheld the Sunne, the Moone, and Starres, and neglected the businesse that lay before their feete. He taunted the Orators because they studyed to speake that was iust, and followed not the same in their liuing: he dispraysed the people, that while they sacrificed, and gaue thankes for their health, would make banquets, which was against their health: he wondred that Seruants could stand and see men eate, and not snatch away their meate. Being mocked because hee annointed his feete with odours, and not his head, he said, the sauour goeth from the head into the ayre, but from the feete vp to the nose. Being asked what time a man should dine, he said, a rich man when hee will, and a poore man when hee may. When one had giuen him a blow vpon the ears, he said, I wist well I had left somewhat vncouered. To young lads that stood about him, saying, We will beware that thou bite vs not: hee said, tush, feare not, for a Dog eateth not beetes. On a fooles house that had written, No euill shall enter here: he wrote, Where then shall the Master of the house enter? When Alexander stood betweene him and the Sunne, and bad him aske what he would of him, he said, I pray thee let the Sunne shine vpon me. When he saw a writing set vpon a riotous mans house, signifying that the house was to be sold, he said to the house, I thought so much, thou wouldest surfet so long, till at last thou wouldest spue out thy Master. When a man that was very superstitious, said, I

can

can cut off thy head at one stroke: Yea (quoth he) but if I stand on thy left side, I can make thee tremble. Being asked what beast biteth sorest, he said, of wilde beasts, a backbiter; and of tame, a flatterer. Being asked why gold looked so wan, because (quoth he) it hath many lying in waite for it. As he beheld a tree whereon many Women were hanged, (he said,) Would God euery tree bare such fruit. When he entred into a very small towne, named Minda, which had mighty great gates, he cryed to the Citizens; Hoe Sirs, shut your gates that the towne run not out. When he saw one, which had beene a weake wrastler, become a Phisitian, what (quoth he) entendest thou now to ouercome them which heretofore haue ouercome thee? When he beheld a Whores childe casting stones amongst a great company, beware childe (quoth hee) that thou hit not thy Father. Beholding Archers shooting, when one that could not skill should shoote, hee ranne to the marke, saying, here will I be for feare lest hee hit mee. To one that asked him a foolish question, he gaue no answere, being asked why hee held his peace, hee said, Silence is the answere of foolish Questions. Innumerable such pretty answeres and taunts he vsed, which who so listeth to heare, may reade the Apothegmes of Erasmus, which is no lesse finely handled in the English then in the Latine: beside that, it is also more plaine and perfect. This Diogenes liued ninety yeeres, and dyed being bit of a dogge, as some write: others say, that hee stifled himselfe with long holding of his breath: after whose death there was great strife amongst his Schollers, who should haue his body to bury, neuerthelesse the strife was appeased by the

the Elders, and they buried him by the gate that leadeth to Isthmus, and made him a faire tombe, and set a pillar with a Dog thereupon, and writ thereon a learned Epitaph. His witty precepts and Prouerbs shall follow in their places.

Of Democritus. Cap. XXI.

DEmocritus was a right excellent, and noble Philosopher. In his childe-hood he learned of the wise men of Caldea, Astronomy, and their diuinity. He went after that into Persia, to learne the Art of Geometry. After he returned into Athens, where he gaue his possessions and riches innumerable, vnto the weale publike, onely preseruing to himselfe a little garden, wherein hee might at more liberty, and with much quietnesse search out the secrets of nature. He wrote many wonderfull and notable workes concerning naturall Philosophy and Physicke. And after he had liued seauenty yeeres, he ended his life.

Of Demosthenes. Cap. XXII.

DEmosthenes was the most excellent Orator among the Greekes: he was first the Disciple of Plato: after that he followed Ebulides, an Orator, and vsed such wonderfull diligence and labour to attaine to the perfection of Eloquence, that where he had a great impediment in his pronunciation, he by putting into his mouth small stones, and inforcing himselfe to speake treatably, attained at the last to a most perfect forme of speaking.

Of

Of Ennius. Cap. XXIII.

ENnius an ancient Latine Poet, was borne in Tarentum, a City in the Realme of Naples: Yet as some suppose, in a towne called Rhudy in Italy, and was brought to the City of Rome by Cato the Censour. For his learning and most honest conditions he was entirely beloued of Affrican. In consideration whereof, he caused his Image to be set on his sepulchre. He made many Bookes in sundry kindes of verses, but the stile that hee vsed was something ancient, rude and homely. Yet notwithstanding, they contained very graue and substantiall Sentences, of great wisedome. Hee dyed also at the age of seauenty yeeres.

Of Galenus. Cap. XXIIII.

GAlenus a noble Phisitian, borne in Pergamo, was the Son of one Nicon, a great Geometrician. He excelled all other (both before and since his time) in the Art of Phisicke: insomuch as in his ministration, counsell, or doctrine, hee neuer at any time sustained reproach. Also liuing as some doe write, an hundred and tenne yeeres, after hee passed the age of eighteene yeeres, vntill the time of his death. hee was neuer vexed with any sicknesse, except the grudge of a Feuer of one day, (as he saith in his worke, De sanitate vendat) and that hapned onely by too much labor: he flourished in the time of the Emperors Marcus, Commodius, and Pertinax, and dyed onely with feeblenesse of age, about the yeere of Christs Incarnation, 160.

Of

Of Hermes. Cap. XXV.

HErmes, otherwise called Mercurius Trismegistus, was not onely the most excellent of the Philosophers, but also the most ancient: whose life, because it is not wholly set forth, nor all agréeing in that which is set forth, therefore giuing credit to the most true Writers, shall be set forth, as they among them by pieces haue preserued it. Of whom Saint Augustine, the Reuerend Doctor saith, Atlas the Astrologian, the Brother of Prometheus the Physitian, flourished & was highly accepted in the same time in which Moses was borne; which Atlas was Grandfather, by the mothers side, to Mercurius the elder, whose Nephew was this Mercurius Trismegistus, which in the Egyptian tongue is called Hermes. Howbeit, some which write of him, hold opinion, that he was Enoch; which, as they say, signifieth the same in Hebrew, that Hermes doth in the Egyptian tongue: & so make him in the seauenth degree from Adam, reckoning after this sort; Adam begat Seth, the Father of Enos, the Father of Caine, the Father of Melalael, the Father of Metusalah, the Father of Iareth, which is the Father of Enoch: which opinion (although it be not vtterly to be neglected) yet it is not sufficient without proofe to be beleeued. For Enoch, whom they take for Hermes, was before Noes flood, in which all the workes which were written, if they had at any time any vse of letters were drowned, but the workes of this Hermes of whom wee treat, are yet appearing in diuers languages: wherefore it should séem that this was not he, except wee should say that he graued it in the stone

stone Pillers, in which in time of the Flood, Astronomy was preserued, which might well bee: (and but that S. Augustine and Pamphilus in his Chronicle, and S. Hierome thereupon, approue the contrary, might bee beleeued: for Iambicus & diuers others write much of Mercurius pillers, and Mercurius was of such fame among the Egiptians, that they put forth all their workes vnder his name. And the Poets for his singular learning, made him a God, and called him a messenger of Iupiter, whom they call the God of heauen, and gouernor of all. And it may be that the pillers which the sonnes of Seth (of whose linage he was) made, were grauen by him, which as many write, are full of learning, out of which, as testifieth Iambicus, both Pithagoras, and Plato, with diuers other moe, learned Philosophie. But those pillers I would take rather to be his two worthy Bookes, which may very well be called Pillers, because they beare both Diuinitie (if with Lactantius I may so call it) and also Philosophy, which were also peraduenture grauen in Seths Childrens pillers, and there-out drawne by some that haue beene since. Of which two bookes, the first called Hymander, is so full of diuinity, as may astonish the wits of such as therein shall read, which causeth S. Augustin to doubt whether he spake such things as he did by knowledge of Astronomy, or else by reuelation of spirits. Howbeit Lactantius doubteth not to count him among the Sibiles and prophets. The other booke called Asclepme, being but small, containeth in it the whole summe of naturall Philosophy: out of which I thinke no lesse, but that the Philosophers haue learned their Science. Tully and

Lactantius

Lactancius (not shewing in what time,) saith that there were fiue Mercuries, and that this is the fift, whom the Egyptians call Theuth, and the Grecians Trismegistus, and that this is hee which slew Argus, and was ruler of the Egyptians, and gaue them lawes, and instructed them in learning, and deuised markes and shapes of Letters after the forme of beasts and trées.

Hee was called Trismegistus, because hee was the chiefest Philosopher, the chiefest Priest, and the chiefest King. He prophesied of the regeneration, and beleeued the resurrection of the body, and the immortalitie of the Soule, and gaue his Subiects warning to eschew sinne, threatning them with the Judgements of God, and shewed that they should giue account of their wicked deedes. Hee taught them also to worship GOD with diuers kindes of Ceremonies, and taught them in all manners to make their Prayer vnto God, and instructed the Ilands in the knowledge of God. And when he had liued vnto a perfect old age, he gaue place to nature. His Precepts, Prouerbes and Parables shall be spoken of in their places.

Of Epimenides. Cap. XXVI.

THeopompus saith, that Phestius was Epimenides father: others say, that Dosiades was: others say, that Agesiarchus. Hée was borne in Crete, in a strete called Gnosus. This Epimenides beeing on a time sent of his Father into the Country to fetch home a sheepe, about noone-tide as he trauelled with the shéepe on his necke, being weary, hée went into a caue, and slept there

fifty and seauen yeares: when he was waked, hée sought for his shéepe, and because he could not find him, he went backe againe into the field, and when he saw that all things were changed, being greatly astonied, hee returned to the towne: and when hée would haue entered into his owne house, they asked who he was, and when he saw his younger brother, he was so old that he knew him not: but at last, after much communication, he told his brother all that had chanced him, which when it was noysed abroad, euery man tooke him for one high in Gods fauour. Wherefore on a time when as the Athenians were plagued with the pestilence, and were counselled of Apollo to purge their Citie, they sent for Nicoas to come vnto Crete, who when hee was come to Athens, purged it in this manner: hee tooke sheepe both white and blacke, and brought them into a sheepe-cote, and suffered them to goe thence whether they would, and commanded those who followed them, to sacrifice them to God in the place where they first lay downe: which done, the plague ceased.

The Athenians deliuered thus from destruction, gaue him a great summe of money, and also a ship to carry him againe into Crete, but hee forsaking their money, onely desired their friendship, and so departed. A little after that hee was come home, he dyed, being an hundred ninety and seauen yéeres old, as saith Phasge: but, as his country-folke say, hee liued two hundred ninety and nine yéeres. He wrote many Workes in Prose, and in Verse, of which somewhat shall be shewed in their places. Some thinke that he died not at that age, but fell asléepe againe vntill another time.

Of Horatius. Cap. XXVII.

HOratius was a famous Poet, borne at Venusium: a man excellent in sharpnesse of wit and quicknesse of sentence. He was addicted to the Epicures sect, and was wanton in manners, though he deliberately noted the vices of other men in his verses called Satiri. In ballads to sing to the harpe (which were in eightéene sundry kindes of verses) he passed all other that wrote in Latine. He was greatly in fauour with the Emperour Augustus, by the meanes of Mecenas the Emperours minion, who tooke in him, for mirth and wit, much delectation: to whom, and to Augustus hee wrote diuers Epistles in verses, comprehending great wisedome in compendious sentences, and died when he was seauen and fifty yéeres old, as Eusebius writeth.

Of Homerus. Cap. XXVIII.

HOmerus the chiefe of all Poets, whose proper name was Malesigenes: but because he was blinde, he was called Homerus; which in the tongue called Jonica, signifieth blinde.

Cicero Tuscula saith, it is written that Homer was blinde, yet we sée his picture and not his poetrie: for what countrey, what marches, what hoast, what nauie, what matters of mindes (as well of men as of beasts) are expressed in such wise, that he maketh vs to sée that he saw not?

Plutarchus, in the booke which he wrote of him, saith, that in his two workes hee comprehendeth both the parts of man: for in the Iliade, hee

describeth strength and vallantnesse of the body: In Odissea hee doth set forth a perfect patterne of the minde. Notwithstanding, for his vndiscréet fabling of Gods and Goddesses, hee was excluded by Plato out of the weale-publique.

Of Isocrates. Cap. XXIX.

ISocrates was a Grecian borne, and came of a good kindred, and was in his youth wel brought vp in all kinde of good manners, and when hée came to age and discretion, hee was a hearer of Gorgias the Orator, whose Disciple hee continued, vntill such time as hee was well learned both in naturall and also in morall Philosophie. And some say he was in the time of Ahasuerus the king, and was of such fame for his learning, namely, for morall Philosophy, that hee seemed to many rather a God then a man. Hee liued vertuously, with such faithfulnesse, and friendship, and continency of his body, and with such pithinesse in his counsels, as very few haue beene like him since. He wrote many good bookes in his youth, which he followed in his age, of which, his good counsels to Demonicum, testifie his wit and his learning in morall Philosophy, beside others which hee wrote of naturall Philosophy. He liued long time, for (as Valerius Maximus saith) when he was ninety and foure yéeres old, he set forth an excellent booke full of Diuinitie. In all his workes hée praysed vertue, as head fountaine of all manner riches, and exhorted all men thereunto. To one that asked him if he would be a King, he answered, that hee would not, and béeing asked wherefore, hee said, If I iudge faithfully, I cannot eschew the

hatred

hatred of many men: & againe, if I iudge wrongfully, I cannot eschew the paine of eternall damnation; wherefore I had rather liue poorely, assured of the blisse of Heauen, then in doubt thereof possessing all worldly riches. Being asked how a man might keepe himselfe from anger, he answered, in remembring that GOD lookes alwayes vpon him. In his time, men delighted much in blacke hayre, wherefore one of his neighbours dyed his head blacke: and when one asked him why his neighbour did so, hee featly taunting his neighbours foolishnesse, answered; Because no man should aske counsell, nor learne any wisedome of him. What would he say now, trow yee, if he saw those women that not onely colour their haire, but also paint their faces? He vsed oft times in his prayers to desire God to keepe and saue him from the danger of his friends, rather then from his enemies, and being demanded of one that heard him, why hée prayed so, hee said, as for my enemy I can beware of, because I trust him not. Beeing asked what a man ought not to doe although it were iust and true, hee answered, prayse himselfe. He liued an hundred and two yeares, and dyed with very age, and was buried honourably. The rest of his sayings shall bee spoken of hereafter.

Of Iustinus. Cap. XXX.

IVstinus comming but of a very base, and poore stocke, hauing a crafty wit, by subtilty and guile obtained the Emperiall authoritie: for with the money which was giuen him to purchase the good will of the Souldiers, that Theocritanus might

be Emperour, he bought the fauour of the Souldiers for himselfe, and of them was made Emperour without resistance. This man in his youth was but a Swin-heard, and after giuing himselfe to warfare, by his towardnesse therein, within few yéeres waxed so expert and cunning in feates of armes, that hee was aduanced to high dignities, and lastly obtained the Empire: which he gouerned with great policy and wisedome nine yeres. He banished in his time all the Bishops of the Arrians, Manichées, and other Heretikes, and endeauoured to restore againe the pure and sincere Christian faith. He raigned in the yeere of our Lord Christ, 521.

Of Iustianus. Cap. XXXI.

IVstinianus, being an Emperour of Constantinople, came of a very poore and base kindred: his mothers brother Iustinus, Emperor before him, was but a Swin-heard, he succeeded his unckle at the age of foureteene yeeres in the Empire, and gouerned it nobly for the space of forty yeeres, augmenting it honourably: he was a right worthy and excellent Prince, but he was not a little corrupted with auarice, and with the heresies of Eutichianus and Pelagian. And not long after was bereft of his wits, and so ended his life when he had liued fifty sixe yeeres.

Of Licurgus. Cap. XXXII.

LIcurgus was the Law-maker of the Lacedemonians, he was a man of great vertue and wisedome, and so moderate and iust, that when he might

might haue raigned after his Brother Poludecta, he would not take it vpon him, but gouerned the Realme to the vse of his young nephew Cabrilaus, to whom, being of age, he restored the Kingdome. And in the meane time garnished the Citie with most honest Lawes.

Of Marcus Aurelius Antonius. Cap. XXXIII

Marcus Aurelius Antonius, was an Emperour of Rome, and a Romane borne, hee succeeded his Father Pius in the Empyre: his Mothers name was Domiclado: hee was a Prince of excellent vertue, wisedome, & learning, and seemed to be prouided for of God against the troubles and miseries which hapned the commonwealth in his time: for vndoubtedly without his great and maruailous wisedome, the Empire had beene sore impayred, or well-nigh vtterly confounded, but hee by his fore-sight and counsell gouerned the same, and kept it from much danger: hee made many worthy Lawes, which remaine yet to this day, hee dyed in Panomy, now called Hungarie, in the eighteenth yeere of his raigne, when he was forty foure yeares of age.

Of Mison. Cap. XXXIV.

Of this Mison is great variance among writers, and all through the doubtfulnesse of Apolloes answere: for when Anacharsis asked of Apollo, who was wiser then himselfe, he answered, Ecius, Mison, Chencus: but some say, that Apollo saide, not Ecius but Eteus, and so they asked what Eteus is? Permenides saith, it is a

village of Laconia, in which Mison was borne. But Sosicrates saith, that his Father was called Eteus, and his Mother Chincum. Ethiphron saith that he was of Créte, and that Heraclides Ponticus was his Father. But Anaxilaus saith, that hee was of Arcadia: thus there is controuersie about him, in which I allow best Sosicrates minde. But after that Apollo had giuen this answere, Anacharsis béeing troubled therewith, came to Mison in the Summer-time, and found him making a share for his plough, and mocking him therefore, said, twis Mison it is not meete to goe to plow now: No (quoth hee) but it is méete to prepare and make it ready. Hee liued solitarily, and when a man by chance met him laughing to himselfe, and asked him why he laughed so, sith no man was present with him, hee answered, euen therefore doe I laugh. He wrote many worthy workes, and dyed when he was seuenty and seauen yeares old: his witty sayings shall be spoken of in their places.

Of Ouidius. Cap. XXXV.

OVidius, surnamed Naso, was borne in Sulmo, brought vp in Rome, and diligently instructed in Latine Letters from his tender age. Hee gaue most diligent study to the making of Verses, from the which he was with-drawne by his Father, and put to learne Rethoricke: where in a while he much profited, and was in the number of the best Orators of that time, and was aduaunced to sundry authorities, and made a Senatour. Notwithstanding, he did much dedicate himselfe to Poetry, wherein by nature hée was excellent, in facilitie and abundance of sentences. Hee was

déerely

deerely beloued of the Emperour Augustus, of whom at the last hee was exiled into Ponthus, where he spent the rest of his life in a towne called Thomos, amongst people most barbarous, who, notwithstanding, greatly lamented his death for his curtesie and gentle manners. The cause of his exile is uncertayne, sauing some suppose, it was for abusing Iulia, daughter to the Emperour Augustus, although the pretence of the Emperour was for making of the Booke of the craft of loue, whereby young mindes might be stirred to wantonnesse. He was before the incarnation of Christ foure yeares.

Of Pithagoras. Cap. XXXVI.

Pithagoras the Philosopher, borne in Samia, was a rich marchant-mans sonne, called Demaratus, howbeit, hee was richer then his Father, who was not able with his marchandise to get so much as his Sonne despised: for hee was both rich in abstinence from couetousnes, and also in wisedome, which is true riches: of which in his youth hee was so desirous, that hee went first to Egypt, and after to Babylon, to learne Astronomie, and the beginning of the worlds Creation: which when he had learned, he returned to Crete, and Lacedemonia, to see Licurgus and Minos lawes: In which when he was perfect, he went unto Cenona, where was a people exceedingly giuen to luxurie and all kinde of vice, amongst whom he so behaued himselfe, that hee reformed them from their euill manners, and in small time brought them to such sobernesse, that men would neuer haue thought it had beene possible: for the wiues that were

were forsaken of their Husbands, and Children cast off by their parents, he so instructed, that they were receiued againe: hee caused the women also to set aside their gorgeous attires, teaching them that chastitie was the chiefest ornament of honest women. This Pithagoras, as saith Boetius, was the inuenter of Musicke among the Grecians, which he found out by the sounds of hammers, whereof he wrote a booke, which Boetius and Apuleius translated into Latine. S. Augustine in his eight booke De Ciuitate Dei, saith, that Philosophy was so named by him, which before was called Sophia. For when it was asked him of what Science hee was, he answered, a Philosopher, which is a desirer of wisedome: thinking it a great arrogancie to haue called himselfe wise. Tullius saith, that Pithagoras spake so wisely, and so elegantly before Leoncius a King, that he wondring at his wit and eloquence, desired him to shew what Science hee knew best, to whom hee answered, that hee knew no science, but was a Philosopher: at which for the newnesse of the name, the King astonished, asked him what was a Philosopher, and what difference was betweene Philosophers and other men. To whom Pithagoras said; Mans life seemeth to me to be like a Congregation of people gathered to see a game, to which men resort for sundry purposes: some by their owne actiuitie to winne the honour of the game, and other some for lucre sake to buy or sell somewhat, and other some minding neither to gaine nor to profit, come onely to behold and see what is done: and in like manner, men which are come vnto this life, as out of another life and nature, occupy themselues with diligence to get praise or profit: or regarding neyther

ther, apply their mindes to search and to know the nature of things: which sort, last named, wee call Philosophers, that is to say, louers of wisedome. Thus by this witty parable he vttered his minde, in the continuance wherof also, he praiseth and proueth his science to be best, saying, like as he which commeth to see the game only, is more liberall, yea, and more to be praised then the rest: so likewise he which in this life giueth his mind to wisedome and knowledge, ought more to be accepted then any of the rest. S. Augustine saith, that he was well skilled in Negromancy, which may be very well, for in that time it was much set by, and none thought wise, that therein was ignorant. Valerius saith, that his hearers worshipped him so much, that they thought it a great sinne to forget ought which they heard of him. In disputing any matter, his words were so esteemed, that it was a cause good and sufficient in any matter, to say that Pichagoras said so. He was so good a Philosopher, as scarce any deserueth to be his match. He kept iustice so much, that after his death, the authority of his name ruled the people of Italy, which in time past was called Magna Grecia. He was so sparing and profitable, that some thinke he neuer eate any dainty meates: he taught many yong men, whose aptnesse hee knew alwayes by their countenance, gesture and manners: and hee with all his disciples liued in common together, as well in loue as in other matters: for he taught them that true friendship was, to make one heart and minde of a great many hearts and bodies: insomuch that Daimon and Phythias, which were of his Sect, loued so together (as saith Valerius Maximus) that when Dionisius the tyrant would haue killed the one of them, which desiring licence to goe and

dispose

dispose his goods before his death, was granted his request, if hee could get another in the meane-while that would be his pledge, who if hee came not againe at the time appointed, should die for him: his fellow not regarding his life so much as his true friendship, became his pledge: And the other beeing let goe, came againe at his time appointed to redeeme his fellow from his death: which faithfulnesse in both, the Tyrant Dionisius seeing, not onely forgaue them both, but also desired that hee might be the third of that fellowship, that had rather die then to faile in friendship: a notable example of most constant friendship, and a good instruction thereto. To one that asked him what hee thought of womens weeping, hee said: There are in womens eyes two kindes of teares, the one of griefe, and the other of deceit. To a couetous man, he said: O foole, thy riches are lost upon thee, and are very poverty: for why? thou art neyther the warmer, better fed, nor richer for them. It was asked him if hee desired to bee rich, to which he answered nay; saying, I despise to haue those riches, which with liberality are wasted and lost, and with sparing doe rust and rot. To one that was gaily apparelled, and spake uncomely things, hee said, eyther make thy speech like unto thy garments, or else thy garments like unto thy language. It chanced a foole in Pithagoras presence, to say, that hee had rather be conuersant among women, then among Philosophers: to which he said, yea, Swine had rather lye routing in durt and in mire, then in cleare and faire water. Beeing asked what new thing was in the world, hee answered, nothing. Being asked what was Philosophy, he said the meditation or remem-

brance

brance of death, labouring daily to get the soule liberty in this prison of the body. Hee was the first among the Grecians that held opinion that the soule was immortall. Hee kept schoole in Italy, and liued vnto a great age, and after that hee was dead the people reuerenced him so much, that they made a Temple of his house, and worshipped him as a God. He flourished in the time of Nabuchadonozar King of Babylon. His Precepts, Prouerbs, and Parables shall follow in their places.

Of Periander. Cap. XXXVII.

PEriander, as saith Heraclides, was borne in Corinth, his Fathers name was Cipcelus: he married a Wife called Licides, which was the daughter of Procleus a tyrant of Epidant, and by her had two Sonnes, the one called Cipcelus, and the other Licophorne, of which the younger was very wise, but the elder was a foole. This Periander was well learned, and wrote a booke of two thousand verses. Neuerthelesse he was a Tyrant, and exercised so much his tyranny, that all men did hate him: he was about the xxxviii. Olimpiad, in Solons time, and hee executed his tyranny lx. yeares. Some say there were two Perianders, the one a tyrant, the other a Philosopher, which might well be: neuerthelesse, this tyrant is he whom Laertius reckoneth for one of the seauen Sages, whose opinion I allow not: for like as hee for his euill doctrine disalloweth Orpheus to bee a Philosopher: so I for his euill liuing, disallow Periander to bee any of the seauen Sages, although hee hath written many wise sayings. For as in Philosophy nothing is lesse allowed then ignorance, so

so in wisedome nothing is more abhorred then tyranny, in which this Periander excelled, insomuch, that when he was demanded why he continued in his tyranny: because it is dangerous (quoth hée) for a man to yéelde himselfe, either of his owne accord, or against his will. Neuerthelesse, he would say, (as wicked Hanniball said of peace) that who so would raigne in securitie, ought to endeauour to haue their Subiects obedient with loue, and not with force; and yet he himselfe sought nothing lesse, For, on a time he being very angry, threw his wife being great with childe, downe a payre of staires, and trode her vnder his féete, and so killed her: and sent away his sonne Licophorne because he mourned for his mother, and draue him into Corcira: and afterward when hée himselfe was very olde, hée sent for him againe, that hée might with his owne hands haue played the tyrant with him: which when the men of Corcira knew, they put him to death themselues, to deliuer him from his Fathers tyranny. And when Periander heard that, raging in his fury, hée tooke all their children and sent them to Aliattes a Tyrant, to be slaine, but when the ship wherein they were, approched vnto Samos, they vowing to Iuno, were saued of the Samnites: which when Periander heard of, he being eighty yéeres olde, what with sorrow, and what with madnesse, dyed. This was his life, which should not haue béene rehearsed, saue that for his good sayings, which shal be spoken of in their places. Neither would wée that any man should take example thereby, but rather should sée how shamefull a thing it is to haue the like conditions.

Of

Of Phericides. Cap. XXXVIII.

PHericides the Sonne of Badis (as saith Alexander) was a Syrian borne, and was an hearer of Pittachus. Theopompus affirmeth him to be the first that euer wrote of Nature, and of the gods, among the Grecians. Many meruailes are written of him: for as hee walked by the Sea side at Samos, beholding a ship sailing swiftly with full sailes, hee prophesied that within a little while it should be drowned, and as hee said, it came to passe, euen in his owne sight. After that he prophesied (as there was indeede) that the third yeere after there should be an earth quake.

Not long after when he was at Massona, in the game-place, hee counselled one Perilaus a stranger, to get him thence, and all his houshold, with as much speed as might be: which counsell he not regarding, was taken not long after (with the towne and all) of the enemies. Hee would say to the Lacedemonians, that neither gold nor siluer ought to bee worshipped, and that Hercules in his sleepe gaue him that commandement: which Hercules also at the same time commaunded the Princes to obey Phericides: Some apply this to Pithagoras. Hirmippus saith, that when there was great warre betweene the Ephesians and Magnesians, he being desirous that the Ephesians might winne the victory, asked of one that passed by, of whence hee was, who confessing himselfe to bee an Ephesian, hee commanded him to draw him by the legs, and to lay him in the Magnesian Field, saying, desire the Citizens, that when they haue got the victory, they bury mee (which am Phericides)

in

in this same place. Which when the Citizens knew, they were in good hope of victory: and the next day they ouer-came the Magnesians in battaile, and found Phericides dead, and buryed him honourably. But some say, that he threw himselfe downe head-long, from an hill called Coriciam, and so to haue dyed, and to be buried at Delphos. Other some say, that he died being consumed with lice. Aristoxenes saith, that when Pithagoras which came to visite him, demaunded how hee did, that hee putting his finger out at the doore, said, Behold thy selfe: which answere afterward among learned men became a By-word. He wrote an Epistle to Thales, wherein hee prophesied of his owne death, saying that he swarmed full of Lice, and that hee had a Feuer: and when any of his friends asked how hee did, hee shewed them his lowsie finger out through the doore, and desired them that the next day after they should come to his buriall.

Of Plato. Chap. XXXIX.

Plato the Sonne of Ariston and Periander, of Solons kindred, was borne at Athens, in the yeare that Apollo was borne, as witnesseth Apollodorus. Which was in the fourescore and eight Olimpiade, and dyed béeing fourescore and foure yeares old. It is said that when hee was borne, there came a swarme of Bées, & hiued in his mouth, which Socrates interpreted to bée a signe of his great eloquence: Hee was a goodly man of person, as saith Alexander, and was therefore called Plato, which some say was for his eloquence, and some for his great fore-head. Hee exercised himselfe

himselfe in his youth to wrastling, and such like feates, and gaue his minde also to painting, and to write Posies, Meeters, and Tragedies. Hee had a small voice, and an eloquent tongue. Socrates dreamed that a swan let fal an egge, which hatched in his lappe, and when it was feathered it flew vp on high, and sung exceeding sweet songs: and the next day when Platoes Father brought him to Schoole to Socrates, O (quoth hee) this is the swan that I dreamed of: and when hee had learned much, and should come before Dionise to a Schoole-game, wherein learned men should shew their witty meeters, and pithy writings, wherein hee that excelled had a good reward: when hee had heard Socrates declare his, Plato threw his owne into the fire, saying, O fire, Plato hath need of thy helpe. And when Socrates was dead, hee went into Italy to Philoleum, who was of Pithagoras Sect. From thence he went into Egypt, to heare the Priests and the Prophets: where being sore sicke, he was healed by one of the Priests with Sea-water, by reason whereof hee said, the Sea ebbeth and floweth all manner diseases. He said moreouer that all the Egyptians were Physitians, hee determined also to goe to the Magitians, but by meanes of the wars that were in Asia, he changed his purpose, and returned to Athens, where hee abode and wrote many worthy workes, and drew together Heraclitus, Pithagoras, and Socrates reasons. And in feasible things hee preferred Heraclitus: and in things that pertayned to diligence, he tooke Pithagoras part: and in ciuill matters, and Morall Philosophy, hee esteemed most his Maister Socrates. And hee drew these three parts of Philosophy into one body. Satirus

saith that he gaue an hundred pound to Philolaum for three of Pithagoras Bookes.

He sailed thrice into Sicill, to see the Country, whereas Dionisius the Tyrant, Hermocrates son, compelled him to talke with him, and when Plato in his communication sayd that a Tyrant ought not to doe that which was for his owne profit, except hee excelled in vertue: the Tyrant beeing angry therewithall, said, thy words sauour of old idle dottrels tayles: and thine also, (quoth Plato) of a young Tyrant. For which this Tyrant would haue slayne him, but hee was entreated otherwise, and he commanded him to be sold; and by chance there was one Annicer, a Cerentake, who gaue thirty pounds for him, and sent him to Athens amongst his friends, who incontinent sent him his mony againe, which hee in no wise would receiue, alledging that other men were as worthy to care for Plato, as they. And when the Tyrant heard how Plato had sped, and was in his Country agayne, he wrote vnto him, praying him not to speake or write euill of him: to which request Plato wrote againe, that hee had not so much idle time as once to remember him. Some say, when the Captaine Cabria, who was guilty of death, fled, that hee (when none else of the City durst) went with him. And when Corbilus a scoffer saw him enter into the Castle with him, hee rayled on him, saying, thou goest to helpe another, as though thou knewest not that wee already owe thee Socrates poyson. To whom Plato answered, saying, when I warred for my Country, hee then suffered perill with mee, wherefore now for friendships sake, I will doe as much for him.

To one, who because he reproued him for playing at dice, sayd, thou chidest for a small matter: indéed (quoth he) the thing is small, but the customable vse thereof is no small thing. To one of his boyes which had displeased him, he said, if I were not angry, I would beate thee. To one of his seruants which had done amisse, and excused himselfe, saying, it is my destiny, I could doe none otherwise, hee said excuse thy selfe no more then, for it is thy destiny also to be punished. Hée dyed in the Schooles, as some say, béeing broken in the middest, and was buried at Athens. His notable Sentences shall be added in their places.

Of Plutarch. Cap. XL.

PLutarch the Philosopher, was a man of wonderfull wit, wel brought vp in his youth, well instructed in manners, and well furnished in all kindes of learning, who growing vp as well in vertue and learning, as in body and yeares, was chosen, & that worthily, to be the instructer of the Emperour Traian, whom he so well instructed, that his glory thereby was greatly augmented, as it is said in Policrato, the fift Booke. He was faithfull in his sayings, and very eloquent in his words, and exceeding diligent and wary in his manners, of a chaste life & good conuersation. He gaue his mind much to instruct & teach others and wrote many Bookes, of which one entituled The education of youth, wee haue in our English tongue (drawne thereunto by the excellent and famous Knight Sir Thomas Eliot, whose good zeale and loue both to further good learning, & to

profit his Country, appeared as well thereby as by many other workes which he hath taken paines to bring into our Language) shewing well the good affection that he had to the Common-weale. He wrote another Booke called The Instruction of Traian: In which hee setteth out the office of a Prince, and what he ought to be, so excellently, as no man can mend it. Hee wrote also another Book, intituled Archigramaton, wherein he teacheth Rulers and Officers how to gouerne themselues, with diuers other things: among which the Letter which he wrote to Traian, what time he was created Emperour, is worthy to be remembred, in the end whereof hee saith thus, Thou shalt rule all things euen as thou wouldest, if thou goest not from thy selfe: and if thou dispose all thy workes to vertue, all things shall prosper with thee. And as touching the gouernement of the Common-weale, I haue taught thee therein already, which if thou dost follow, thou shalt follow mee thy Master Plutarch, as an example of good liuing; but if thou dost otherwise, then shall this my Letter be my witnesse, that I gaue thee neither counsell, nor any example thereunto. When hee was aged hee dyed, and was buried honourably. His worthy Prouerbes, Adages, Parables and Semblables shall follow in their places.

Of Photion. Cap. XLI.

PHotion was scholler to Plato, and to Zenocrates: hee was one of the chiefe gouernours of the City of Athens, and a man of such wonderfull grauity and constancy, that hee was not lightly

lightly séene to change his countenance, either to laugh or to mourne, nor to haue his hands out of his bosome, except in war: & when hée was in the Country, he went alwayes bare-footed, except it were in the cold Winter, whereof there was no better token then to see Photion goe shod. His speech was short, graue, vehement, and full of darke sentences, and therefore the most eloquent Orator Demosthenes called him the hatchet that did cut his words: hée alwayes kept himselfe in pouerty and base estate, and refused infinite treasure sent unto him by Alexander. And although he had been the generall Captaine of the Athenians in sundry wars, and honourably atchieued his enterprises, yet was he best contented to liue poorely. Finally, euen of his own unkinde Country-men he was condemned to death, whereunto hee went with the same countenance that hee had in authoritie.

Of Philip. Cap. XLII.

PHilip King of Macedone, Son of Amintas, Father of great Alexander, he was from his childe-hood a Prince of excellent wit & power, of whom these excellent things following are to bée remembred. After hée had vanquished the Athenians at Cheronea, he began to reioyce in his felicity, but to the entent that he therefore should not be the more prone to iniuries towards his subiects, nor to haue indignation at them whom he had vanquished, he then, & euer after, caused a childe to come to his Chamber-doore in the morning, and cry unto him with a loud voyce: Philip, thou art a man mortall. Which hee obserued so

 constantly

constantly, that he neuer went out of his chamber, or receyued any Counsellors or Sutors till the childe had thrice spoken those words, notwithstanding he was a Panim.

Of Plinie the second. Cap. XLIII.

PLinie the second, was famous, and a man of great vertue and excellent learning (as was the other Plinie) he wrote to Traian of the persecution of the Christians, certifying him, that there were many thousands of them put to death, of the which none did any thing contrary to the Romane Lawes, worthy persecution, sauing that they vsed to gather themselues together in the morning before day, and sung Psalmes to a certaine God whom they worshipped, called Christ: all other their actions being very vpright, godly, and honest. Wherefore the persecution, by commandement of the Emperour, was greatly lessened. Hee wrote (as it is supposed) the most excellent worke called, The Historie of Nature. He liued in the dayes of the Emperour Traian, and dyed in the yeare after Christs Incarnation one hundred and tenne.

Of Plautus. Cap. XLIV.

PLautus was a right worthy & excellent Poet, borne in Umbria, in the country of Italy. He had a great felicity and pleasure to spend his time in making and setting forth Comedies, and when he spent all his substance on Players garments, he was brought to such want, that he was fayne for his liuing to serue a Baker in turning a

querne

querne, or hand-mill. When he was vacant from his labour, he would write eloquent and pleasant Comedies: wherein he was reputed so excellent that Eupius Strabo saith of him, hee doubted not but that the Muses would speake as Plautus did write, if they should speake Latine. He was in the time of Cato Censorius.

Of Pittachus Mittilenus. Cap. XLV.

Pittachus Mittilenus was a noble and excellent man: hee was one of the seauen wise men of Greece. In his time he did exceede all men, both in learning and martiall feates. He was also of the Citie of Mittilene.

Of Pirrhus. Chap. XLVI.

Pirrhus King of Epire, was a valiant & fierce warriour, sterne of countenance, and a man terrible to behold, he seemed to be framed and naturally inclined to Martiall prowesse. He was induced by a doubtlesse answere of Apollo, to aide the Tarents against the Romanes, whom hee ouerthrew in two great Battailes, but with such losse of his owne Captaines, friends, and Souldiers, that he said, if we ouer-come the Romanes once againe, we shall be vtterly vndone. Wherefore greatly maruelling at the man-hood and prowesse of the Romanes, hée said with a loud voyce to his friends: O how easie were it for mee to subdue the whole world, eyther to my selfe, by the ayde of the Romane Souldiers, or to the Romanes if I were their King? He was receiued of the Macedonians for their King seauen months.

He warred against Demetrius King of Asia, vnto whom he gaue a great ouerthrow. He raigned before Christ, two hundred eighty and eight yeeres.

Of Pacuuius. XLVII.

PAcuuius was a famous and excellent writer of Tragedies, borne at Brundusium in Calabria, hee was sisters son to Ennius the poet, he is commended of Quintilian for the grauity of his sentences, the ponderousnesse of his words, and the authority of the presages which are in his Tragedies and Comedies: and that his stile seemeth somewhat rude, is to be ascribed to time, and not to his fault. Hee liued vnto the age of ninety yeares.

Of Pompeius. Cap. XLVIII.

POmpeius, called Magnus, for his incomparable victories, (whose father was called Pompeius Strabo) had so good a grace in his visage that from his childe-hood hee moued the people of Rome most entirely to fauour him, for his singular beneuolence, continency of liuing, martiall experience and knowledge, pleasantnesse of speech, fidelity of manners, and easinesse in speaking too. Hee neuer required any thing without shamefastnesse, nor granted any thing but with a glad countenance. In his visage appeared alwayes both nobility and gentlenesse, so that in his flourishing youth there shined in him manners both Princely and reuerend. He was of a liuely, stout, and noble courage. He fortunatly preuailed, & had commonly good successe in all his enterprises: hee greatly

triumphed

triumphed for his victories in Africke: béeing almost but a childe, he vanquished the valiant Captaine Sertorius, a man at that time most famous in prowesse: he vanquished also Methridates the great King of Ponthus. And when a great number of the concubines of Methridates, women of excellent beautie were taken and brought vnto him, hee would not company with any of them, but sent them to their friends. He subdued Armenia, Capadocia, Phlagonia, Medis, Scilicia, Mesopotamia, and sundry other Realmes. Hée brought to Rome (by reason of his triumphs & victories) innumerable treasure of gold & siluer: hée afterward tooke to wife Iulia the daughter of Iulius Cesar, who liued not long. And when the amity betwéene Pompey and Cæsar decreased, hée was at the last by Cæsar vanquished, and priuily fled by sea into Egypt, where being vnder the conduct of Ptholomeus, he was slaine in a boat, his head being stricken off, and the body cast on the strand, where it was poorely buried, when hee had liued aboue thréescore yeeres, and from his youth in most high honour, wealth, and prosperitie, on whom it did seeme that Fortune had powred all her treasures most prodigally.

Of Quintilian. Cap. XLIX.

Quintilian in his time was a worthy and famous man, and beeing a perfect Rethoritian, taught Rethoricke in Rome, and receiued his salary and stipend out of the Emperours Exchequer. He flourished in the time of Ignatius, who gouerned the Congregation of the Christians at Antioch.

Of

Of Solon Salaminus. Cap. L.

LIke as there is among Wꝛiters great variance (as I said befoꝛe) about the first Philosopher, euen so is there great contention, which were the seauen Sages, but as their variance maketh doubtfull which were the persons, so their whole consent assureth that there were such. And foꝛ because wee intend not so much to shew the persons and names, as their good doctrine: therefoꝛe it shall be sufficient that a wise and apꝓoued Philosopher hath said such things as to them are attributed: yet as foꝛ good causes I haue allowed Socrates foꝛ the first moꝛall Philosopher after Laertius minde, so doe I best allow Laertius iudgement in this matter, which saith that these were they, Thales, Solon, Periander, Cleobulus, Chilon, Bias, and Pittachus. Of whom although Periander was a tyꝛant, yet because that foꝛ his good doctrine, hee hath of the learned long time beene allowed, therefoꝛe hée shall enioy that name which they haue all giuen him. Of Thales ye haue heard already, after whom Solon is next, who was son to Existides, and was boꝛne in Salamina, & therof was called Salaminus, he wꝛit many good Lawes, and did many noble deedes woꝛthy to be remembꝛed: among which this is very notable; after that the Athenians and Megarenes had made great warre, and soꝛe slaughter betweene them, to haue had the signioꝛitie of his country Salamina, and both were soꝛe wearied with warres, they made a Law at Athens, that no man on pain of his head should speake oꝛ perswade ought to challenge the Iland any moꝛe. Then Solon being troubled and thought-

thoughtfull for his country, fearing lest with holding his peace he should do small good to the common-wealth: and againe, if hee should speake, it should be for his hurt, sodainely fayned himselfe mad, thinking thereby not onely to speake, but also to doe such things as were forbidden. And disguising himselfe, he ran abroad among the heartlesse people, and there in the manner of a Crier, he perswaded the people to that that was forbidden, and stirred vp their mindes so much, that incontinent they began war to obtaine the Iland, and to at last they got it. He perswaded them also to chalenge Chersonesum, a City in Thraci, affirming that it was their right: & by this meanes so wan the peoples loue, that they gladly would haue made him Ruler: but, as saith Sosicrates, he had a neighbour called Pisistratus, who trayterously endeuoured to hurt him, whereof as soone as hee had knowledge, he armed himselfe and went into the streete, and when hee had called a great company about him, hee discouered Pisistrates treason, & not onely that, but sayd also that hee was ready to amend it, and would be glad to fight for his liberty, saying, Ye men of Athens, I am wiser then some, and valianter then other some. I am wiser then those that marke not Pisistratus, & I am valianter then those which know him and dare not for feare shew what he is. But the Senate that tooke Pisistratus part, said he was mad: and when he saw he could haue no redresse, he laid downe his armour before them, and said; Country, I haue alwayes holpe thee with word and deede: and then sayled into Cypres, and there met with Cresus, who demanded of him whom he thought happy, hee said, Thales of Athens, and Bito, and such other,
which

which all men speake of. Another time when Cresus had arrayed himselfe richly, and was set on his high throne, he asked him if he had euer séene a more gorgeous sight? Yes (quoth he) both Capons, Phesants, and Peacocks, for their goodly colours are naturall. From Cresus hée went into Scilicia, and there builded a Citie, and after his owne name called it Solons. Hee made many good Lawes, for such as were warriours: for if any had got victory, he should haue a great reward for his labour; and such as were slaine had their Wiues and children found of the common purse euer after. Hée made a Law that no Executours should dwell with any Orphanes mother, nor that any should bée Executour, to whom, after the heires death, the goods should belong. And that no ring or seale-maker, should keepe the print of any old seale. And that whosoeuer had put out a mans eye, should leese both his owne for it. And that whosoeuer tooke ought that was not his owne, should dye for it. And that if any Gouernour were found drunken, to die for it. And that no man should giue any dowry with his Daughter: with many moe good Lawes. When hée was demaunded, why he made no Law against such as killed their Father or Mother, he answered, because it is a desperate mischiefe. Being demanded how men might best kéepe them from breaking the Law, hee said, if such as haue no wrong, be as sory and carefull as those that are wronged. Hee would say to rich men, abundance groweth from riches, and disdaine out of abundance. He wrote many Bookes both of Verses, Lawes, & other matters, besides many witty Epistles. Hee flourished in the fortie sixe Olympiade, and was Prince of Athens the third

third yéere, which was from the worlds creation 4675. yéeres, he liued eighty yéeres, and dyed in Cipres, commanding his Seruants to carry his bones to Salamina, and there being beat to pouder to strew them about the city. Dioscorides writeth, that when hée was asked why hée wept for his Sonnes death, sith it profited him nothing, hee answered, euen for this cause I weepe, because I can profit him nothing. Thus much of his Life and Answeres: the rest of his sayings shall be spoken of in their places.

Of Socrates. Cap. LI.

SOcrates, as saith Plato (the Sonne of Sophroniscus, a Lapidary, and his Mother Phanareta a Myd-wife) was borne at Athens, a man of a wonderfull wit, and as some say, was an hearer of Anaxagoras, and of Damon. But Duris saith, that he was a seruant, & that he graued in stone, and that in Gracy thrée goodly Images were of his caruing: wherefore Timon calleth him a caruer of stones, a vaine Gréeke Poet, and a subtle Orator: for in his Orations he was sharpe and prompt, & was therefore forbidden to teach it by thirty tyrants, as saith Xenophon. But (as saith Fauorinus) he with his Disciple Eschenes opened the fields of Oratories craft. Hee got money to finde himselfe withall by his handy-worke, from which Crito deliuered him because of his wisedome, and became his scholler, as Bizantius saith, But after that Socrates perceiued that there was no fruit in the speculation of naturall Philosophy, and that it was not greatly necessary to the outward manners of liuing, hee brought in the

kinde

kinde called Ethnicke, that is, Morall Philoso-phy, and taught it daily both in the Shops and streetes, and exhorted the people chiefely to learne those things which should instruct them in man-ners, which were needefull to bee vsed in their houses. He vsed sometime through vehemency of his communication to shake his head, and stirre his finger; yea, and to pull himselfe by the hayre also, and was therefore mocked of many, which hee suffered patiently, and was so patient, that when one spurned him, hee suffered him: and be-ing asked why he strucke not againe, hee asked, if an Asse had kicked him, if he should kicke againe? When Euripides had giuen him a worke of Hera-clitus to read, and asked him what hee thought by it, he answered, such things as I vnderstand are very mysticall, and so I thinke those be which I vnderstand not: but surely they lacke some Apol-lo to expound them. He tooke great care to the ex-ercise of his body, and was of a comely behauiour. He was also a good warriour, for when Xenophon was in the wars fallen from his Horse, he caught him and saued him. Another time when the Athe-nians fled away hastily, he himselfe went leasure-ly alone, looking backe oftentimes priuily, and watching to reuenge him, if any man with his sword durst venter to inuade his fellowes: hee warred also by sea, & when he had valiantly fought and ouercome his enemies, hee gaue willingly the victory to Alcibiades, whom (saith Aristippus) he lo-ued greatly: hee was of a constant minde, and in-uincible reason, & exceeding carefull for the com-mon-weale: he was also thrifty & continent. When Alcibiades would haue giuen him much Lime and Sand to build him a house, hee said, if I lacked

shooes

shooes, and thou wouldest giue me a whole hide to make mee a payre, should I not be mocked, if I tooke it? When he beheld many times the multitude of things that were sold, he would say, Good Lord, how many things there be that I need not? He would say commonly, that gold, silke, and purple, and other such things, were more meet to set forth Tragedies, then necessary to be vsed: hee liued so sparingly & temperately, that many times when they were plagued in Athens, he onely himselfe alone was neuer sicke. Aristotle saith, that hee had two wiues: the first Xantippe, of whom he begat Lamprocles: and the other, Matrone, Aristides daughter, whom he tooke without dowry, of whom hee begat Sophroniscus, Meneximus, Satirus, and Hieronimus. Rhodus saith that he had both at once: for the Athenians being consumed with warres and mortalitie of people, to augment the City, decreed that euery man should haue two wiues, the one a Citizen, & the other what hee would, to beget children of both, which Law Socrates obeyed. He despised greatly such as were proud and high minded, and wranglers. Hee gloried greatly in poore fare, and said that such were most like vnto God that lacked fewest things: he had a great gift both in perswading, and also in disswading: for he (as saith Xenophon) perswaded a young man which was mercilesse and cruell against his mother, to reuerence her: hee disswaded also Platoes brother, who was desirous to haue come into the Common-wealth, and caused him to leaue off, because he was rude and ignorant in things. Being asked what was the honour of young men, hee answered, to attempt nothing too much. To him that asked him whether it were better to marry

or

or no? he said, which soeuer thou doest it shall repent thee. Hee would say that hee wondred much at men which with great diligence endeauoured to carue and make stones like men, and tooke so little heede to themselues, that they both seemed and were like vnto stones. Hee exhorted young men to behold themselues oft in a looking-glasse, to the intent that if they were beautifull and well formed, they should doe such things as becommed their shape, but if that they were ill fauoured, then they should with learning and good manners hide their deformitie. When he on a time had bidden many rich men to dinner, and his wife Xantippe was ashamed of the small preparation that hee had made, he said, Be content Wife, for if our guests be sober & honest men, they will not dispise this cheere: and againe, if they be riotous and intemperate, wee shall be sure they shall not surfet. Hee said, some liued that they might eate; but hee did eate that he might liue. Being on a time reuiled, and asked why hee spake nothing: because (quoth hee) that which he speaketh, pertaineth not to me. O that men could now a dates so take such matters Another time when it was told him that one had spoken euill of him, hee said, hee hath not learned as yet to say well. When Alcibiades told him that hee could not suffer the frowardnesse and scolding of Xantippe, as hee did: no, (quoth he) but I can, I am so vsed thereto: canst thou not at home suffer the gagling geese? yes, (quoth Alcibiades) for they lay me egges: marry (quoth Socrates) and so doth Xantippe bring mee forth children. On a time when his wife in the open streete plucked his cloake from his backe, and some of his acquaintance counselled him to haue strucke her

therefore,

therefore he said, yes sirs, yée say well, that while we are brawling and fighting together, euery one of you might cry, now to it Socrates, yea, well said Xantippe, the wittiest of the twaine. He counselled that men should so goe to their wiues, as horse-men goe to their fierce horses: with a pretty simi-litude he coloured his patience, saying, like as an horse béeing broken of an horse-keeper, suffereth euer after any man to ride vpon him, so I by the vse of Xantippe, can suffer all other folke.

Finally, he daily saying and doing such things, was praised of Apollo to be the wisest man that liued: at which diuers béeing displeased, and because that hee reproued some that thought themselues very wise men, to be very fooles, they not content conspired against him, and accused him, saying, Socrates breaketh the Lawes of the Citie, which haue beene giuen of the Elders, teaching that there are no Gods, and bringing in new Spirits: (for Socrates held opinion that there was but one God, who was without beginning and ending, who hath made and gouerneth all things, and that the soule of man was immortall, and that euery man had two spirits assigned him of GOD, and therefore he despised their Gods, and would not worship them,) and against right and Law hee corrupteth our youth, wherefore let him dye.

When this was put vp against him, Lisias a Phylosopher wrote an Apologie for him, which when hée had read, hée sayd, Lisias the Oratour is good and excellent, but surely it is nothing méete for mee, (for why? it was more iudiciall then should séeme méete for a Philosopher. And when Lisias demanded of him sith it was so good, why it

was not meete for him, hee said, Garments and shooes may be both good and fayre, and yet unfit for mee. But while he was iudged, it is said that Plato stood up in his defence, and could not be suffred: and so he was condemned by eighty Iudges and cast into prison, for whom the Prince of Athens was very sorry, but the sentence which the Iudges had giuen unto him, which was that hee should drinke poyson, could not be reuoked.

The King had a Ship fraught with sacrifices, which he offered to his Idols, which then was abroad, and hee would giue no sentence upon any mans death before it came to Athens: wherefore one of Socrates friends, called Inclites, counselled him to giue a certaine summe of money to the keepers, to let him escape away secretly, and so to goe to Rome: but Socrates said he had not so much. Then sayd Inclites, I and thy friends haue so much, which we will gladly giue to saue thy life if thou wilt.

To which Socrates answered, I thanke you and my friends, but sith this Citie wherein I must suffer my death, is the naturall place of my birth I had rather dye here then else-where: for if I die here in my Country without deseruing, onely because I reproue their wickednesse, and their worshipping of vaine Idols, and would haue them worship the true God: if these men of mine owne Nation persecute me for saying and maintayning truth, euen so will strangers wheresoeuer I become: for I will neuer spare to say the truth, and surely strangers would haue lesse mercy on mee then mine owne Country-folke. Being thus minded, hee continued still in prison, teaching his

Schollers

Schollers which resorted to him, many things, both of the composition of the Elements, and also of the Soule, but would write nothing, for he said that wisdome ought to be written in mens hearts and not in beasts skins, neuerthelesse his scholler Plato wrote well nigh all that he taught. A little before he should be put to death, he desired that he might bath himselfe, and say his Orisons: which he did, aad calling his wife and children, he gaue them good instruction. And when he went toward the place where hee should finish his life, his wife went after him, crying, alas, my husband dyeth guiltlesse: to whom he said, why woman, wouldest thou haue mée dye otherwise? and sent her away. So when the cup of poyson was deliuered him to drinke, his friends began to wéepe, wherefore he blamed them, saying: I sent away the woman because she should not doe as you doe. Then Polidorus proffered him a precious garment to dye in, to whom he said, hath not mine owne coat serued mee to liue in, why then may it not well serue mee to dye in? And then after he had commended his soule to God, hee dranke the confection. And as he was in trauaile of death, one of his Disciples, said, O Socrates, full of wit, yet teach vs somewhat while thy speech lasteth, to whom hée answered, I can teach you no otherwise now dying, then I taught you in my life time. Thus finished hée his most godly life, béeing seuenty yéeres old. His godly sayings shall be spoken of in their places.

Of Seneca. Cap. LII.

SEneca the Philosopher, an excellent well learned man was borne in Corduba, and therefore called Cordubencis: he was scholler to Stratus, the Stoicke, and was Lucane the Poets countryman. Hee flourished at Rome in the time of the Emperour and Tyrant Nero, whom he taught in his youth in learning and manners, which afterwards was cause of his death. In the time of this Seneca, Peter and Paul came to Rome and preached there: and when many of Nero the Emperors house gathered together to heare Paul, Seneca, among the rest, was so familiar with him, and delighted so much to heare the diuine seruice, & wisdome which hee saw in him, that it grieued him to be separated at any time from his communication, insomuch that when hée might not talke with him mouth to mouth, he vsed communication by Letters oft sent betweene them. He read also the writings and doctrines of Paul before the Emperour Nero, and got him the loue and fauour of euery body, insomuch that the Senate wondered much of Paul. This Seneca was a man of very chaste life, and so good, that S. Hierome numbred him in his bed-roll of Saints, prouoked thereto by his Epistles which are entituled, Seneca to Paul, and Paul to Seneca. After he had liued vnto a middle age, hée was slaine by Nero the Tyrant, two yeeres before Peter and Paul suffered their glorious Martyrdome: for Nero on a day beholding him, and calling to minde, how hée when hée was his Master did beate him, hee conceyued hatred against him, and beeing desirous to reuenge himselfe,

himselfe, and to put him to death, gaue him license to choose what kinde of death he would: Wherefore Seneca seeing that his tyranny could not be appeased, and supposing that to dye in a veyne was the easiest kinde of death, desired to bee let bloud in the veynes of his arme, and so dyed: which death (as some thinke) was fore-shewed in his name, Seneca, that is to say, Se necans, which signifieth in English, A killer of himselfe. He wrote in his life time, many good bookes, out of which shall be picked some of the most pithy sentences, both of Precepts and Counsels, and also of Prouerbs, Adages, Parables, Semblables, which in their places hereafter shall follow.

Of Sigismund, Emperour. Cap. LIII.

SIgismund was the sonne of Charles the fourth, King of Boheme, and of Hungarie: hee was ordayned Emperour, and was a prudent, wise, learned and noble Prince, in person and countenance of such Maiestie, as was comely and meete onely in a great Monarch, & Ruler of the world. But in war and deedes of armes vnfortunate; for he was oftentimes ouerthrowne and chased of the Turkes and other enemies. And for that he was King of Boheme, he had it by succession after the death of his brother Vincestaus. He raigned twentie and seauen yeeres, and departed this life.

Of Thales Milesius. Cap. LIV.

THales (as saith Herodotus, Democritus, and Duris) had to his Father a noble man, called

Examius, and to his Mother Cleobulina, of the stocke of Cadmus and Agenor. And was borne (saith Plato) vnder Damasius Prince of Athens, and is the first that euer was called a Sage, or wise man. He flourished at Miletum, what time Oseas was Judge of Israel, and Romulus Emperour of Rome: what time Senacherib King of the Chaldes, sent the Assyrians to inhabit Jewry, which by the counting of Eusebius was the 4550. yeere from the creation of the world. This Thales was very well learned both in Astronomie and Physicke, and wrote many worthy works, & was a Citizen of Miletum, (as Phalerius writeth) & was come of a noble linage, who after hee had dispatched his businesse belonging to the Commonweale, gaue himselfe to the searching of naturall causes, and surely, hee was a profitable Counseller to the common-weale: for when as Crœsus demanded to haue had his fellowes, he would not grant to it, which afterward when Cyrus had gotten the victory, was cause of sauing their Citie.

Heraclitus saith, that hee liued solitarily: but some say, hee tooke a wife, and had a childe called Cidistus: but others say that he liued chast all his life long: and when it was asked him why he would not get Children, hee answered, because he would not be bound to loue them. When his mother cryed on him continually to take a Wife, he would say he was too young, and afterward when his youth was past, and his Mother still importunate, he would say, it was out of season and too late. Hee would say alwayes hee was bound to thanke Fortune, but for three causes chiefely: first because hee had reason, and was not a beast: secondly, because he was a man, and not a woman: thirdly,

thirdly, because he was borne a Grecian, and no Barbarian.

He said there was no difference betweene death and life, and being therfore asked why he died not: because (quoth he) I should then make a difference. When he was asked whether GOD knew mens euill workes: yea, (quoth he) & their thoughts too. To an adulterer that asked him whether hee might sweare that hee was no adulterer, hee said, periury is not worse then adultery. When he was asked what thing was hardest, he answered a man to know himselfe: and what was easiest, he sayd, to admonish others: what was sweetest, for a man (saith he) to vse that he hath: what is God, that which lacketh beginning and end: and when he was asked what was the rarest and seldomest seene thing, hee answered, an old Tyrant: a seldome seene thing indeede; for God eyther taketh them away before they be old, or else then their old age changeth their hearts. Being demanded how a man might best suffer aduersitie, to see (said he) his enemies in worse plight then himselfe. It was asked him how he might liue best, and most rig teously, to which hee answered: In flying those things our selues which wee reproue in others. Being asked who was happy, hee said, hee that hath his bodily health, is fortunate in riches, not of a vaine minde, but learned. These are part of his wise answeres: his precepts, prouerbs, and semblables shall be spoken of in their places.

This Thales (as witnesseth Appolidorus) liued seauenty eight yeeres: Socrates saith ninety yeeres, and that he died in the eight and fifty Olympiade, and flourished in Cæsars time, to whom he promised, that hee would cause the Riuer Alin to runne

backwards against the streame. There were many more of this name, as testifieth Demetrius, Durus, and Dionisius: But this Thales Milesius the sage, being old and worne with age, dyed of heate, whiles he beheld a triumph. Some say, that as he went forth of his house to behold the Stars, he fell downe sodainely into a pit, and was therefore mocked of an old Wife that hee kept in his house, with this saying: O Thales, how thinkest thou to comprehend those things that are in heauen, when thou canst not see such things as are before thy eyes?

Of Theopompus. Cap. LV.

THeopompus was an historiographer after the time of Herodotus and Thucidides: hee was also an ancient Poet, and a King of Lacedemonia.

Of Tyranus, otherwise called Theophrastus. Cap. LVI.

THeophrastus Eresius, as sayth Athemodorus, was a Fullers son, and was first an hearer of Leucippus, a citizen of his owne Country: Afterward when he had also bin an hearer of Plato, hee got him to Aristotle, whose successor he was in keeping of his schoole after his departure vnto Chalcides. He was a man of exceeding wisdome, and of singular study, & Schoolemaister (as saith Pamphila) of Menander, the Writer of Comedies: he was a very friendly man, and gentle to be communed with, Cassander tooke him to him, and Ptolemeus sent for him: He was so beloued of the Athenians,

Athenians, that when Agnonides had accused him of heresie, they would haue killed him for his accusation. There came from all places to heare him at least two thousand men, who became his schollers, all which notwithstanding, hee was neuer the prouder or higher minded, but continued one in vertuous humblenesse. In his time Sophocles, Amphicides sonne, made a Law, that no Philosopher should keepe Schoole vpon payne of his life, without the agreement and decree both of the Senate and the people: wherefore he with many moe of the Philosophers departed for a time: but the yeere following, when according to their good order, Philo called Sophocles to the account of his doings, they returned againe, and the Athenians abolished the Law, and fined the maker thereof in fiue Talents, and restored to Theophrastus the regiment of his Schoole. And whereas before time his name was Tyranus, Aristotle named him Theophrastus, because of his diuine and witty vtterance. He vsed oft these notable sayings: Wee may better trust an vnbridled horse then a disordered word. Time is the most pretious experience. He dyed being fourescore and fiue yeares old, when hee had a while taken himselfe to ease. When his Schollers before his departure, asked if hee would command them any thing, hee said, I haue nothing to say vnto you, saue that this life makes many things seeme sweete through the shew of glory, but we all dye as soone as we enter into this life; for nothing is more vaine then desire of glory: but endeuour to be happy and blessed, and either regard not the performance of this precept, because the labor therof is great, or else diligently endeuour to follow it, for thereby you shall attaine

exceedingly,

exceeding great glory. Moreouer, the vainenes of this life is greater then the profit. But seeing I am not able to counsell you what to doe, consider you among your selues what is best to doe. As he thus said, he gaue vp the ghost. The Athenians kneeling before him after his death, worshipped him openly. He wrote many notable works, whereof at this day wee haue but a few, so many good things haue been lost through negligence of men, and iniury of time. He dyed very rich, as may appeare by his testament, which Laertius hath written out at length: with diuers other things, which to auoyd superfluity I haue omitted. His vertuous sayings shall follow in their places.

Of Xenophon. Cap. LVII.

XEnophon, the Son of Grillus, was borne at Athens: he was shamefast and exceeding beautiful. It is said that Socrates met him in a narrow lane, & would not let him passe till he had answered him to diuers questions, & when he asked him wherein men were good and bad, whereat hee stayed and could not tell; Socrates said, come with me and learne: and so he did, vntill such time as he went to Cyrus, whose fauour hee obtained, and became in great reputation with him, and wrote all his actes. He had a woman called Philecia, which followed him, by whom hee had two children. Hee had much trouble in his life, and was banished, & fled from place to place till hee came to Corinth, where he had an house. And when the Athenians entended to succour the Lacedemonians, hee sent his two Sons, called Diodorus and Grillus to Athens to fight for the Lacedemonians: from which battell

battell Diodorus returned, without doing any great feate: but Grillus fighting manfully among the horse-men, dyed about Mantinia. And when Xenophon (who was offering Sacrifice with his crowne on his head) heard that his son was dead, hee put off his crowne: but when hee afterwards heard that he dyed fighting valiantly, he put it on againe, not so sorry for his death, as ioyfull of his valiantnesse. He died at the Citie Corinthum, as saith Demetrius, being very old: a man both good and valiant, expert in riding and hunting, and greatly skilled in martiall affaires, as appeareth by his workes. He was also religious, & much intentiue about sacrifice, & was a follower of Socrates. He wrote xl. bookes, intituled euery one by a sundry name: and Thucidides works, which by negligence were lost, hee brought to light. And was himselfe so pleasant in his stile, that he was called the Muse of Athens There were more of this name, of whom this is the chiefe, whose good sayings and precepts hereafter shall be touched.

Of Xenocrates. Cap. LVIII.

XEnocrates, the Son of Agathenos, was borne in Calcedony, hee was Platoes Scholler euen from his youth. Hee was blunt witted & slow, insomuch that Plato speaking of him and Aristotle, would say, that the one had need of the spur, and the other of the bridle. Hee was graue and earnest, and dry in his communication. Hee was much in the Schooles, and if at any time he went into the Towne, boyes and foolish people would cry after him for the nonce to anger him. He was so chaste, that when some of purpose had hyred an harlot

harlot to meddle with him, who lying with him many nights could not obtayne her purpose, she said hee was an Image and no man. When his fellowes once cast into his bed Lais (which was at that time the fayrest strumpet in Athens) when she would entice him with her whorish conditions hee cut a part of his owne members, because she should not ouercome him. Being sent with other Ambassadours to Philip, when all the rest tooke rewards and banketted with him, hee would not: Insomuch, that when Philip many times would talke with him, hee refused. For which cause Philip admitted him not for any Ambassadour. And when hee, with the rest of his fellowes, was returned to Athens, they sayd that hee went with them in vaine: and when (according to the lawes) he should therefore pay to forfait, he counselled the Rulers to take good heede to the Common-weale, saying, that Philip with gifts had corrupted all the other Ambassadours, but could not make him grant by any manner of meanes, which they hearing, esteemed him more then euer they did before. Beeing sent another time to Antipater to redeeme the prisoners which he had taken in battell, Antipater desired him to dine with him, which he denying, sayd, I came not to dine and banket, nor to take pleasure with thee, but to redeem my fellowes from the sorrowes which they suffer with thee. And when Antipater heard the wisedome, and saw the constant minde of the man, he gently entertayning him, deliuered his prisoners. When Dionisius in his presence sayd to Plato, some body shall take from thee thy head, hee sayd, that they shall not, except they take away mine first. He liued holily, and wrote exceeding many goodly works, and

dyed

dyed being fourescore and two yéeres olde. His good counsels shall be spoken of in their places.

Of Zeno Eloates. Cap. LIX.

Zeno Eloates, the son of Piretus, by adoption became Permenides son: he was of body large and tall, and learned of his adopted father his Philosophie, wherein he became so excellent, that as Plato and Aristotle say, hee was the first deuiser of Logicke. He was a noble man both in gouerning the Common-weale, and also in teaching of Philosophy. There was in his time one called of some Nearchus, of others Diomedes, which vsurped the gouernment of the Country, and there according to his lusts, without respect eyther of Law or Justice, vsed all points of Tyranny. Wherefore Zeno with others conspiring to put him downe or driue him thence, were preuented of their purpose, & Zeno taken. And when the tyrant inquired of him what confederates & prouision of weapons they had, he, minding to make him afraid, confessed that all those whom the Tyrant trusted most, & tooke for his chiefest friends, were of counsell in his conspiracie. And when hee told him certaine things openly of some of them, hée fained that he would secretly shew him greater matters. And when the tyrant therfore went néere him, and bowed his head to him, he with his teeth caught him by the eare, or (as Demetrius saith) by the nose, and left not his hold till he tare it quite away. But when the Tyrant, the more incensed herewith, brought him to the rack, as saith Antisthenes, he would confesse nothing more then what he did at the first. Wherefore, as saith Hermippus, he

he was by the Tyrant put into a morter of stone, and there pounded with a pestle to force him to bewray his confederates.

And when he was therewith almost killed, hee cryed out to the people, fie upon you cowards, that yee can suffer a Tyrant, the destruction of your countrey, thus to deale with you, and though nothing else might moue you, mee thinkes this cruelty which I sustaine of him for my countries sake, and yours, were sufficient. And when hee had so said, because he would confesse nothing, hee bit of his owne tongue, and spat it out in the tormenters face. who therefore killed him, as Hermippus saith. But Antisthenes saith, that the people moued partly with his words, but more with his man-hood and grieuous torments, fell immediately into a rage, and with stones killed the Tyrant He despised all pompe and glory, & for iustice and truth sake, suffered all kinde of torments. When men rayled at, and slandered him, he would bee angry, and when diuers Philosophers would therefore reproue him, he would make this answere: If I should not bee mooued with reproaches, then should I neither delight in prayses. His other sayings shall be noted in their places.

The summe of all.

In this first Booke of Philosophers I briefely declared,
The right order of their liues and godly conuersation:
Whose examples of vertue ought ioyfully to be embraced,
And to be followed of all men without exception.
Their counsels are comfortable in euery condition,
And next diuide Scriptures there is nothing more true,
Then their godly doctrine, to leade men to vertue.

THE

THE SECOND BOOKE.

Of Theologie Philosophicall. Cap. I.

BEcause the name of Philosophers, or Heathen, is a thing very odious to ignorant eares, who will not onely suspect, but also despise whatsoeuer the Heathen teach, taking them for Infidels and misse-beleeuers, therefore I thought it good before I came to their Precepts, to shew their opinion concerning religion, that it may be knowne what they beleeued of GOD, of themselues, and of his workes: all which they themselues call philosophy: for no doubt the common-weales wherein they dwelt, had sundry Religions, and those most vile and shamefull: some worshipping their owne deuices, as Idols and Images of men, beasts, diuels, and other things: Other some the Creatures themselues, as Spirits, Diuels, Sunne, Moone, Starres, Elements, Men, Serpents, Onions, and other like, and with fond and detestable Ceremonies, seruing them with drunkennesse, lechery, & sacrifice of all kindes of Cattle and Fowle; yea, murdering children, men, and women, yea, euen their owne selues to doe their Gods homage. But the Philosophers of whom I treate, although for feare, obedience, and quiet sake they seemed to doe as the common people did, yet they knew by the search of Nature, that there was but one

one God, and that all their religions were wicked and abhominable. And therfore some of them cryed out vpon them, and rather suffered death, then agreed to allow them, as for example, Socrates, whose life you haue before in Fol. 33. For as S. Paul saith the consideration of the Creatures which they saw, draue them to confesse there was a Creatour, who as by his wisedome and power he had ordained all things, so by his prouidence and goodnesse, ordered and preserued them. They perceiued also that there was in themselues a reason and minde, which attained to the knowledge of God, and had power to comprehend and command Spirits, which sith they be immortall, their soule must needes also be immortall, because it had power ouer immortall things. But although they knew God and themselues in this wise, yet ouercome with worldly pleasures, many of them worshipped him not as they ought, but fell with the world to Idolatry, for their bodily commodity, following the lust and sensuality of the flesh. But none of these heathen Philosophers (or sure very few) were of that sort, but like true, wise and constant men, both knew God, and serued him with puritie of life, which is his true seruice: wherof what they thought, and what they taught is declared in this Booke, which I call their Theologie, because it concerneth specially their doctrine of God, which when it shall be read and duely considered, I doubt not but the odiousnesse of their heathen names shall so little trouble any man, that their precepts shall the rather be accepted, considering that they be both honest and naturall, and come from such men, whose heathen liues doe stayne in vertuous perfections (I am

sorry

sorry to say it, but more sorry to see it,) our honest professors that now be or ought to be Christians.

Of God, of his Workes, of his Mercy, and Iustice. Cap. II.

The order of all things that are visible in this world, declareth that there must needes be one principall cause and beginning, which wee call God, and also that the same order cannot be without prouidence, and one perpetuall Gouernour. Aristippus

That is God which lacketh beginning and ending: which God, being made of none, hath by his owne power created all things. Hermes.

God is the beginning of all things.

He onely is to be knowne and taken for a God which is not onely a creator, but also a comforter, a preseruer, a sauiour, and a deliuerer. Plato.

There is a God that doth rule and gouerne all things, who maintaineth the course of the Stars, the changes of times, the alteration and order of things, beholding both sea & land, & who playnely seeth both the liues and doings of all men. Cicero.

There is a liuing God, who onely knoweth, who onely remembreth, who fore seeth, gouerneth, and moderateth all things, and hee it is that liueth for euer. Cicero.

There is no kinde of men so rude, or so dull, who though they be ignorant what God we ought to haue, yet that knoweth not there is a God.

This seemeth to be a most sure and principall occasion why we should thinke there is a GOD, because that there is no Nation so sauage and bestiall, nor any man so barbarous and rude,

whom the opinion of God hath not truely touched.

He surely is vtterly mad, who when hee looketh vp into heauen, doth not thereby know that there is a God: or thinketh those things to be done by chance which are made by so great power the order and alteration whereof no man is almost able by any Art to conceiue?

What can be so plaine and manifest, when we looke vp into Heauen, and behold the Sunne, the Moone, and the Starres shining with glory in heauen, as that there is some, God who ruleth & gouerneth them?

Let all men in this be truely perswaded, that God is the moderator & gouernor of all things, & that all things also be done by his onely power, and appoyntment, and that hee it is, who most cleerely beholdeth euery man, both what he doth, and what hee admitteth in himselfe, with what minde and godlinesse he doth loue and fauour religion, and that he hath also a regard both of godly and wicked men.

Plato. God is without any body, inuisible, and also immortall: whose forme cannot be comprehended with the eyes of mortall men, nor yet described by any sensible knowledge.

Plato. GOD in power is in all things, and in euery part of the world, & by his prouidence all things are preserued, gouerned and moued. And he himselfe is of none other eyther moued or gouerned, but is the first comprehensible mouer.

God is the principall and chiefest God aboue all nature, whom all creatures honour and looke for.

The diuine nature & substance of God suffreth

neyther

neyther change nor end: for it is both immutable and infinite.

In God, or about God, can be no euill: therfore all euill is far from God: for all goodnesse proceedeth from him, and he is the onely fountaine and principall goodnesse. Plato.

God as he is almightie, so may hee worke in all things after his owne minde and will, except in Iustice.

There is nothing that God cannot bring to passe, and that without labour and trauaile.

God is all goodnesse, all charitie, all loue.

The God immortall hath made all things communicable to men mortall, except immortallity, & therfore he is called immortall, because hee neuer dyeth, and wee also be called mortall and fayling, because we all take an end. Mar. Aur.

God the author of all goodnesse, hath created all good things.

God is carefull for all, as well small as great. Plato.

God is pitifull, for though hee giueth vs paine yet he keepeth the fault close. Mar. Aur.

In all thy troubles commit thy selfe onely and altogether vnto the most high and mighty God, and feare not men that threaten, nor trust men that speake fayre, but trust him that is mercifull, true of his promise, and able to make his word good.

To looke for no helpe of man bringeth the help of God to all them that seeme to be ouerthrowne in the eyes of the wicked.

Onely God forgiueth & pardoneth vs our sins.

God knoweth and seeth both the deedes and also the thoughts of all men, from whose knowledge nothing may be hid. Peter. Lumber.

Diogenes. God presently beholdeth all things.

God knoweth all men, hée loueth the iust, and hateth them that worke wickednesse.

Hermes. No man may escape the iust iudgement of God.

Alex.Scu. God is our onely Iudge: who being in heauen faileth not to punish all them that abuse his image.

Photion. As God findeth thée to be when he calleth thée, so doth he iudge thée.

Mar.Aur. God is so righteous that his fierce and cruell chastisements neuer fal vpon the earth, but by our owne cruell shrewdnesse: and our secret sinnes in such wise awaketh vs, that wee acknowledge to haue but iust and due punishment.

Hermes. God will reward euery man according to his workes.

Mar.Aur. The iust God neuer appeaseth his ire against vniust men, except the requirers be vtterly innocent and méeke: God is so iust, that he will not giue iust things but by the hands of iust men.

Diogenes. If thou wouldest obtayne any thing of God, frame thy workes according to his will.

Pithagor. Desire nothing of God saue that which shall be rightfull, for hee will grant nothing vniustly asked.

Socrates. Be carefull in such things as appertaine vnto God.

Anacharsis. Though God exalt thée in this world, be not proud, nor despise any man therefore, nor thinke not thy selfe better then another: but remember that God by creation hath made all men alike.

Antisthen. Forasmuch as all men, although they be great sinners, receiue daily great benefits of God, they are therefore much the more bound to thanke him for his grace, and most heartely to aske him forgiuenesse for their sinnes and trespasses.

God

God greatly esteemeth vertuous people, though in the world they be little set by. Socrates.

All the world is the Temple of God.

A good man is the similitude of God.

When thou wilt fast, purge thy soule from filth, and abstaine from sinne, for God is better pleased therewith, then with abstaining from meates. Hermes.

Seauen things are to be noted concerning God: The first is, let man neuer leaue Gods helpe for any mortall mans, lest that God depart from him in his greatest necessity. The second is, that it more auayleth to rest vpon the helpe of the immortall God that is in heauen, then vpon all the mortall men in the whole world. The third is, that men should beware to displease God, for the ire of God doth much more damage then the enmity of all men. The fourth is, that God neuer forgetteth man at any time, except God be forgotten of him a thousand times. The fift is, that God doth suffer that one should be persecuted of another that is euill, if he haue first persecuted one that is good. The sixt is, if men will haue God fauourable vnto them in time of warre, they must serue him in time of peace. The seauenth is, that God is a pittifull God, not sending to any Realme any kind of extreame chastisement, except it be for some extreame offence committed in the same Realme. As God is full of mercy, so is he also a iust God. As well in aduersity as in prosperity, reioyce and thanke God. Mar. Aur.

God supplyeth where our power lacketh. Phocion.

Be mindefull of God, for the remembrance of him keepeth men from euill.

Like as God surmounteth all other creatures, so the remembrance of him surmounteth all other imaginations.

The summe of all.

God is a substance, euer durable,
Eterne, omnipotent, mercifull and iust:
Which guideth all things in order conueniable,
A God, in whom each man ought for to trust.
Who by prayer giueth grace to mortifie our lust,
In whose feare and loue all that here shall endure,
Shall after this life of a better life be sure.

Of Man, and what he is. Cap. III.

Chilo. There is nothing so hard a matter, as for a man to know himselfe: for we be so blinded with selfe-loue, that we flatter our selues in many things.

Agapetus. Let vs learne first of all this commandement of God, Know thy selfe, and let vs follow it: for he that knoweth himself shal know God, & he that knowes God, shall be made like God. He shall be made like God, that is worthy Gods fellowship: he is worthy of Gods fellowship, that doth nothing vnworthy of God, but thinketh on godly & heauenly matters, & speaketh that he thinketh, & doth that he speaketh.

Pithagor. Thou shalt know thy selfe according to Gods commandement, if thou considerest what thou art, what thou wert, & what thou shalt be: by this last both the first are knowne, because the last is most euident. Thou knowest thy body shall putrifie and become earth, then was it earth before it was thy body, for looke wherein any thing ceaseth, thereof be sure it had the beginning. And seeing that neyther in, nor with the earth of thy body is any wisedome, discretion or knowledge left after thy death, it is euident that those things (which while thou

wert

wert aliue were in thee) came not of the earth, for whatsoeuer commeth naturally of any thing, is so ioyned therewith, that it cannot be seuered. And therefore the growing and sensible mouing life that came of the earth, remaineth so with it, that by putrifaction plants and wormes doe engender thereof, which encrease, moue and feele as thou didst, but wisedome, discretion, or knowledge they haue not: whereby thou mayest know thou hadst them from some other thing, and not of the earth or bodily mixture. If wisedome, discretion, or knowledge come not of the body, then seeing they be the best things in man, then must they come of a better thing And better then the Elements (whereof man is made) is nothing sauing God, and the spirit and power proceeding from God. Then is thy reason or soule, (which I call knowledge, discretion and wisedome,) eyther of God or his Spirit, and so of it selfe immortall and incorruptible.

Man is a creature made by God of two parts, of a soule euerlasting, immortall, of substance materiall, wherein is reason, wisedome, and knowledge: and of a body, fraile and corruptible, made of the foure Elements, whereof commeth life, lust and senses. Plato.

Because God made man to his owne likenesse and similitude, he therefore loueth him according to the common Prouerbe: All things loue that which is like themselues. Plato.

Mankinde, whom God hath onely endued with the great gift of wit, vnderstanding & reason aboue all other creatures, may not (most of all) sticke still or abide in this grosse appetite, to trauaile for nothing else, but for pleasures and profits of this fugitiue and vaine world, but insuing slowly Tullius.

the heauenly guide of our nature, must be led to the desire of truth, honour and seemelinesse: wherewith the more that we be decked, adorned, and beautified, the further off we shall be from the brutishnesse of beasts, and approach the neerer unto the nature diuine, which of it selfe is onely most excellent, and therefore most specially to be embraced.

Tullius. As all things (whatsoeuer they be) that are bred upon the earth, are all created and bred for the commodity and vse of man: so man for the commodity of man is begotten into the world, that they may, (as men among themselues should) be helpers one to another.

Aristotle. Man is the patterne of frailty, the spoyle of time, the play of Fortune, the image of inconstancy, the tryall of enuy and misery, and all the rest of him fleame and choller.

Herodotus Miseries haue power vpon man, not man vpon miseries.

Democrit. There is no stablenesse in ought that belongeth to man, but all things are guided with a disorderly course, men neuer can almost finde any good thing, seeke they it neuer so diligently, but euill things fall vpon them vnsought for.

Socrates. The chiefe cause of all euils that happen to man is man himselfe, for hee through his greedy lusts and desires troubleth both himselfe and all other creatures.

Hermes. O man vnkinde, more cruell then wilde beasts: all things hate thee, because thou destroyest all things: death watcheth ouer thee euery houre: if thou flyest into the earth, wolues and wild beasts will deuoure thee, if thou climest into the trees, Birds

Birds and wormes will assault thee: if thou take the water, the Crocadiles and Ewts will destroy thee, which beasts nature hath iustly ordained, to take vengeance vpon vniust men.

Men dwelling vpon the earth, glad of reason, able to talke, and hauing soules immortall, their members subiect vnto death, they are both of merry and carefull minds, they haue brutish and vile bodies, not like in all conditions, but all like in errors: all of peuish boldnesse, stiffe in hope, vaine in labour, brittle of fortune, euery one mortall, and yet euer continuing together their whole kind, by mutuall succession of their brood, changeable, their time euer flying away, long before they be wise, some dead, some forgotten, and in their liues are neuer sufficiently contented. Apulcus.

Man is vncertaine of any thing all his life, finding nothing that he may leane or trust vnto, hee wanders euer among doubtful chances, with vaine hope alwayes comforting his minde, for no man knoweth certainely what shall betide him, or where he shall leaue his carkasse. Thales.

Man is onely a breath and shadow, and all men are ignorant, and as fraile and vnconstant as the shadow of smoake. Eurip.

God hath so ordained for mankinde, that wee must liue in care: for among all things that liue and creepe vpon the earth, none is more miserable then man. Homer.

All beasts are happier and far wiser then man: for behold the Asse, of beasts no doubt most miserable, yet hath he no harme through his owne fault saue what doth hap him by nature, but wee beside our naturall euils, procure our selues many other, for wee be sorry for euery misfortune, angry for Menander

euery

euery euill word, if any strange thing happen wee are amazed, and afraid of euery shadow.

Bias. Griefes, opinions, greedy desires, and lawes are euils of our owne procuring, not sent by nature.

Diogenes. Men in the beginning accompanied themselues together, and builded Townes to saue them from wild beasts: but now contrary, for their safegard they were glad to flye all company, and to liue in the wildernesse, safer abroad among wilde Tygers, then in any Towne among tame Officers.

Plato. All men are by nature equall, made all by one workeman, of like mire, and (howsoeuer we deceiue our selues) as deere vnto God is the porest begger, as the most pompeous Prince liuing in the world.

Herodotus To them that be greatest in worldly wealth, the greatest mischiefes euer approach.

Seneca. It may chance to each man, that chanceth to any.

Hermes. My sonne, the ends and disposition of all things are in the hand of Almighty God, and he ordereth them as hee list, man hath no power ouer his life, but we liue like beasts, alwayes ignorant, doing and suffering that God hath appointed, notwithstanding wee comfort our selues still with good hope and confidence.

Plato. There be in euery man two powers drawing and leading him: A desire of pleasure, which is bred in the body: and a good opinion coueting onely good things. Betweene these twaine, there is continuall strife in man, and when the opinion hath the mastery, it maketh a man sober, chast, discreete, and quiet: but when desire getteth the vpper hand, it maketh him a lecher, a rioter, a surfetter, a brauler, couetous, and vnquiet.

Socrates. Wo be to him, which contemning the excellency of his owne nature, and the dignity that is in him

serueth

serueth onely his bodily lusts, defiling his owne soule, through his vile desires & beastly delights.

Nature is a certaine strength and power put into things created by God, who giueth to each thing that which belongeth vnto it. Augustin.

The nature of a man (properly of it selfe) is, neither apt to keepe measure in displeasure, nor yet in gladnesse and pleasure: for he is driuen by the violence of affection, sometime with pitty, & sometime with fury, & his desire present doth gouerne him. Aminitas.

He ceaseth to be a man, and is indeede but a brute beast, that leaueth the rules of reason, and giueth his mind onely to the fulfilling of his bodily lusts. Zeno.

The summe of all.

Man that consisteth of body and soule,
Is Gods good creature, specially made
To know his Maker, also to controule,
Such lusts in flesh as Elements perswade:
A beast, if that his life be beastly lead,
An earthly God, if voide of hope and hate
He liue content, and know his owne estate.

Of the Soule, and gouernment thereof. Cap. IIII.

The most precious and excellent thing that God hath created here on earth, is a man, and the richest thing to him is his soule and reason: by which he keepeth iustice, and escheweth sinne. Hermes.

The soule is an vncorruptible substance, apt to receiue either ioy or paine, both here or else-where. Solon.

By the Iustice of God the soule must needes be immortall, and therefore no man ought to neglect it, for though the body dye, yet the soule dyeth not. Plato.

The

Socrates. The ſoules of the good ſhall liue in a better life, but the euill in a worſe.

Pithagor. When a reaſonable ſoule forſaketh his diuine nature, it becommeth beaſt-like and dyeth. For although the ſubſtance of the ſoule be incorruptible, yet lacking the vſe of reaſon, it is imputed dead, for it looſeth the intellectiue life.

Plato. If death were the diſſoluing both of body and ſoule, then happy were the wicked, which being rid of their body, ſhould alſo be rid of their ſoule and wickedneſſe: but foraſmuch as it is euident that the ſoule is immortall, there is left no comfort for the wicked to truſt in.

The ſoule when it dyeth carryeth nothing with it, but her vertue and learning, and hath it ſelfe none other helpe, wherfore all ſuch as for the multitude of their ſinnes and miſchiefes are hopeleſſe, and ſuch as haue committed Sacriledge, ſlaughters, with ſuch other like wickedneſſe, the iuſtice of God and their owne deſerts damne vnto euerlaſting death, from which they ſhall neuer be deliuered. But ſuch as haue liued more godly then other, being by death deliuered from the priſon of the body, ſhall aſcend vp into a purer life, and dwell in heauen euerlaſtingly.

Leginon. The immortality of the ſoule excludeth all hope from the wicked, and eſtabliſheth the good in their goodneſſe.

Socrates. The ſoule that followeth vertue ſhall ſée God.

Boëtius. The ſoule deſpiſeth all worldly buſineſſe which being occupied about heauenly matters, reioyceth to be deliuered from theſe earthly bands.

Ariſtotle. The delights of the ſoule are to know the maker, to conſider the workes of heauen, and to know her owne eſtate and being.

A clean soule delighteth not in vnclean things. Solon.

The night séemeth tedious vnto a man & darke; how much rather a soule destitute of the light of God, and darkened with sinne? The goodly beauty of the body pleaseth the eyes, but how pretious a thing is the beautie of the soule?

A deformed visage séemeth an vnpleasant thing, Socrates. but how odious a thing is a minde spotted and defiled with vices? So onely shall the soule happely depart from the body at the last end, (as afore hand shee hath diligently (thorough true knowledge) recorded and practised death: and also hath long time before, by the despising of things corporall, and by the contemplating and loue of things spirituall, vsed her selfe to be (as it were in a certaine manner) absent from the body.

The Soule knoweth all things: wherefore hee that knoweth his soule, knoweth all things: and hee that knoweth not his soule, knoweth nothing.

Little teaching sufficeth the good soule, but to Plotinus. the euill much teaching auayleth not.

The well-disposed Soule loueth to doe well, Seneca. but the euill desireth to doe harme.

The good Soule graffeth goodnesse, the fruit Boëtius. whereof is saluation; but the euill planteth vices, whose fruit is damnation.

The good soule is knowne in that it gladly receiueth truth, and the euill by the delight that it hath in lyes.

The Soules of the good be sorrowfull for the workes of the wicked.

A good soule hath neyther too great ioy, nor too Pithagoras great sorrow, for it reioyceth in goodnesse, and it sorroweth in wickednesse: by the meanes wherof, when

when it beholdeth all things, and seeth the good & bad so mingled together. It can neyther reioyce greatly, nor be grieueth with ouer much sorrow.

Plato. Soules be lost that delight in couetousnesse.

Who so desireth the life with the soule, ought to mortifie it with the body, and giue it trouble in this world.

Hermes. It is better for the soules sake to suffer death, then to loose the soule for the loue of this life.

Hermes. While the soule is in company of good people, it is in ioy: but when it is among the euill, it is in sorrow and heauinesse.

Hee is in great danger that looketh not to his Soule.

Sickenesse is the prison of the body, and sorrow the prison of the soule.

Socrates. A wise man ought to looke more carefully to his soule then to his body.

It is better to haue a Soule garnished with vertue and knowledge, then a body decked with gorgeous apparell.

Wisdome, vertue, and vnderstanding, are the garnishings of the soule.

Pithagor. Order thy selfe so that thy soule may allwayes be in good estate, what soeuer come of thy body.

Dispose the Soule to all good and necessary things.

Plato. Euill men by their bodily strength resist their misfortunes: but good men, by vertue of the soule suffer them patiently, which patience commeth not by might of arme, by strength of hand, nor by force of body, but by grace of the soule, by which wee resist couetousnesse, and other worldly pleasures, hoping to be rewarded therfore with eternall blisse,

Blessed

Blessed is the soule that is not infected with the filthinesse of this world.

The vanities of the world are an hinderance to the soule.

Woe be to the sinfull soule that hath no power to returne to her owne place, whose filthy workes of bodily pleasure doe hinder her from the blissefull state, & keepeth her downe from the presence of God. Plato.

No dead carrion so loathsomely stincketh in the Nose of an earthly man, as doth the abhominable and dead stincking soule of man in the presence of God.

The soule of man is dead, & hath lost both his life, his beauty, and sweetnesse, when there proceedeth wickedly from it, detractions, blasphemies, lyings, filthy communication, and such like.

If the soule of Man (through sin) be once dead, it is neuer againe reuiued, but by the onely meere grace and mercy of the most gracious and liuing God: whose vẽgeance (by his iustice) stil wayteth the destruction of wicked and wilfull sinners.

As the body is an instrument of the soule, so is the soule an instrument of God. Plutarch.

The body was made for the soule, and not the soule for the body.

Mans soule being decerpt or taken of the portion of Diuinity called Mens, may be compared with none other thing (if a Man might lawfully speake it) but with God himselfe. Tulius.

The minde of man is not a vayne, or idle substance of Man, but is a liuely substance, which endeauoureth it selfe iustly to set forth and expresse in word whatsoeuer it doth contayne in it selfe (by the meanes of the Spirit) which is, (as it

were)

were) the conduit whereby the word is brought forth, from the déepe secret parts of the minde.

Cateline. We vse specially the rule of the soule, and seruice of the body: the one wee participate with God, and the other with beasts.

Socrates. The Soule passeth out of this World more swiftly then any bird that flyeth.

Diogenes. Looke how much the Soule is better then the body, so much more grieuous are the diseases of the soule they the griefes of the body.

The soule cannot but euer liue, it hath none end of liuing: yet we may say that the soule liueth, and dieth: It liueth in the grace and fauor of God, and dyeth in the malice of the deuill.

The soules life is the light of vertue, and his death is the darkenesse of sinne,

The summe of all.

Of all the good creatures of Gods creating,
Most pure and precious is the soule of man;
A perfect substance at no time abating,
Which with the body passion suffer can,
In vertue ioyous, in vice both woe and wan:
Which after death shall receyue the reward
Of Workes, which in life time it most did regard.

Of mans life, how full of miseries and wretchednesse it is. Cap. V.

Hermes. LIfe is nothing else, but as it were a glue, which in a man fastneth the soule and body together, which procéedeth of the temperament of the elements, whereof the body is made, which if it be not violently melted before through our owne

owne distemperance, or loosed with the moysture of our owne merits, or sodainly consumed with the loue or hate of God, weareth away through age of the body, & so at length comes to nothing.

Life is a bridle and miserable fetter, which chaineth the pure and euerlasting soule, to the vile, sinfull, and corruptible body. Plato.

Life is of his owne nature a grieuous thing, most miserable, and full of innumerable cares. Menander

Life is a perillous passage, for wee be therein troubled with stormes & tempests, far more miserable then those that make shipwrack: for we saile as it were in the Sea, alwaies in doubt, hauing Fortune our liues gouernor, some hauing prosperous winde, othersome contrary: but wee arriue altogether at one hauen, vnder the ground. Socrates.

O life, how may a man get from thee without deaths helpe? thy euils be infinite, and yet no man is able eyther to auoid, nor yet to abide them. Onely the Sunne, the Moone, the Starres, the Sea and Land are pleasant, because they are by nature beautifull, all other things are doubtfull and grieuous. And if any good thing happen to any man, he feeleth also therewith tribulation and sorrow. Pithagor.

Consider that mans life is weake & frayle, fulfilled with many froward and troublesome businesses in prouiding for it meate, sustinance, and things needfull to saue it from miserie. Democrit.

There is no kinde of life but may be exceedingly discommended, as hauing in it no notable, worthy or honourable thing: but all mingled with frailty, weakenesse, and many grieuances. What life then should a man leade? Abroad, (that is to say in offices,) are strifes & troublesome actions: Menander

at home, cares: in the field, great labour: in the sea, feare: in wandering or iournying, if it be voyd of ieopardy, yet it is painfull and tedious. Art thou marryed? then canst thou not be without cares: wilt thou not marry? then thy life is vaine and solitary.

Children bring sorrowes, but lack of them make the life unpleasant. Youth is wild and foolish, age weake and feeble. Wherefore one of these two things is to be chosen, eyther never to be borne, or to dye immediately after our birth.

Heraclit. Alas, alas, what a sort of divers euill chances, & how strangely they happen to us in this life! One bewayleth the losse of his children, his wife, and goods: another weepeth for lacke of health, liberty, & necessary living. The work-man maymeth himselfe with his owne toole, while he earnestly applieth his busines: the idle man is pined with famin, bitten with dogs, imprisoned, & whipped in every good Towne: the gamer breaketh his leg in dancing, his stones in vaulting, his lungs in running, his armes, shoulders, or necke in wrastling. The adulterer consumeth himselfe with botches, and leprosie. The dicer is suddenly stabbed in with a dagger. The Student wrung continually with the Rhewme or the Gout. Who is free from the strokes and murder of theeues, or from the wounds, rapine, and slaughters of Souldiers, worse then theeues? besides that, iust and innocent men are oftentimes wrongfully punished, imprisoned, banished, and cruelly put to death: children are smothered in the cradle, fall into the fire, are drowned in the water, over-run with beasts, poysoned with Spiders, & murdered, or plagued with infection of the ayre, besides divers sicknesses,

and

and other casuall haps: as falling of houses, dearth, famine, thunderbolts, lightning, flouds, and many moe troublesome changes, which sodainly alight vpon all men indifferently.

Whosoeuer thinketh in this life to liue without labour and sorrow, is a Foole: for God hath so appointed our state, that we by vertue of our soule should suffer and subdue all kinds of aduersities. Solon.

Little would we regard the true life of the soule which entereth after it is losed from this life, if this life had any pleasure in it: notwithstanding the innumerable sorrowes and griefes that wee sustaine thereby, we are loth to be rid of it. Zeno.

How can life be of any great value when euery Souldier will sell it for sixe pence? Life is like one dayes imprisonment: for the whole time of our life is but a day, vpon which the night of death commeth. Diogenes.

God hath purposely ordained the griefes, miseries, and sorrowes of this life to be so many and great, and the pleasures thereof so small and few, to make vs the more desirous of the heauenly life which is nothing but ioy and pleasure.

There is none either so great an Orator, or else so mighty an enchanter as life is, for it perswadeth vs the contrary of that which both wee see and feele. For notwithstanding that we know our owne frailtie, and that wee must needes dye, yet what wrongs, what hatreds, what labours, and what greedy deuises, begin we daily and fresh, in hope, or rather assurance of life, to finish and enioy the fruite of our enterprises? Plato.

The flowers of life, which are lusts and pleasures, are false shewes, shadowes, & vanities, and the Seneca.

the fruits thereof, labour, care sicknesse, and te dioušnesse, the tree it selfe, corruption and frailty.

Theophr. What a shame is it for men to complaine upon God for the shortnes of their liues, when as they themselues as short as it is, doe through riot, malice, murthers, cares, and warres, make it much shorter both in themselues and others.

The summme of all.

Life which chaineth the body and soule in one,
Is fraile and vaine, more slipper then the slime,
Heapes full of care, but quiet it hath none:
Ordained of God a prison for a time,
To plague and purge the body and soule from crime,
Which who so spendeth vertuously and well,
Shall after it in ioyes and glory dwell.

Of the world, the pleasures, and dangers thereof. Cap. VI.

Aristotle. The world was created by the diuine prouidence of God.

Plato. The goodnesse of God was cause of the worlds creation.

Hermes. God created this world a place of pleasure and reward, wherefore such as suffer in it aduersity, shall in another world be recompenced with pleasure.

Seneca. This world is a way full of sharpe thistles: wherefore euery man ought to beware how hee walketh for pricking of himselfe.

Hee is not wise, knowing he must depart from this world, that boasteth himselfe therein to make buildings,

This

This world is like a burning fire, whereof a little is good to warme a man, but if hee take too much, it will burne him altogether. Pithagor.

We may vse this world, but if we abuse it, we breake the loue that we haue to God.

He that loueth the world hath great trauaile, but he that hateth it hath great rest.

Print in thy mind, and execute with liuely diligence, the effect of this counsell following: wherein is contained the life and death, the ioy and sorrow, as well in this present miserable world, as also in the other euerlasting world to come. Socrates. Three things thou must diligently note, that is to say: the soule, the body, and the substance of this world. The first place of these three (by good reason) hath the soule, seeing it is a thing immortall, Soule. that is created and made after the figure & shape of the almighty and euerlasting God. The next Body. and second roome hath the body, as the case and sepulchre of the soule, and neerest seruant to the secrets of the spirit. The third roome and place occupieth the riches and goods of this world, as the Goods of this world. necessary instruments or tooles of the body, which cannot want nor lacke such needefull things. Let then the eyes of thine inward minde first, chiefely, and diligently behold the first and best thing in thee, that is thy soule: next vnto that, haue respect vnto thy body: and thirdly, consider the world.

Hee that happily (through grace of the liuing God) keepeth these three in their degrees and due order, shall surely content God, please himselfe, & satisfie the world: first therefore, care for thy soule as thy chiefest iewell and onely treasure: care for thy body, for thy soules sake: care for the world for

thy bodies sake. Take heede aboue all things that thou goest not backeward, as hee doth that first careth to be a rich man: next to be a healthfull man: a thirdly, to be a good man: where he should doe cleane contrary: first, to study for goodnesse: next for health: and last for wealth.

We see by experience so great blindnesse among men that they in such wise care for riches, that very little they care for the health of the body, and nothing at all they minde the state of the soule.

He that loueth the world shall be sure either to displease God, or else to be enuied of mightier men then himselfe.

Mar. Aur. This world is but a passage into the other: wherefore he that prepareth him things necessary for that passage, is sure from all perils.

The world is so mallicious, that if we take not good heed to prepare against his wrinches, it will ouerthrow vs, to our great losse and hurt.

Behold well this world, take warning in time, and marke how they fall that vse to climbe.

Plato. Beware that for the variable and vain delights of this wicked world, thou loose not the ioyfull and euerlasting felicitie.

Periander The man that is mindfull of this world, a hath no consideration of the world to come, must needs be wicked in the sight of God, and a gracelesse man in the sight of men.

Socrates. The loue of this world stoppeth mens eares from hearing wisedome, and blindeth their eyes from seeing through it: also it causeth men to be enuied, and keepeth them from doing any good.

Mar. Aur. The world and the flesh doe nought else but fight against vs, and wee haue neede at all times to defend vs from them.

Man

Man hath neuer perfect rest nor ioy in this world, nor possesseth alwayes his owne winning. Seneca.

O World, thou hast so many countenances in thy vanity, that thou leadest all wandring in vnstablenesse. Mar.Aur.

Trouble not thy selfe with worldly carefulnes, but resemble the birds of the Ayre, which in the morning seeke their foode but only for the day. Socrates.

Fixe not thy minde vpon worldly pleasures, nor trust to the world, for it deceiueth all that put their trust therein.

He that seeketh the pleasures of this world, followeth a shadow: which when he thinketh hee is surest of, vanisheth, and is nothing. Hermes.

This seemeth an vnhappy and cruell destiny, which is giuen vnto this world of misery: that those things which are most excellent and of greatest price in this world, are soonest with violence taken away, as vnworthy for so euill a world. Menander

The children of vanity do abide in the dungion of this world: which is founded vpon the sand. Mar.Aur.

He that delighteth in this world, must needs fall into one of these two griefes, eyther to lacke that which hee coueteth, or else to lose that which hee hath gotten with great paine. Aristotle.

Hee that loueth this world is like one that entereth into the sea, for if he escape the perils, men will say hee is fortunate: but if hee perish, they will say he is wilfully deceiued. Pithagor.

Trust not the world, for it neuer payeth that it promiseth.

He that trusteth to this world is deceiued, and he that is suspitious is in great sorrow.

This world giueth to them that abide, an example, by them that depart. Seneca.

Archelaus. He that yéeldeth himselfe to the world, ought to dispose himselfe to thrée things, which hée cannot auoid. First, to pouerty, for he shall neuer attaine to the riches that he desireth: secondly, to suffer great paine and trouble: thirdly, to businesse without expedition.

Solon. This world hath euer a multitude that honoreth, worshippeth, and magnifieth nothing, besides tedious and short life, and those things that pertaineth to this life.

Euery mete choketh a worldly man, euery little sound maketh a worldly man to tremble & shake.

He is to be called a worldly man that giueth all his care to vse his wits in this world: that creepeth vpon such things as be seene, heard, felt, tasted and smelt: that climbeth not in consideration aboue the midst of this valley.

Hermes. This world is the delight of an houre, and sorrow for many dayes: but in the other world is great rest and long ioy.

Alex. Scu. He that in this world hath a good name, and the grace of God, ought not to aske any other thing.

The vanities of the world are an hinderance to the soule. There is no new thing in this world.

Aristotle. He that fixeth his minde wholly vpon the world léeseth his soule: but hee that thinketh vpon his soule, hateth the world.

The summe of all.

The world is a Region diuers and variable,
Of God created in the beginning
To containe his creatures of kindes innumerable.
Wherein each one should liue by his winning:
But many pleasures are cause of much sinning.
Wherefore all that gladly as vaine doe them hate,
Shall after the world haue a permanent state.

THE

THE THIRD BOOKE.

Of Policie, and gouernment of Common-weales.

Cap. I.

Of the necessity of Order.

SEeing the quietnesse, peace, and bodily wealth (which by meanes of mens vnruly lusts) cannot bée had nor maintayned héere in this world without politike order and gouernment, (for order is the onely preseruer of worldly quietnesse:) seeing also all order standeth in ruling and obeying, wee will in this Booke following, shew whom the Philosophers doe allow for a ruler, and what kind of ruler is best allowed of them: what Policie and Lawes are best to be admitted: and what ministration of obedience thereunto belongeth: that such as be in authority may heereby see the Offices, and that all subiects may know their duties, and performe the same, for the attayning of the said peace, wealth, and quietnesse.

Of

Of Kings, Rulers, and Gouernours, and how they should rule their Subiects. Cap. II.

Aristotle. KIngs, Rulers, and Gouernors (in consideration of their high estate, authoritie, and calling, to the setting forth of vertue and true obedience, and winning to themselues immortall prayse,) should first learne to rule themselues, and then those that be in subiection to their high authority.

Plato. Hee is vnmeete to rule others that cannot rule himselfe.

Phil. Rex. None ought to rule, except he first haue learned to obey.

Mar. Aur. As the life of a Prince is but as a white for all others to shoote at, and as a glasse wherein all the world doth looke: So wee see by experience, that whereunto a Prince is inclined, the people trauelling to follow the same, haue not the grace nor power to eschew the euill, and follow the good.

Mar. Aur. It is a great offence and an immortall infamy to a Prince, that in stead of giuing his hand of good liuing to relieue others, he casteth backward his foot of euill example, whereby he ouerthroweth all others.

The vniuersall Schoole of all this world, is the person, the house, and Court of a Prince.

It behoueth a Prince, or Head-ruler, to be of such zealous and godly courage, that hee alwayes shew himselfe to bee as a strong wall for the defence of the truth: and that hee suffer it not to be abused, nor once to fall vnder his hand.

Those

Those rulers sinne exceedingly, that doe giue others license to sinne.

The greatest that a Prince is of power aboue others, the more ought he to be vertuous aboue all others.

The counsailours and houshold seruants of the Prince, being well tryed, and by his owne examples brought in good order: also the head Officers, Iudges, and all other that haue authoritie in the publike weale, being well chosen and instructed by the example of the Princes court: it would be wonderfull to behold, with how little difficulty and how soone the residue of the weale publike would be brought into a good fashion, all men delighting in vertue, and praising the beautie and commoditie thereof in their superiours: also reioycing at the possibility and gentlenesse of so vertuous & noble a Prince, & semblably dreading his seueritye, they shall (at the last) in such wise bring vertue in custome, whereby it will happen, that such vices as before seemed but little and were nothing regarded, shall become to all men, or at the least to the most part, most filthy and detestable. Alex. Seu.

The Princes pallace is like a common fountaine or spring to his citie or countrey: whereby the people by the cleannesse thereof, be long preserued in honesty, or by the impurenesse thereof are with sundry vices corrupted. And vntill the fountaine be purged, there can neuer be any sure hope of remedy.

A King ought to refraine the company of vicious persons, for the euill which they doe in his company is reputed his. Plutarch.

If thou be a Gouernour, or hast ouer other soueraignty,

soueraigntie, know thy selfe, that is, know that thou art verily man, compact of soule and body, and that all other men be equall vnto thee.

Know also, that euery man taketh with thee equall benefit of the spirit of life: nor hast thou any more of the dew of heauen, or the brightnesse of the Sun, then any other person. The dignitie or authoritie wherein thou differest from others, is as it were but a weighty and heauy cloake, freshly glittering in the eyes of them that be purblinde, where vnto thee it is painful if thou weare it in his right fashion, and as it shall best become thee: and from thee it may be shortly taken of him that did put it on thee, if thou vse it negligently, or that thou weare it not comely and as it behoooueth. Therefore, whiles thou wearest it, know thy selfe: know that the name of a Soueraigne or Ruler, without actuall gouernement, is but a shadow. Gouernment standeth not by word onely, but principally by act and example. By example of gouernours men doe rise or fall into vertue or vice.

Aristotle. Rulers more grieuously doe sinne by example, then by their Act: and the more they haue vnder their gouernance, the greater account haue they to render, that in their owne precepts and ordinances they be not found negligent.

And to put them the more in remembrance of their high estate, authoritie, and calling (and their right order of life, due vnto the same,) here is the minde of Claudianus (a noble Poet, of famous memory) set forth, by the right worthy and worshipfull Sir Thomas Eliot, Knight: in his booke called, The Gouernour.

These

The verses following.

Claudio.

THough thy power stretch both farre and large,
Through Inde the rich, set at the worlds end:
And Mede with Arabia be both vnder thy charge,
And also Seres, that silke to vs doth send,
If feare thee trouble, and small things thee offend,
Corrupt desire thy heart hath once imbraced,
Thou art in bondage, thine honour is defaced.
Thou shalt be deemed then worthy for to raigne,
When of thy selfe thou winnest the masterie,
Euill custome bringeth vertue in disdaine.
License superfluous perswadeth much folly,
In too much pleasure set not felicitie:
If lust or anger doth thy minde assaile,
Subdue occasion, and thou shalt soone preuaile.
What thou mayest doe, delight not for to know,
But rather what thing will become thee best,
Embrace thou vertue, and keepe thy courage low,
And thinke that alway measure is a feast,
Loue well thy people, care also for the least,
And when thou studiest for thy commoditie,
make them all partners of thy felicitie.
Be not much moued with singular appetite,
Except it profit vnto thy subiects all,
At thine example the people will delight,
Be it vice or vertue, with thee they rise and fall.
No lawes auaile, men turne as doth a ball,
For where the ruler in liuing is not stable,
Both Law and Counsell is turn'd into a fable.

Those that haue any authority and gouernment committed to them, ought to know the bounds of their estate and calling, their office and dutie, being

being themselues but men mortall among men, and instructours and leaders of men. And that as obedience is due vnto them, so is their study, their labour, their industry, with vertuous example due to them that be subiect to their authority.

Alex. Seu. Authority ought to be giuen to such as careth least for it: and kept from them which presse fastest towards it: for hee that desireth it would haue it for his onely commoditie: hee that looketh not for it, considereth that he is chosen for others necessitie. Therefore how diuers their ministration is, it euer appeareth whereas both happeneth?

Socrates. A King ought not to trust him that is couetous, which setteth his minde to get riches: nor him that is a flatterer, nor any to whom hee hath done wrong, nor in him that is at truce with his enemies.

Aristotle. It is better for a Realme, Countrey, or Citie to be gouerned by the vertue of a good man, then by a good law.

Plato. Except wise men be made gouernours, or gouernours be made wise men, mankinde shall neuer haue quiet rest, nor vertue be able to defend her selfe.

Happy is that Citie or Countrey, that hath wise men to gouerne it.

Aristotle. Men ought not to be chosen for their age, nor for their riches, but for their wisedome and vertuous conditions.

When wretched worldlings and fooles for their wealth, are rather chosen to rule and gouerne in the common-wealth, then the vertuous, wise, and learned men, it must needes follow, that in steed of fame and honourable report, that should

worthily

worthily redound to the godly and wise Electors, graue and ancient Fathers of the city or country, for their dutifull, carefull, and fatherly choyse, tendring the state of the common-wealth, and the honour of their Prince, vnder whom they haue authority to rule and choose rightly: (For who louing dearely their Prince, whom they know to be wise and vertuous, will choose to rule vnder him a foolish man, hurtfull and vicious?) shame shall then be spoken of them, the buckled browes of maiestie shall be bent against them, the vertuous and wise shall eschew them worthy credit is not to be giuen vnto them, an horrible crime is committed by them: for the Prince and the people are abused by them, the fierce fury of God hangeth ouer them, and the Prince by Gods iustice ought sharpely to punish them: for they are not as they ought to be, faithfull fathers, friends, and fauourers to their country: but step-fathers, very aduersaries, wicked conspirators, and traitors to their Prince and Country. Chilon.

Most miserable is the state of that country and common-wealth, where rich men that be fooles are more commonly chosen, then rich wise men, or poore men enriched with wisedome, to gouerne in the Common-wealth. Protagen.

Reason and godlines deny not, but that it were better that the goods of wicked worldlings or rich foolish men should beare (by true hands, or else by the common treasure) the charges of the poore and vertuous Gouernor (by whom great goodnesse and much honour shall be encreased) rather then the vicious and rich faulty fondling should rule, by whom Common-weales are destroyed, or at the least hindered and defamed. Legmon.

For

For as the Wiseman hath his wisedome vpholdeth the state, and purchaseth wealth, fame, and honour to the City: so the foolish or vngodly man ouerthroweth the state, bringeth losse, shame and dishonour to the City. And if custome (viciously) be the ground of euill choyce to gouerne among a few affectionate, fond, or corrupted persons, that are wealthy, not respecting duely (as they ought) the straight office and dutie of a gouernour: the high state himselfe of most Princely Maiestie ought speedily to redresse that foule enormitie, whereby due obedience is neglected, Godly lawes infringed, iustice not executed, sinne not duely punished, his owne honor impaired, his people with penury impouerished, and the roote is daily nourished, whereby is increased heapes of Gods fury for the plaguing most bitterly both of Prince and Country.

The mis-doings of the Prince are a scourge to the Commons.

What greater ground of disglory? What greater occasion of dishonour? What greater and more huge heapes of mischiefes and inconueniences can be attempted and raised vp against the Maiesty of God, or against the Prince, and the people of God, (in godly common-wealths) then by putting vaine, wicked, and rich worldlings, or only a rich foolish idiot in the Roome of Maiesty, and godly authority, whereas hee himselfe should of all others be most straightly bridled and restrained from his wicked attempts and foolishnesse.

Iustinian. Imperat. It is required in a godly ruler or Magistrate, to be in his calling wise, learned in Gods Law, and in life and conuersation vpright and pure.

An

An vnworthy person to be exalted in dignitie is great wickednesse. Mar. Aur.

Three things are to be pittied, and the fourth not to be suffered: a good man in the hands of a shrew: a wise man vnder the gouernance of a foole: a liberall man in subiection to a caitife: and a foole set in authoritie. Hermes.

Where good order and gouernance faileth, obedience decayeth, boldnesse encreaseth, deceit scapeth, iniurie preuaileth, auarice corrupteth, and the estate of a weale-publike soone after perisheth. Alex. Seu.

Those men that should rule and haue authoritie ouer others, ought to be such persons as neuer were infamed with any notable vice, and whose liues be inculpable, and therewith sufficiently furnished with wisdome and grauitie, void also of all priuate affection, feare, auarice and flatterie: who like Chirurgious shall not forbeare with corrosiues and medicines to draw out the festered & stinking cores of old marmoles, and inueterate sores of the weale publike, engendred by the long custome in vice.

It becommeth a king to take good heed to his counsailors, to finde who follow their lusts, and who intend the common-weale, that hee may then know whom for to trust. Plutarch.

Glorious is that common-wealth, and fortunate is that Prince, that is Lord of yong men to trauaile, and ancient persons to counsell.

Unhappy is that Prince that esteemeth himselfe happy to haue his coffers full of treasure, and his Counsaile full of men of cursed and euill life. Mar. Aur.

All that haue authoritie should temper it with wisedome and purenesse of liuing.

If a King be mercifull his estate shall prosper, and his wisedome shall helpe him in his neede: if he be iust, his subiects shall reioyce in him, and his raigne shall prosper, and his estate continue.

Hermes. The strength of a King is the friendship and loue of his people.

Mar.Aur. When a Prince is greatly beloued of his comminaltie, and is vertuous of his person, then euery man saith, (if he haue not good fortune) although our Prince want good fortune, yet his worthy vertues faile not, and though hee be not happy in his intents, yet at the least hee sheweth his wisedome in the meane season.

And though fortune denieth him at one houre, yet at another time shee agreeth to his wisedome. And contrariwise, an vnwise Prince, and hated of his people, by euill Fortune runneth into great perill.

The Prince is in great perill, and the commonwealth is in euill aduenture, where many intentions be among the Gouernours.

Aristotle. It is a great happinesse to the people, to haue a righteous Prince, and it is a great corruption vnto them to haue a corrupt and vicious Ruler.

Plutarch. A King ought to be of a good courage, to be courteous, free and liberall: to refraine his wrath where he ought, and to shew it where it most needeth: to keepe himselfe from couetousnesse: to execute true iustice, & to follow the vertuous examples of his good Predecessors. And if it chance that the strength of his body faile, yet ought hee to keepe the strength of his courage.

Mar.Aur. Princes liue more surely with the gathering to them men of good liuing and conuersation, then with treasures of money stuffed in their chests.

The

The most secret counsaile of a King, is his owne conscience, & his good deeds are his best treasure. Assaron.

A King most surely gouerneth his Realme, if he raigne ouer his people as a Father doth ouer his children.

A man shall not well gouerne a City or Countrey, and set in good order manners of the people, except hee be well and sufficiently furnished with eloquence, wherewith onely hee may perswade effectually, stirre, incline, and leade where hee listeth the mindes of the grosse multitude. Agesilaus.

Whosoeuer prouideth but for part of the people, and is vnmindfull of the rest, they bring in sedition and discord, a thing most hurtfull to the common-wealth, whereby it commeth to passe, that some doe seeme flatteringly to fawne vpon the people, some affectionate to the Nobilitie, but very few to please and content the whole. Tullius.

Gouernours of the weale publike must obserue these two precepts: the one is, that they so maintaine the profit of the commons, that whatsoeuer in their calling they doe, they must refer it thereunto: alwayes forgetting their owne commodity: the other is, that they be (in any wise) carefull ouer the whole body of the Common-weale: lest while they vphold some one part alone, they leaue all the rest miserably destitute. Plato.

Modestie is a vertue most necessary for all Rulers and Magistrates: whereby in the handling of all matters, they yeeld nothing to affections: but doe follow most aptly that same, which seemeth to be comely, vpright, and allowable. And it is also a meane to restraine them, that in following the rigor of the Law, they doe not ouermuch pinch, or impouerish their poore subiects.

Tullius. A prudent, graue and vpright Gouernour of the Common-wealth, without respect of persons, or part-taking, will rather giue himselfe wholy to the profit and commoditie of the same, then to hunt for riches, or the encrease of honour: for hee wil very gladly and vprightly seeke to defend the whole state, and to make prouision (as wee may) for all men indifferently.

Alex. Sex. He that would be a Ruler or Gouernour should first learne to bee a subiect: for truly a proud and couetous subiect, shall neuer be a gentle and temperate Gouernour.

Next vnto God, who is so great a father, as he who is the Father of a whole country? that is, Father of them that be Fathers, their Children, and whole Families? how much then ought the care of him to exceed the cares of all others, the charitie of him, the loue of all others? the wisedome of him, the prudence of all others?

Democrit. Rule and authority in a good man doth publish his vertue, which before lay hid: in an euill man, it ministreth boldnes and licence to do euill, which by dread was before couered.

Alex. Seuerus. He that exerciseth his office duely, vprightly and circumspectly in the Common-weale, at the end, when he shall depart and leaue his office, the publike weale shall be bound to pray for him, & to render vnto him most due and hearty thankes.

The office of Kings is to heare the complaints and causes of all persons without exception.

Phil. Rex. So great is the person and dignity of a King, that in vsing his power & authority as he ought, he representeth among men here vpon the Earth the glorious state and high Maiesty of God in Heauen.

Vnder

Under the King are both free and bondmen, and they be both subiect to his power, and are all vnder him: and he is a certaine creature that is not vnder man, but onely vnder God.

The King hath no Peere or equall in his Kingdome: he hath no equall, for then he should lose his dignitie and authority of commanding, since that an equall hath no rule nor commandement ouer his equall.

The King himselfe ought not to be vnder man, but vnder God & the Law, because the Law maketh a King. Let the King therefore attribute that vnto the Law, that the law attributeth vnto him, that is, dominion and power: for he is not a King, in whom Will, and not the Law, doth rule; and therefore he ought to be vnder the Law, seeing he is the Vicegerent of God here vpon the Earth.

Who so commeth to the office of a King, armed aforehand, with the Precepts of Philosophy cannot lightly swerue from the right trade and pathway of vertue.

The chiefe act of a King is to reiect no person, but to make all persons profitable to the Common-weale.

Wise Princes may make very profitable instruments, as well of the euill persons as of the good.

A Kings good word is better then a great gift of another man.

Kings must loue honest persons, and punish the vnhonest.

Nothing can be to a Prince more royall, then if he make the state of the Realme better then it was before it came into his hands.

Malicious and euill men make Princes poore,

and one perfect good man sufficeth to make an whole Realme rich.

A Prince that is godly and vertuous, is the glory of his fathers age.

Zeno. A good Prince differeth nothing from a good father.

Protogeus. An euill disposed King is like corrupted carren that maketh the earth to stincke round about it: and the King that is good and vertuous, is like the fayrest swéete running riuer, that is commodious and comfortable to euery creature.

Pithagoras Subiects are to their King as the winde is to the fire, for the stronger that the winde is, the greater is the fire.

Plato. As a small spot or freckle in the face, is a greater blemish then a scar or knot in the body: so a small fault in a Prince séemeth worse then a greater in a priuate person.

As a shepheard among his shéepe, so ought a King to be among his subiects.

Hermes. Like as a small disease, except it be looked to in time and remedied, may be the destruction of the whole body: so if Rulers be negligent, and looke not to small things whereupon greater doe depend, and sée them reformed in due time, they shall suffer the Common-weale to decay, and not be able to reforme when they gladly would.

Socrates. Like as the rule ought to be straight and iust, by which other rulers ought to be tryed, so ought a Gouernour who should gouerne others, to bee good, vertuous, honest, and iust himselfe.

Plato. Like as the Sun is all one both to poore and rich: so ought a Prince not to haue respect to the person, but to the matter.

Euen as a good gardiner is very diligent about his

his Garden, watering the good and profitable hearbs, and rooting out the vnprofitable weedes: so should a King attend to his Common-weale, cherishing his good and true subiects, and punishing such as are false and vnprofitable.

Ye kings, remember first your King the Gouernour of all: & as you would be honoured of your Subiects so honour you him. Use no familiaritie with any vicious persons. Trust none with your secrets before you haue proued them. Sleepe no more then shall suffice the sustentation of your bodies. Loue righteousnesse & truth. Embrace wisedom. Feed measurably. Use no excesse in apparel. Hermes.

Remember that good gouernance is in vertue, and not in beautie and costly apparell. Reward your trustie friends. Fauour your comminaltie, considering that by it your Realmes are maintained. Loue learned men, that the ignorant may thereby be encouraged to learning. Defend the true and iust, and punish the euill doers, that others admonished thereby, may flie the like vices. Cut off stealers hands. Hang vp Theeues and robbers, that the high wayes may be sure. Burne the Sodomites. Stone the adulterers. Beware of lyers and flatterers, and punish them. Suffer not swearers to escape vnpunished. Visit your prisons, and deliuer the vnguilty persons: punish immediatly such as haue deserued it.

Follow not your owne wils, but be ruled by counsaile: so shall you giue your selues rest, & labour vnto others. Bee not too suspicious: for that shall both disquiet your selues, and also cause men to draw from you.

The authoritie of Princes & gouernors (which properly depend vpon the authoritie of God, is

truely to be called Temporarie, that is, but for a time, because of the alteration and weakenesse of worldy matters, and the ordering of them: when that hee which is this day greatly aduanced for his authoritie, is sodainely the next day ouerthrowne, as appeareth to be nothing at all.

The summe of all.

A King which in earth is euen the same
That God is in heauen, of Kings King eterne,
Should first feare God, and busily frame
Himselfe to rule, and then his Realme gouerne
By law, by loue, by iustice, and by right:
Cherishing the good, and punishing the stubborne,
The lengthening of his raigne, doubling of his might.

Of Counsell or Councellors. Cap. III.

Aristotle. Counsell is an holy thing.

Counsell is the aduise particularly giuen by euery man, for that purpose assembled.

Plato. Counsell is the key of certainty.

Socrates. There cannot be in man a more diuine thing, then to ask counsel how he should order himselfe.

It is to be diligently noted, that euery counsell is to be approued by three things principally: that is, that it be righteous, that it be good, and that it stand with honestie. That which is righteous is brought in by reason: for nothing is right that is not ordered by reason. Goodnesse commeth of vertue: of vertue & reason proceedeth honestie, wherefore counsell being compact of these three, may be named a perfect captaine, a trusty companion, a plaine and vnfained friend.

The

The reward for diuers seruices a man may make, but the reward for good Counsell God had neede to doe it. Mar.Aur.

The greatest reward that one friend may doe to another, is in great and waightie matters to succour him with good counsell.

Hee that giueth good counsell to another, beginneth to profit himselfe. Isocrates.

The most easie thing in the World is to giue good counsell to another, and the most hard and highest thing is, a man to take it for himselfe.

There is no man so simple but hee may giue good counsell though there be no neede, and there is none so wise, that will refuse counsell in time of necessitie.

When thou dost amisse take better counsell. Titus Liu.

Many things be impeached or let by nature: which by counsell be shortly atchieued.

Without counsell see thou doe nothing, and then after thy deede thou shall neuer repent thee.

Follow rather dangerous honestie, then secure vtilitie: albeit that indeede vtilitie can hardly be discerned from honestie. Seguuins.

Be not ashamed to take counsell in small matters euery houre. Legmon.

The end of all doctrine & study is good counsell.

When counsell is taken of diuers, then if any fault bee, it shall be diuided amongst them all. Mar.Aur. Though the determination might be done by a few, yet take counsell of many: for one will shew thee all the inconueniences, another the perils, another the damages, another the profit, and another the remedie. And set thine eyes as well vpon the inconueniences that they say, as vpon the remedie that they offer.

The

Mar. Aur. The Counseller that hath his minde ouercome with ire, and his heart occupied with enuie, and his wordes outragious to a good man: it is reason that hee loose the fauour of God, his priuity with his Prince, and his credence with the people: for hee presumeth to offend God with his euill intention, to serue the Prince with euill counsell, and to offend the common-wealth with his ambition.

Mar. Aur. That publike weale is in better state where the Prince is void of grace, then where the Kings counsailors and companions be euill and wicked.

Protogeus. It is not conuenient that he which is called to the high estate of a Counsailer should spend all the night in sleepe, or whole day in pastime.

Aug. Cæs. Hee is to be called a good Counsailour, which while he consulteth in doubtfull matters, is voyd of all hate, friendship, displeasure, or pitty.

Wrath and hastinesse be very euill counsailors.

Alex. Seu. Those counsailours seeme to be vertuous, wise, and honourable, which can content themselues and reioyce, that they haue so wise and vertuous a Prince that preferreth the weale of his people before any priuate affection or singular appetite.

Where there is a great number of counsailours, they all being heard, needes must the counsell be the more perfect.

Tullius. In things most prosperous, the counsell of friends must be vsed.

Protogeus He that giueth counsell, and praiseth himselfe, would faine be called a wise man.

Isocrates. If thou wouldest know a mans counsel in any matter, and wouldest not haue him to know thine intent, talke as the matter were another mans, so shalt thou know his iudgement therein, and hee neuer the wiser of that thou intendest.

Take

Take no counsell of him that hath his heart all set vpon the world, for his aduice shall be after his pleasance. Seneca.

When thou wilt take counsell in any matter, marke well thy Counsailours how they order their owne businesse: for if they be euill counsailours towards themselues, they will bee worse counsailours towards other men.

Their counsailes must needes be alwayes full of perturbations, which are onely embracers of their owne aduice. Cobarus.

Good counsell is the beginning and ending of euery good worke. Zenoph.

Consult and determine all things with thy friend, but first with thy selfe. Seneca.

Giue blamelesse counsell, and comfort thy friends.

He is discreete that keepeth his owne Counsell. And he is vnwise that discouereth it.

Make not an angry man, nor a drunkard of thy counsell, nor any that is in subiection to a woman, for it is not possible they should keepe thy secrets. Socrates.

Hee that keepeth secret that which hee is required doth well, but hee that keepeth secret that which he is not required, is to be trusted. Aristotle.

Hee which shall giue counsell, specially to the making of lawes, ought to consider foure things: that his counsell bee honest, that it be necessary, profitable, and possible. Alex.Seu.

A wise man ought to take counsell, for feare of mixing his will with his wit. Socrates.

They that consult for part of the people, and neglect the residue, doe bring into the Citie or Countrie a thing most pernicious, that is to say, sedition and discord. Tullius.

Ambition

Alex.Seu. Ambition and flattery are vtterly to be abhorred in a Counseller.

Homer. Like as Calchas (as Homer writeth) knew by diuination things present, things to come, and things that were passed: So Counsellours garnished with learning, and also experience, shall thereby consider the places, times, and personages, examining the state of the matter then practised, and expending the power, assistance, and substance: also resoluing long and oftentimes in their mindes, things that bee passed, and conferring them to the matters that bee in experience studiously doe seeke out the reason & manner, how that which is by them approued may be brought to effect: and such mens reasons would be throughly heard, and at length. For the wiser that a man is, in tarrying, his wisdome increaseth, his reason is more liuely, and quicke sentences aboundeth. And to the more part of men, when they bee chafed in reasoning, arguments, solutions, examples, similitudes, and expediments, doe resort and (as it were flow vnto their remembrance.

Hermes. As a Phisician cannot cure his patient except he knoweth first the truth of his disease: euen so may a man giue no good counsell, except he know thorowly the effect of the matter.

The summe of all.

Counsell is a thing so needfull and holy;
That without it no worke may prosper well,
Wherefore it behoueth him that hateth folly,
Nought to begin, without he take counsell.
Which who so vseth shall neuer him repent,
Of time, of trauell, that he therein hath spent.

Of

Of Honour, Glorie, Nobilitie, and Worship. Cap. IIII.

First, and aboue all things, let men consider that from God onely proceedeth all honour, glory, nobility, and worship, and that noble progenie, succession, nor election, to be of such force, that by them any estate or dignitie may bee so established, that God being stirred to vengeance, shall not shortly resume it, and perchance translate it, where it shall like him.

All things liuing both in Heauen and Earth, oweth vnto God due Worship and Obedience. There be two most speciall and weighty causes why God ought to be honoured and worshipped, the one is, because he ought of duty to be worshipped: and the other, because it is for our commodity, yea rather for our necessity. Solon.

To worship God, and to serue him truely, is, to gratifie him, or to be thankefull vnto him. And no man can rightly gratifie him, but by doing that which pleaseth him. Wherefore all kinde of worship which is rather grounded vpon the will of man, then vpon the will of God, it is to bee vtterly refused in his sight: and imputed as vaine before him, ingratefull, hurtfull, and void.

Who will say that he serueth well which serueth not according to his masters will, but as he lusteth himselfe, doth not the very instinct of nature it selfe, the reason also of seruice, the subiection of Seruants, and the common opinion of all men shew, that as the bodily Master ought to be reuerently serued and obeyed, much rather the

high

high and puissant God that ruleth ouer all.

Socrates. God ought to bée worshipped and serued as he himselfe commaundeth to be worshipped and serued.

They are to be counted but foolish, that doe estéeme the seruice of GOD to consist in those things which be rather instituted by the deuice of man, then of God himselfe. Let therfore the wise and godly consider wel with themselues, whether the seruice and worship they doe vnto God (as a worke of holinesse and dutie) be worthy his will and acceptation, and whereby the conscience of a faithfull man may be quieted and assuredly well perswaded of the onely good will of God.

August. The sincere and vncorruptible seruice of God is done but in a few. He cannot be a true seruer of God, which serueth him not in the spirit of his minde, and in truth, but fantastically, and in hipocrisie, as a beastly slaue and a counterfayter of Gods seruice.

True worship of God (which is done in spirit and in trueth) requireth not any outward or worldly beauty, but rather a spirituall beauty and comelinesse.

Plato. Honour is the fruit of vertue and trueth, and for the truth a man shall be worshipped.

Mar.Aur. That thing is honourable and good, which commeth of good kinde. He is to bee honoured among them that be honoured, that fortune abateth without fault: and he is to be ashamed among them that be ashamed, that Fortune inhauncheth without merit.

The worthy honour resteth not in the dignities that we haue, but in the good workes whereby we merit.

Honour

Honour ouer great, wherein is statelinesse and too much pride, be euen like great and corporate bodies, sodainely throwen downe. Plutarch.

Honour, glory, and renowne, are to many persons more sweet then life. Phil Rex.

The neerest way to attaine glory, is, for a man to endeauour himselfe to be such a one indeede as he would be counted to be. Socrates.

True glory taketh deepe roote, and spreadeth abroad, but all counterfait things doe wither as little flowers: neyther can there any forged thing be durable. Tullius.

He that to his noble linage addeth vertue and good conditions, is highly to be praised.

Humilitie is the sister of Nobilitie.

He is worthy to be honoured that willeth good to euery man: and he much vnworthy honor, that seeketh his owne wealth, and oppresseth others.

Honours, riches, pleasures, and others of the same kinde) which seeme profitable) are neuer to be preferred before friendship. Tullius.

Nobilitie is not onely in dignitie and auncient linage, nor great reuenewes, lands, or possessions: but in wisedome, knowledge and vertue, which in man is very nobilitie, and that nobilitie bringeth man to dignitie.

Honour ought to be giuen to vertue, and not to riches. Anacharsis.

All men haue care ouer their owne honour: but as for Gods honour, no man at all regardeth it.

It is a shame for a man to desire honor, because of his noble progenitors, and not to deserue it by his owne vertue. Chrisost.

They that be perfectly wise, despise worldly honour.

Where

Plato. Where riches are honoured, good men are despised.

Hee that honoureth rich men despiseth wisedome.

An asswager of wrong ought greatly to be honoured.

Mar. Aur. Hee is worthy to be honoured that deserueth honour.

Pelion. They are to be counted chiefely honourable, that in their high estate and calling, first seeke the honour and glory of God, by whom they are called to honour: secondly, the honour of their Prince, vnder whom they haue authoritie to rule: and thirdly, for the comfortable state of their Country and common-wealth, for whom they are called to office and dignitie.

It is very honourable, excellent, and praiseworthy, for a man of honour, to ioyne to his high office and calling, the vertue of affabilitie, lowlinesse, tender compassion and pittie, for thereby he draweth vnto him (as it were violently) the hearts of the multitude.

The true honour and worship is the vertue of the minde, which honour no King can giue thee, nor no flattering nor money can purchasse thee. This honour hath in it nothing fained, nothing painted, nor nothing hid. Of this honour there is no successor, no accuser, nor defiler. This honour is not varied nor it esteemeth not the fauour nor dis-fauour of Princes.

Diogenes: Vaine pleasure lightly perisheth, but true honour is immortall.

Socrates. Glory, Honour, Nobilitie, and Riches, are to cloake maliciousnesse.

Mar. Aur. The glory of one, among great men, maketh

strife

strife, suspition among them that be equall, and enuy among them that be meane.

Neuer commit thine honour to the mishaps of Fortune, nor neuer offer thy selfe to perill with hope of remedie. For suspitious Fortune keepeth alwayes her gates wide open to perill. All her walles be high, and her wickets narrow to finde any remedie.

Noble men, and such as are rich and wealthy in this world, are to be compared to a merchants Compters, that is to day worth thousands, and to morrow not worth two-pence halfe-penny.

The glory of the ancestors, is a goodly treasure to their children.

Immortall honor is better then transitorie riches.

Aboue and before all things worship God.

The worship of God consisteth not in words but in deedes.

It is a right honourable and blessed thing to serue God and sanctifie his Name. Pithagor.

Worship good men, so shalt thou haue the peoples fauour.

Nobilitie is not after the vulgar opinion of men, but it is only the praise and surname of vertue.

The sufferance of Noble men to be spoken vnto, is not onely to them an incomparable suertie, but also a confounder of repentance (an enemie to prudence) whereof is engendred this word, Had I wist: which hath beene euer of all wise men reproued.

The perfect and most principall glory consisteth in these three things: If the multitude loueth vs, if also as it were meruailing at vs they thinke vs worthy to haue honour giuen vnto vs. Tullius.

The summe of all.

The honour and glory that worldlings desire,
Surmounting others in riches and dignitie
Cannot long flourish, but they with small hire
Shall end their dayes in wofull miserie.
But vertue sustayneth no such calamitie,
Therefore or euer thou desire honour,
Call for grace to be thy gouernour.

Of Law and Lawyers. Cap.V.

Iustinian. The Law (as Iustinian saith, lib. 1. Pandect) is a facultie or science of the thing that is good or right.

Celsus. Celsus defineth that the law is a rule to doe well by: which ought to be known, and kept of all men.

Cicero de lege, saith, that the law is a certaine rule, proceeding from the minde of God, perswading right and forbidding wrong.

Alex.Seu. Lawes be nothing else then rules of Iustice, whereby is commanded what should be done, and what ought not to be done, where a weale publike should prosper.

Hermes. Law is the finder and tryer out of truth.

Aristotle. The law of the Spirit is to be vnderstood by faith, or the law of faith by which a man is deliuered from the second death, wherein sinne is condemned, and whereunto life may be ascribed, because that in remitting of sinne, it deliuereth from death, and giueth life.

The grace & law of the spirit, furnished with the strength of God, doth iustifie the wicked, reconcileth the damned, and giueth life to the dead.

Nature

Nature is the fountaine, wherof the Law springeth: and it is according to nature, no man to doe that whereby he should make (as it were) a pray of another mans ignorance. Tullius.

Such lawes by men are sometimes made, which rightly may be called the lawes of God. As when a law being made by man, taketh his principall ground vpon the law of God, and is made for the declaration or confirmation of mans true faith: and to remoue from the godly all wicked opinions and heresies, or such light lawes, Canons, or other lewd ordinances, reared vp in darkenesse and ignorance by vngodly men, or by the common people vnlearned in the Law of God, to the hinderance of the said faith, or stopping the way to vertue, and that letteth the procéedings or spéedy prospering of rightfull and holy lawes. And to such godly purposes they are rather called the lawes of God, then the lawes of man.

Whatsoeuer is righteous in the Law of man, the same is also righteous in the Law of God. For euery law, that by man is made, must euer be consonant to the Law of God. And therefore the Lawes of Princes, the commandements of Prelates, the statutes of comminalties, ne yet the ordinances of the godly multitude, are neither righteous nor obligatory, vnlesse they be aptly consonant to the Lawes of God: For by it is truely knowne to whom right belongeth in any respect, and whereunto also Iustice orderly beareth his full force and sway.

The law of God is left vnto all posterities, to touch the consciences of all men without respect: because they cannot (by Gods iudgement) be excused which doe sinne against right and equity. Horace.

Law and wisedome are two laudable things, for the one concerneth vertue, and the other good conditions.

The Law necessary for a common wealth, is, that the people among themselues liue in peace and concord, without discord or dissention.

Tullius. It shall be expedient for gouernours to haue in remembrance, that when according to the Lawes they doe punish offenders, they themselues be not chafed nor moued with wrath: but be like to the Lawes, which be prouoked to punish, not by wrath or displeasure, but onely by equity.

Law is the Quéene of mortalitie.

Socrates. Lawes ought to be made for no mans pleasure.

S. Bridget. in lib. 40. Cap. 129. Euery good law is ordained to the health of the soule, to the fulfilling of the lawes of God, to induce the people to flée euill desires, and to be fruitfull in all good workes.

The Law must be correspondent to the originall decrée of nature, or the first example of honestie.

Tho. Aqu. The Law of nature is nothing else, but the participation of the eternall Law in the reasonable creature.

God hath grauen the law of nature in euery mans minde, to frame (as it were) thereby a shew and comelinesse of manners.

Where good law and order is, all things prosper well.

Where the order of the law may serue, weapons hath no place.

Plato. A law-maker ought to be godly, learned, and wise, and such a one as hath béene subiect to other lawes.

God

God is the causer that lawes be made. Antist.

God is the law of sober men.

Wise men liue not after the lawes of men but after a rule to vertue. Anaxag.

Lawes of men may be likened to copwebs, which doe tie or hold the little flyes fast, but the great flies breake forth and escape.

Cities must néedes perish, when the common lawes be of none effect.

An euill law, and the loue of a shrew, are like vnto the shadow of a cloud, which vanisheth away as soone as it is séene. Seneca.

The Law that is perfect and good, would haue no man condemned nor yet iustified, vntill his cause were both throughly heard and knowne. Boëtius.

The whole body of the Law ciuill hath these thrée principles, (that is to say) liue honestly, hurt no man, and giue vnto euery man his due.

He that maketh his realme subiect to a law shall raigne, and he that maketh the law subiect to a Realme, may hap to raigne a while, but he that casteth the Law foorth from his Realme, casteth foorth himselfe. Iustinian.

Breake not the lawes made for the wealth of the Countrey.

Indeauour thy selfe so to kéepe the Law, that God may be pleased with thée. Aristotle.

The Law of God cannot be truely kept with heart, if by déed it be despised: For no man kee-peth the Law with heart, vnlesse he loue the law: and he that loueth the Law, doth according to the nature of loue, and fulfilleth it to the vttermost of his power. Pithagor.

There is in the law two points, first doctrine to teach, and next an authority to command & compel.

The way to blisse is to loue all men, and to be subiect to the lawes, but to obey God more then man.

As a sicke man is cured of his disease by vertue of a medicine: so is an euill man healed of his malice by vertue of the Law.

The summe of all.

Lawes be the rules of Iustice and equitie,
Whereby we vnderstand our charge and duetie,
To loue with due order, with peace, and amitie,
As God and nature our hearts hath bound:
And that praise also may worthily redound
To such as make lawes through wisedome and vertue,
Authorizing ministers both faithfull and true.

Of Iudges. Cap. VI.

Mar. Aur. The authority of a Iudge giuen to him by his Prince, ought to be his accessary, and his good life his principle, in such manner, that by the rectitude of his iustice the euill should feele execution thereof.

It is better for a man to iudge after law and learning, then after his owne mind & knowledge.

Diogenes. A Iudge sitting in iudgement (being wise) ought to remember that he is but a man: and to consider also that so much as is committed vnto him, is at all times lawfull for him to accomplish.

Cicero. And to remember that not onely power, but credit is also giuen vnto him, and not to appoint that which is not according to the Law: and therewith diligently also to marke what matter it is which is in controuersie. Both these things are much

to

to bée noted. And also, it is the poynt of a iust Judge, to entertaine néere about him these foure very noble and worthy Counsailors, namely, the Law, Fidelitie, Religion, and Equitie: and to separate farre from him these false deceiuers, that is to say, concupiscence, feare, enuie, and all vnlawfull desires.

He is an vniust Judge, that doth things eyther of enuy, or of fauour.

Judges inclined to gréedinesse and corruption, are oft times pulled away from their presences by the multitude of bribes and gifts.

What thing can be more monstrous, then that Judges should ordaine men to put away euill customes from them that be euill, when they themselues be the inuenters of new vices. Mar. Aur.

Such persons are to be chosen for Judges as are learned in the Lawes, as be ancient, and such as be knowne to be of good conscience, and vnto them is to be appointed an honourable stipend. Alex. Seu.

We be admonished to iudge our selues, not according vnto the reckoning of mans iudgement, but according to the infallible censure of God.

When the Judge giueth sentence, hee must remember that God is his sure witnesse, that is to say, the beholder inwardly of his owne secret conscience, then the which, God hath giuen nothing vnto man that is more diuine and heauenly. Cicero.

The iudgements of God are many and secret, but they are all true, holy, and good.

Both hatred, loue, and couetousnesse, causeth Judges oftentimes to forget truth, and leaue vndone the true execution of their due and straight charge. Aristotle.

They are worthy to bée accounted wicked

Iudges, who eyther of errour, affection, corruption or negligence doe discharge the wicked, and condemne the iust and innocent.

Socrates. Whatsoeuer it shall chance thee to heare, thine eye not consenting and knowledging the same, beleeue not, nor hastily credit thine eare, but beleeue and giue iudgement rather by thine eye.

Bias. It is better for a man to be a Iudge among his enemies then among his friends. For of his enemies hee may make one his friend, but among his friends he shall make one his enemie.

Mar. Aur. Certainly the Iudge that winneth more good-wils then money, ought to be beloued: and he that serueth for money, and loseth the good-wils for euer, ought to be abhorred as the pestilence.

Alex. Scu. Couetousnesse and wrath in Iudges are to be hated with extreame detestation.

Mar. Aur. The Iudges to whom is giuen authoritie to redresse and amend wrongs, be they that otherwhiles cause more griefes, and stirre vp greater mischiefes.

He that is not deceiued by flatterers, that is not corrupted with gifts, and not forgetfull of his vnderstanding, that man may rightly be called a good Iudge.

The summe of all.

Iudges to whom authoritie is giuen,
From their liege Lord and most deere Soueraigne,
To rule rightly his Lawes they should be driuen:
By wisedome and learning chiefly to refraine
From couetise that hath truth in disdaine
For Iudges that should ease and asswage many griefes,
Are sometime th'occasion of great mischeifes.

Of

Of Iustice and Iniustice, Cap. VII.

IUstice properly is nothing else then a confor-mitie of all things in the reasonable creature to the law of Gods minde, by which is commanded that God be loued aboue all things, and that a man loue his neighbour as himselfe. Mar. Cels.

Iustice is not onely a portion or piece of vertue, but it is entirely the same vertue, and thereof onely (saith Tully) men be called good men: as who saith, without iustice all other qualities and ver-tues cannot make a man good. Aristotle. Tullius.

Iustice is a will perpetuall and constant, which giueth to euery man his right. In that it is na-med constant, it importeth fortitude in discerning what is right or wrong, Prudence is required. And to proportion the iudgement or sentence in an equalitie, it belongeth to temperance: all these together conglutinated, and effectually executed, make a perfect definition of iustice. Seneca.

The most excellent and incomparable vertue called Iustice, is so necessary and expedient for a ruler and gouernor of a publike weale, that with-out it none other vertue can be commendable, nor wit, nor any manner of doctrine profitable.

The foundation of perpetuall praise and re-nowne is Iustice: without the which nothing can be commendable. Which sentence is verified by experience: for be a man neuer so valiant, so wise, so liberall or bounteous, so familiar or curteous: if hee be seene to exercise Iniustice or wrong, it is often remembred: but the other vertues bee seldome reckoned without an exception. Which is in this manner: as in praising a man for some Tullius.

good

good qualitie, when hee lacketh iustice, men will commonly say, He is an honorable man, a bounteous man, a wise man, a valiant man, sauing that he is an oppressour, an extortioner, or is deceitfull, and of his promise vnsure. But if he be iust, with the other vertues, then it is said: he is good and worshipful, or he is a good man and an honorable good and gentle, good and hardie: so that Iustice onely beareth the name of good, and like a Captaine or leader, exceedeth all vertues in euery commendation.

These be the words of a Prince that sendeth forth any person with the charge of Iustice.

Aug. Cæs. I put not the confidence of mine honour into thine hands, nor commit to thee my Iustice, to be destroyer of innocents, nor an executioner of sinners, but that with one hand, thou shalt helpe the good, to maintaine them therein, & with the other hand to helpe to raise them that bee euill from their wickednesse. And mine intention is, to send thee forth to be a protector of Orphants, and an aduocate for Widdowes, a Chirurgion for all wounds, a staffe for the blinde, and a Father to euery person, to speake faire to mine enemies and to reioyce my friends.

Would God these wordes were well planted in the hearts of all Princes, Rulers, Iudges, and Iusticiaries

Mar. Aur. Euery Prince committing charge of Iustice to him that he seeth vnable to execute the same, or doth not principally for iustice sake accomplish iustice, but doth it for his owne profit, or else to please the partie, thinke surely, when the Prince doth not regard this, by some way that he thinketh least of, hee shall see his honour infamed, his credence lost, his goods deminished, and some great chastisement come to his house.

Mar. Aur. It is an vngodly thing to commit the authoritie of

of iustice into the hands of an vniust man.

The vniust men doe great iniustice to speake euill of them that be iust, and specially of God, for he is most iust.

As God doth neuer vniust things, so man neuer lightly doth any iust thing.

Nothing ought to be promised, which should be in any wise contrary to iustice. Tullius.

Aray thy selfe with iustice, and cloathe thee with chastity, so shalt thou be happy, and thy workes prosper. Seneca.

Use iustice, and thou shalt be both beloued, and also feared.

All that is done by iustice, is well done: but all that is done otherwise, is euill.

Iustice is a measure which God hath ordained vpon the earth to defend the feeble from the mighty, and the true from the vntrue, and to roote out the wicked from among the good. Plato.

No man can be iust that dreadeth death, paine, banishment, oppression, or pouerty: or any that before equity preferreth the contraries. Tullius.

Sweet hope followeth him that liueth holily and iustly, nourishing his heart, and cherishing his old age, and comforting him in all his miseries. Alex. Seu.

None delighteth in iustice, but the iust man.

If thou haue alwayes respect vnto iustice, and consider the causes with a prudent minde, the great knowledge of the Law ciuill shall not much trouble thee. Homer.

Hee that vprightly intendeth to the common weale may well be called iust: but he that intendeth to his owne onely profit is a vicious person.

Without iustice no Realme may prosper.

Without iustice no city may long be inhabited.

We

Bee not ashamed to doe iustice, for all that is done without it, is tyranny.

Two manner of wayes all iniuries are done: the one is with-holding anothers right: and the other in taking away anothers right.

Mar.Aur. Euery man in generall loueth Iustice, yet they all hate the execution thereof in particular.

Zeno. There is neither iustice nor friendship in them among whom nothing is common.

Alex. Seu. The rigour of Iustice which seemeth to bee in Princes, in punishing offenders against the weale-publike, is but a forme of discipline conuenient & necessary, hauing regard to such persons as be found corrupted with all kinds of vice, and hauing their mindes and wits all disposed to folly, which being a generall detriment, Princes should vse therein a more sharpe remedie, and therefore consequently, it should bee found the more conuenient and speedie.

Mar.Aur. It is a great custome, and righteous iustice, he that willingly draweth to sinne, against his will should be drawne to paine.

Phil.Rex. Haynous transgressions must of necessitie bee suppressed by due iustice, correction, and punishment.

The chiefe cause why euill and mischieuous men ought to be punished in this life is, that other being restrained with the feare of the penalty, may abstaine from sinne, and that the quietnesse also and safety of mans life may be preserued.

Iustice exalteth the people: but sufferance to sinne, maketh the people most wretched and miserable.

Like as a good Prince is allwayes most gratious, most fauourable, and bounteous vnto all such

as

as bee sincere in their ministrations, and suppor-ters of equity: so is the rigorous, sharpe and terrible to such as be corrupt Judges, and oppressours of Justice.

There is nothing to bee more abhorred then the selling of Justice, which knoweth no reward: How much more intollerable is the selling of iniustice, or wrong, whereby the one part suffereth dammage by sustaining of wrong, to other is more indammaged by leasing of his good name, and also his money (if it happen) as it hath done oftentimes by a good and righteous Gouernour, that he which hath done wrong, bee compelled to make restitution. Alex. Seu.

There bee two kindes of iniustice, the one is of such as doe wrongfully offer it, and the other is of those, who although they be able, doe not defend the wrong from them vnto whom it is wickedly offered. Tullius.

Like as extortioners and bribers are to be impouerished, so good men & iust are to be inriched.

As the cutting of Vines, and all other Trees, is cause of better and more plentifull fruit: so the punishment of the bad, causeth the good to flourish

There is nothing more impossible to correct, then the manners of him who will seeme to know all things, and yet contemning the good, will only imbrace those things that be euill.

Men that haue not in themselues a perfect and sound minde, are to be vtterly reiected, as corrupted both in iudgement and in minde. And if there come from them any appearance of wisdome, it shall tend rather to the doing of mischiefe, then to the doing of any goodnesse.

As the vertue of Justice maketh clemency the

more

more excellent and noble: so on the other side clemencie also maketh Iustice the more amiable and seemely.

Alex.Seu. Iustice maketh lawes and not lawes Iustice: also he that readeth the law seeth the commandement of Iustice, but seeing the Law onely in that, that he seeth it, he doth know Iustice. But contrariwise, he that knoweth Iustice, by her may he discerne what is right, or what is wrong: what is equall or vnequall, and by the patterne of Iustice may inuent a remedy proper or necessary, which expressed in word or writing may be called a law.

The knowledge of Iustice eyther happeneth by speciall influence from the high God, or else it is gotten with the studie of wisdome, comprehended in the Bookes of wise men: who of Pithagoras were called Philosophers, which doth signifie the louers of wisdome: wherefore they which by diuine inspiration, or by study of the workes of excellent wise men, haue the true knowledge of Iustice and haue best vnderstanding what is iust, and consequently can prouide remedies according to Iustice. Which remedies if they once be made vniuersall, they bee Lawes, howsoeuer they bee pronounced, be it by a multitude, or by one person.

The summe of all.

The vertue of Iustice both precious and incomparable,
Should be fast fixed in the hearts of all Gouernors,
Without which vertue nothing may be commendable.
Before God the King, and the higher powers,
Or otherwise reliefe to base inferiours.
For the wicked and vniust man that hath iustice to keepe
To defraud the poore righteous, full closely doth creepe.

Of

Of Parents, and bringing vp of youth. Cap. VIII.

VVhat manner children shall be borne lyeth in no mans power, but the right bringing vp that they may prooue good lieth in his power. Licurgus.

Parents that indeed are good parents, ought to know how to bring vp their children. Mar. Aur.

If thou hast vnder thee a charge of children and family, bring them vp reuerently, in obedience and chastitie.

So prepare for thy children in their youth, that they afterwards fall not to wickednesse, and then their sinne to be imputed vnto thee,

It is to be imputed vnto bringers vp of children if afterwards they prooue to be well mannered, or otherwise, Philip.

Those parents are to be blamed, that are very carefull to heape vp riches, and take no care for the good bringing vp of their children.

Good bringing vp is the head of good manners. Socrates.

Good bringing vp maketh a man well disposed.

Hee is perfect which to his good bringing vp ioyneth other vertues.

It is not possible for him to be of vertuous disposition, that is wealthy and wantonly brought vp in rioting and pleasures. Seneca.

Noble wits corrupted in bringing vp, prooue more vnhappy then other that be more simple. Plutarch.

The childe is not bound to his parents of whom hee hath not learned some good thing.

This all men (naturally) receiue of their parents, and to be alwayes remembred of them for their comfort: which is, that no man liueth so poorely in this world as he poorely came into it. Plato.

The

Socrates. The better of birth that a childe is, the better ought his bringing vp to be.

Alex. Seu. Children by their laſciuious and remiſſe education, grow in time to be perſons moſt monſtrous and filthy in conuerſation of liuing.

Diogenes. Children ought of congruence to be trained and framed to vertuous diſpoſition.

Tullius. Parents ought to rebuke and chaſtiſe their children, and that ſecretly in their houſes.

Seneca. Wee teach our children liberall Sciences, not becauſe thoſe Sciences may giue any vertue, but becauſe they make the mind apt to receiue vertue.

The ſtudious father careth more how to bring vp his children in honeſty, then how to liue plea-
Alex. Seu. ſantly. The wiſe Father more conſidereth what his Son ſhall be in eſtimation of other men, then how he may content his ſingular affection.

Mens children be diuers and of ſundry conditions; ſome be of nature apt to vertue and towardneſſe, and ſome of nature not ſo prompt and beneuolent, wherefore by education they muſt thereunto be formed. Some be quicke of wit, ſome dull in capacitie.

Of ſharpe wits, ſome doe moſt reſplendiſh in acts that be honeſt, and others ſeeme quickeſt in malice and ſhrewdneſſe.

The good und diligent Father or Maſter, eyther of them is equally carefull, and aſſayeth firſt by education, to make them all conformable to his good
Pithagor. intention and appetits.

Vſe examples, that ſuch as thou teacheſt may
Plato. vnderſtand thee the better.

Be ſober and chaſt among young folke, that they may learne of thee, and among old that thou maiſt learne of them.

He ought not to lye that taketh vpon him to teach other.

Children must euen from the very youth bee fruitfully trayned in their exercising and doing of the best and most godly things, sith nothing sticketh more fastly, then that which is receyued and taken of pure youth, not yet infected with peruerse and crooked manners or opinions. Quintilian.

Nothing either sinketh deeper, or cleaueth faster in the minde, then that which in the youth and tender yéeres is powred in. Fabius.

What thing a man in tender age hath most in vre, Eurip.
The same to death alwaies to keepe he shall be sure,
Therefore in age who greatly longeth good fruit to
In youth he must apply himselfe good seed to sow. (mow
As long as a tunne or a vessell may last, Horace.
Of the first liquor it keepeth the tast:
And youth being seasoned in vertuous labour,
Will euer after thereof keepe the sauour.

Like as waxe is ready and pliant to receiue any print or figure: so is a yong child apt to any kinde of learning. Hermes.

Like as there is no beast so wilde, but diligence may make tame: so is there no child so vntoward, nor no wit so vnruly, but that good bringing vp may make gentle and vertuous. Aristotle.

Like as there is no trée but will waxe barren and grow out of fashion, if it be not well attended: so there is no wit so good but will waxe euill, if it be not well applyed. Plutarch.

Like as they which bring vp horses well, teach them first to follow the bridle: So they that teach children, should first teach them to giue eare to that which is spoken. Socrates.

He that teacheth good to other, and followeth it Seneca.

not himselfe is like him which lighteth a candle to others, and goeth himselfe darkling.

Alex.Mag. We are no lesse bound to our Schoolemaisters that rightly teach vs, then we are to our very naturall parents.

Quintilian. It is most méet to be instructed by them that be best learned, forasmuch as it is difficult to put out of the minde that which is once setled: the double burthen being painefull to the Maisters that shall succéede, & verily much more to vnteach then to teach.

Horace. What instructions soeuer thou intendest to giue, be not too tedious therein, that the mindes of the hearers may the more easily perceiue it, and the better retayne it.

Mar.Aur. The teachers to Princes, and maisters to disciples, profit more in one day with good examples, then in a whole yeare with many lessons.

The maister that instructeth, ought first to giue to his scholler a strong bridle, and a sharpe bit, to the intent he may be well mouthed, so that no man take him with lyes.

Iuuenal. Those that be yong, and with-hold due reuerence vnto their elders, are not worthy of life.

Chilon. The honor due vnto our parents, is none otherwise to be vnderstood, but to iudge discréetely, reuerently, and honorably of our parents, and to esteeme well of all their things, not onely as of elders, but principally because they be parents, whom God vsed as instruments to the entent that by them wee might haue naturally in this world our first beginning and entrance into life, and by whom after our birth wée be most tenderly brought vp, carefully attended vpon, naturally beloued, and most daintely fed and nourished.

In

In honouring of our Parents, we doe not onely honor the great vertue and power of God, but also the excellency of his goodnesse, whereby we are made and borne men, euen of the bloud of man.

It is the first Law euen of Nature, that wee should dearely loue our Parents. Valerius max.

If children vse to eate and sleepe ouermuch, they be therewith made dull to learne.

It appertaineth to Princes to see that their children be well brought vp, informed in wisedome and instructed in manners, that they may be able after them the better to rule and gouerne their kingdomes. Solon.

The summe of all.

Parents and Masters that haue charge ouer youth,
Ought well to regard their office and duty,
And bring vp their children in Gods holy truth;
By word and example, both honest and godly,
Rebuke, chastice, and instruct them gently:
For as they shall order themselues hereafter,
It shall be imputed vnto their teacher.

Of Obedience. Cap. IX.

Obedience is a vertue of high and great estimation before God, who willeth it to raigne in the hearts of all men, to shew and set forth the loue and amity due to God and man. As the Philosophers writeth: be fauourable to all men, be obedient and in subiection to all lawes, but aboue all things obey rather God then man. Socrates.

Plotinus doth also write, that obedience is an incomparable vertue, and due both to God and man: Plotinus.

 that

that is to say, first and chiefly unto God, and then to those that be sent of him and set in authority, also to Parents, Masters, and Officers.

Plato. Thou fallest into disobedience and great presumption, when thou grudgest against thy rulers, although they be worthy of all dispraise.

Princes being by God put in authority are his vice-gerents, and should therefore require obedience, which we must doe unto them with no lesse will for Gods sake, then we should doe it (what honour soeuer it were) immediately unto God himselfe.

And in that place he hath set Princes, whom (as representers of his image unto men) he would haue to be reputed the supreme and most high, and to excell among all other humane creatures, as the holy Ghost witnesseth, and that the same Princes doe raigne by his authority, the holy prouerbs maketh true report: By me (saith God) Princes doe raigne, &c. 1 Peter 2.

Reuerence thine elders with obedience.

Prou.8. Obey lawes, for he that is obedient to the law, obeyeth God. Aristotle.

Alex. Seu. Where any obedience is due, there ought to be excluded all kinde of reproach, all rebuking or mocking, considering that thereof ensueth contempt, which like a pestilence consumeth all lawes and authorities.

Pontanus. What manner of obedience may be there where vice is much made of, and Rulers not regarded: whose contempt is the originall fountaine of all mischiefe in euery weale publike?

Thopon. Where reason ruleth, appetite obeyeth.

A man obedient to nature, cannot hurt a man.

That country is well kept where the King doth

not

not onely know how to gouerne it, but rather because also the people know how to obey him.

The people owe obedience to their Prince, and to his person great reuerence, and to fulfil his commandement: and the Prince oweth equall iustice to euery man, and meeke conuersation to all men. Mar.Aur.

The King obeyeth no man, but the Law onely.

The publike weale is there perpetuall, and without any sodaine fall, where the Prince findeth obedience, and the people findeth loue with the Prince, for the loue of the Lord or Prince breedeth the good obedience of the subiect: and the obedience of the subiect, breedeth the good loue of the Prince. Iustinian.

Wicked men obey for dread, and the good for there goodnesse.

The wicked and disobedient persons seeke confusion.

Loue him that obeyeth God and his Prince, and seeke not his fellowship that disobeyeth them.

The inferiour person or subiect ought to consider, that albeit in the substance of a soule and bodie he is equall with his superior, yet forasmuch as the powers and qualities of the soule and body with the disposition of reason, be not in euery man equall, therefore God ordained a diuersity of preheminence in degrees to be among men, for the necessary preseruation of them in conformity of liuing.

Reuerently obey thy Parents.

Vanquish thy Parents with sufferance.

Striue not with thy father and mother, although thou say the truth.

Looke what obedience thou rendrest to thy Parents, looke for the like againe of thy children. Aristippus

Tullius. It is the part of a young man to reuerence his elders, and of such to choose out the best and most commended, whose counsell and authority hée may leane vnto, for the vnskilfulnesse of tender yeeres must by old mens experience be ordered and gouerned.

Socrates. Seruants (in word and déede) owe due obedience vnto their bodily maisters.

Alex. Seu. A seruant made malapart, will kick at his duty: and labour by custome becommeth easie.

Gentle masters haue commonly proud seruants, and of a master sturdy and fierce, a little winke to his seruant is a fearefull commaundement.

Solon. He obeyeth many that obeyeth his lusts.

He doth himselfe wrong, which obeyeth them whom he ought not.

Hermes. He that at one instant another will defame,
Will also at another to thee doe the same,
For none are so dangerous and doubtfull to trust,
As those that are readiest to obey euery lust.

Nothing obtayneth fauour so much as diligent obedience.

The summe of all.

Obedience is a vertue that God dearely loueth,
Which mightely doth extoll the glory of his name,
And to the effect of Gods loue it directly looketh,
As the Philosopher full worthily writeth the same,
Gods holy loue and obedience excludeth all shame.
Obey the King, thy parents, all lawes and authority,
Then doubtles thou shalt lead thy life most quietly.

THE

THE FOVRTH BOOKE.

Of Sorrow and Lamentation, or *vexation of the minde.*

Cap. I.

Sorrow is a griefe or heauinesse for things that be done and past. Aristotle.

Sicknes is the prison of the body, but sorrow the prison of the soule. Hermes.

Sorrow is next friend to solitarinesse, & enemie to company, & heire of desperation. Mar. Aur.

It is a great sorrow for an auaraticus man to see his goods lost.

The suspitious, the hastie, and the Jealous man liueth euer in sorrow. Plato.

The hastie man is neuer without trouble. Socrates.

Of sorrow commeth dreames and fantasies.

By sorrow and thought, the hart is tormented.

Sorrowfull sighs shew the griefe of the heart.

There is no comparison of the great dolor of the body, to the least paine that the spirit feeleth.

Sorrowfull hearts liue with teares and weeping, and be merry, and laugh in dying. Cicero.

It must needes be that the mindes of men bee oftentimes mooued with vexations & griefes: but yet a meane must be had, beyond the which no man that is wise ought of right to passe.

The easing of sorrow consisteth in two poynts: the one is to deuise meanes not to thinke of griefe, and the other is in the inioying of honest delights and pleasures.

Mar. Aur. Sweet words comforteth the heart but little that is in tribulation, except they be mingled with some good workes.

Of thought commeth watching and bleared eyes.

Hermes. There be sixe kinds of men, that be neuer without vexation. The first, is he that cannot forget his trouble. An enuious man dwelling with folke newly inriched. Hee that dwelleth in a place and cannot thriue, whereas another thriued before him. A rich man decayed and falne in pouertie. Hee that would obtayne that he cannot get. The last is hee that dwelleth with a wise man, and can learne nothing of him.

Securitie putteth away sorrow, and feare hindereth gladnesse.

If thou wilt be counted valiant, let neyther chance nor griefe ouercome thee.

Plato. If thou desire to haue delight without sorrow, apply thy minde to study wisdome.

Accustome not thy selfe to be heauy and sadde, for if thou doe thou shalt be thought fierce: yet be thoughtfull, for that is a token of a prudent man.

Mar. Aur. To friends afflicted with sorrow wee ought to giue remedy to their persons, and consolation and comfort to their hearts.

Aristotle. The multiplying of friends, is the asswaging of cares.

A wise man in torments is euermore happy: but he that is troubled either for Faith, for Iustice, or for the liuing Gods sake, the sufferance of paine bringeth that man to perfect felicitie.

Plato. The Rodde of God, or his Scourge of affliction (whereby the proud flesh of man is pinched and brought low) is the most ready and necessary

meane

meane whereby they shall be driuen to remember themselues, and to liue the more honestly and vertuously in the sight of God.

The greatest easement to ease him that is in heauinesse, is to exercise the wauering heart with some good occupation. Mar. Aur.

There is no sorrow but the length of time may asswage, and make more easie. Sulpitius.

As a wise marriner in calme weather prepareth himselfe looking for a tempest: euen so doth the minde when it is most at quiet doubt of some tribulation. Plutarch.

Wise men quietly beare their griefes and sorrowes, as things that are very sweet & commodious to them, assuredly knowing, that if they shall patiently suffer, they shall not lose their reward.

As in battaile the cowardly and fearefull Souldier, so soone as hee beholdeth the face of his enemie, leaueth his armour, and with all speed possible betaketh him to his feete, and trudgeth away, and is therefore by his enemie most mercilesly slaine, whereas to him that stoutly fighteth, no such extremitie happeneth: euen so they which cannot suffer the frowning face of sorrow and lamentation, being thereat amazed, tormented, or made afraid, doe in faintnesse of courage dye, when they which do manfully resist, oft times with triumphant ioy depart as lustie conquerours. Cicero.

Sorrow commonly taketh not place in him that abstaineth from foure things: that is, from hastinesse, willfull forwardnesse, pride, and slouth. Pithagor.

Counsell, exhortation, and perswasion, to him that is in trouble, giueth small consolation when there is no remedie. Mar. Aur.

He

Seneca. He is not worthie to liue, that taketh not care to liue well.

Hermes. He is wicked, and most to be dispised of all men, that careth and studyeth for none but for himselfe.

Seneca. In all thy trouble remember this reason: hard things may be mollified, straight things may be loosened, and heauie things shall little grieue him that can handsomely beare them.

Lactantius As euerlasting felicitie doth quickly follow the godly in the short race of their misery: so euerlasting misery quickly followeth the vngodly in the short race of their worldly felicity.

The summe of all.

Sorrow is a griefe, for things done and past.
Which by painfull sighs appeareth from the heart.
Sorrow secretly worketh mans life to waste,
Sorrow and sicknesse together taketh part,
Sorrow must be thought on when felt is no smart,
And as after a calme, tempests doth follow,
So after quietnesse there followeth sorrow.

Of Wit and Discretion. Cap. II.

Plato. Mans wit is the instrument of God, whereby is declared vnto the world that all vertue commeth of him.

Seneca. There is no greater treasure then discretion and wit.

Wit without learning is like a Tree without fruit.

By reading, wit and vnderstanding increaseth.

Mans wit (by the will of God) is naturally nourished and fed with the gift of learning and knowledge: and by time spent in studie, it eyther diligently searcheth, or doth alwaies somewhat, and is fed with the delight both of seeing and hearing. Tullius.

Thou shalt much profit in reading, if thou doe as thou readest.

Wisedome cannot be profitable to a foole, nor wit to him that vseth it not. Solon.

Wisedome is the treasure of wit, wherewith euery man ought to enrich himselfe. Plato.

Dispose not thy wit both to vertue and vice.

The wit of man is apt to all goodnesse if it bee applyed thereunto. Diogenes.

Mans wit is of it selfe so corrupt and peruerse, that by counterfaiting and dissembling, one may easily beguile or abuse another, hauing one thing secretly hid in his heart, when outwardly hee saith and doth cleane contrarie to the meaning of his heart.

Many excellent and goodly wits are not a little hindered, through the fault of many Instructors and teachers. Alex. Seuerus.

The wit is made dull with grose and immoderate feeding. Diogenes.

A wise hart possesseth knowledge, and a prudent care seeketh vnderstanding.

A wise man seeth the plague, and hideth himselfe: but the foolish goe on still, and are punished.

Neither wit, strength, or courage (in any man) can become liuely and excellent, where the minde Alex. Seu.

it

is addict to superfluous féeding, to beastly idlenes, or wanton pastimes, but onely by temperance in liuing, vigilant prouidence, and continuall exercise, whereby strength is nourished, and wits be encreased, like as by the other, strength of body is desolued, and the wits be consumed, or vnprofitably dispersed.

Sigism. The ornaments of wit are much more fayre, then the badges of outward nobility.

Hermes. Ambitious men haue vngracious wits.

A méeke witty man is hard to be found.

Through lacke of wit springeth much harme.

Celsus. That man that is void of wit and faith, there is in him no hope of redresse, neyther by any comfort nor counsayle that shall be giuen vnto him.

Polion. He that hath least wit is most poore.

Socrates. He séemeth to be most ignorant, that trusteth most his owne wit.

Stablish thy wit both on thy right hand, and on thy left, and thou shalt be frée.

Socrates. A bondman to wrath hath no power to rule by his owne wit.

Xeno. If thou shalt at any time be constrained to fight in warre or else where, trust more to thy wit then thy strength: for wit without strength much more preuayleth, then strength without wit, to attaine the victory.

To sée is but a small matter, but to foresée is a token of a good wit.

Pitacus. Excellent things ought to be done wittily, and with great circumspection.

Photi. It is better to want riches then wit.

Seneca. Shamefastnesse in a child is a token of wit, but in a man, a token of foolishnesse.

A witty woman bringeth forth wise children.

Recreation of wits are to be suffered: for when they haue a while rested, they spring vp oftentimes the better and more quicker.

That pastime is to be abhorred, where wit sléepeth, and idlenesse with couetousnesse is onely learned. Alex.Seu.

A quiet wit and cléere vnderstanding, taketh right great héede of things that be past: prudently waying things present and things to come.

The wits which in age will be excellent, may be knowen in youth by their honest diligence. Alex.Seu.

No wit can make straight that which nature hath made crooked.

He best perceiueth his owne wit: that though his knowledge be great, yet thinketh himselfe to vnderstand little. Protogeus.

Authority and fauour doth not onely shew a good wit, but it doth also polish that which is rude.

God truly giueth wisedome, but fauour and authority doe shew it most chiefly in a Weale publike.

Like as the earth nourisheth the root of the trée, but yet the Sunne bringeth foorth the blossomes: and if the stormes let not, hée with his wholsome heate ripeneth the fruit, and maketh it pleasant: euen so, study and labour bringeth in knowledge, which by the comfort of Princes appeareth abroad in some ministration. And if enuye or displeasure bring not impediment, the increase of fauour maketh both wit and learning fruitfull and profitable vnto the weale publike.

As empty vessels make the loudest sound, so they that haue least wit, are the greatest bablers. Socrates.

Like as narrow mouthed vessels which are Hermes.

longest

long in filling, keepe their liquour the better, so wits that are slow in taking, are best of all to retaine that they learne.

As yron and Brasse are the brighter for the wearing, so the wit is most ready that is most occupyed.

The summe of all.

The greatest treasure without comparison,
For mans felicity heere in this life,
Aboue gold and siluer, is Wit and Discretion,
To temper the ioyfull and comfort the pensiue,
Or otherwise to instruct man in peace or strife,
Wit also is increased by often reading,
And like the fruitlesse tree is wit without learning.

Of Friends, Friendship, and Amitie. Cap. III.

Aristotle. Tullius.

FRiendship is a vertue, or ioyneth vertue. Friendship cannot be without vertue, and that in good men onely.

Friendship is none other thing but a perfect consent of all things, appertaining as well to God as to man, with beneuolence and charitie. And there is nothing giuen of God (except wisedome) that is to man more commodious.

Friendship in good men, is a blessing and stable connexion of sundry wits, making of two persons one, in hauing and suffering. And therefore a friend is properly named th'other I, for that in them is but one minde, and one possession. And that which is more, a man reioyceth more at his friends good fortune, then at his owne.

This is a iust law of friendship, that the friend in all

all things trusteth to his friend, first regarding who is his friend. Mar. Aur.

It is small pleasure to haue life in this world, if a man may not trust his friends.

Beware that thou takest not them for thy friends whom thou subduest and bringest to subiection. Diogenes.

Friendship is to be preferred before all worldly things, because there is nothing more agreeable with nature, nor that helpeth man more, eyther in prosperitie or in aduersitie. Tullius.

True and perfect friendship is to make one hart and minde, of many harts and bodies. Pithagoras

He that would endeuour to take away friendship from the fellowship of mans life, should seeme to take away the Sunne from the World. Cicero.

Friendship is the louer of loue. Plato.

It is the propertie of friends to liue and loue together. Aristotle.

Good wit is the beginner of friendship, which by vse causeth friendship to follow. Plato.

Friendship ought to be ingendred of equalnesse, for where equality is not, friendship may not long continue.

Where any repugnancie is, there can be no amitie, since friendship is an entire consent of wils and desires.

Therefore it is seldome seene that friendship is betweene these persons: namely a man sturdy, of opinion inflexible, & of sower countenance, and betweene him that is tractable, with reason perswaded, and of kind countenance and entertainment. Also betweene him which is eleuated in authority, & another of very base estate or degree: yea, & if

they

they be both in an equall dignitie, if they be desirous to climbe, as they doe ascend so friendship for the most part decayeth.

Isocrates. Distance of place seuereth not, neyther hindereth friendship, but it may let the operation therof.

Mar. Aur. In friendship fayned is great doubtfulnesse, doublenesse, faintnesse, coldnesse to doe good, much hardnesse, slipperinesse and inconstancie.

Cicero. Whereas true friends be, there paynes are in common.

Seneca. A true friend is more to be esteemed, then kinsfolke.

Plato. Hee is a good friend that doth his friend good, and a mightie friend that defendeth his friend from harme.

Aristotle. Get friendship of them that follow truth.

Periander. Admit none thy friend, except thou first know how hee hath behaued himselfe with his other friends before, for looke how he serued them, euen so he will serue thee.

Hermes. Be slow to fall into friendship, but when thou art in continue.

Mar. Aur. Who so loueth good manners, perseuereth in friendship.

Put no trust in friends in thy present prosperitie, for it is an euident token and prognostication of euill fortune.

He is a very friend that lightly forgetteth his friends offence.

Scornefull men are dangerous friends.

Socrates. There is no man that would choose to liue without friends, although he had plenty of all other riches.

Phocion. It is a sweet pleasure for a man to helpe and be holpen of his friends.

One

One friend ought not to require any vniust thing of another. Mar. Aur.

Friends ought to be like good horses, that is, they ought to haue a little head, by humble conuersation, quicke of hearing, to the intent that they be quick when they are called: a soft mouth, to the end that their tongue be temperate; the houe of the foot hard, to suffer trauaile: and their hands open to doe good deedes: their feet sure to perseuere in amity: a bay colour for his good renowne: also that he be without curbs and bits, and that he may goe where any fatall Destiny turneth the bridle and reine of Fortune.

There is so little difference betweene our enemy and our friend, and so hard to know the one from the other, that there is great ieopardy, lest we (somewhat rechlesse or negligent) defend our enemy in stead of our friend, or hurt our friend in stead of our enemy. Plato.

The agreement together of euill men in mischiefe is not friendship: for friendship is of it selfe so pure, that it will not be vsed in euill. Aristotle.

Proue not thy friend with damage, nor vse thou him vnproued. This mayest thou doe, if when thou hast no need, thou faine thy selfe to be needy: in which if he helpe thee, thou art neuer the worse, but if he refuse, then knowest thou by fayning how for to trust him.

Be as mindfull of thine absent friends, as of them that be present. Isocrates.

Friends in aduersity are a refuge, and in prosperity a pleasure and delight, to communicate our pleasures withall. Aristotle.

If thou desirest to be thought a friend, doe thou the workes that belong to a friend. Hermes.

Pithagoras If thy friend misorder himselfe towards thee, breake not off friendship therefore immediately, but rather assay by all meanes to reforme him, so shalt thou not onely retaine to thee thy old friend, but shalt double his friendship.

There be many which lacke no friends, and yet lacke friendship.

A wise man though he be contented and satisfied with himselfe: yet will he haue friends, because he will not be destitute of so great a vertue.

Beare witnesse rather against friendship, then against truth.

Plato. There cannot be friendship betweene a seruant and his master, inasmuch as their states are vnequall: but for as much as they be both men, they may, because that in manhood they be both equall.

Mar. Aur. New amities or friendships be weary in three dayes.

We see oftentimes proued by experience, that friends lightly taken, are likewise lightly left againe.

Doe good to thy friends, that they may be more friendly: and to thine enemies, that they may be thy friends.

Socrates. The iniury of a friend is much more grieuous, then the iniury of an enemy.

Mar. Aur. He that promiseth, and is long in fulfilling, is but a slacke friend.

Plutarch. He that casteth away his kinsfolks, and maketh him friends of strangers, doth as the man which would cast away his fleshy leg, and set on another of wood.

Seneca. As fire and heat are inseparable, so are the hearts of faithfull friends.

Like

Like as a Physition cureth a man secretly, hee not seeing it: so should a good friend help his friend priuily, when he knoweth not of it. Aristotle.

The summe of all.

Friendship, which is the agreement of mindes
In truth and loue, is the chiefest vertue
Of morrall vertues, that in the world man findes:
Wherefore in the world to liue who so mindes,
Ought Friendship to get, and got to ensue
By loue, not by lucre, that true Friendship blinds,
Knit with an heart where rancour neuer grew,
Which knot estates equalitie so binds,
That to dissolue in vaine may Fortune sue,
Though malice helpe, which two, all glory grindes:
So strong is Friendship as no stormy windes
Haue might to moue, nor feare force to subdue,
Where all these poynts be setled in their kindes.

Of Giuing and Receiuing. Chap. IV.

As giuing and receiuing are contrary the one to the other, so the one is more commonly vsed then the other. Catiline.

In giuing these things must bée considered, what thing, and to whom, how, where, and wherefore thou giuest. Photion.

God will increase that little that thou hast, if thou purposest to giue of that little.

In receiuing be thankfull, and at the least haue a good will to requite a friendly benefit. Tit. Liu.

When thou friendly dost intend to giue, choose (as néere as thou canst) such a person as is playne and honest, of good remembrance, thankefull,

abstayning from the goods of others, no niggard of his owne, and specially to all men beneuolent.

Alex. Seu. Whom peruerse Fortune, long sicknesse, seruice, friendship, disloyaltie of them that were trusted, or whom theeues & oppressors haue brought vnto pouertie, to those let men extend forth their compassion and charitie.

Tullius. The greatnesse of a benefit is declared eyther by the commoditie, or by the honestie, or by the necessitie.

Mar. Aur. He that may giue, and giueth not, is vtterly an enemie: and he that promiseth forthwith, and is long ere he doe, is but a suspitious friend. What needeth words to our friends, when wee may succour them with workes? It is no right that wee render him onely our tongue, which is the worst thing without, of whom we receyue the heart, which is the best thing within.

Those friends are but slender, & scant friends, that in promising many things, will be slacke to giue any thing.

A vertuous hand is not bound to make the tongue a foole.

Promise is an ancient custome among the sons of vanitie: and of custome the tongue speaketh hastily, and the hands worke at leasure.

Promise and performe.

Socrates. Giue vnto the good, and he will (if hee can) requite it againe: but giue to the euill disposed, and he will still beg and aske more.

If thou bestowest a benefit, keepe it secret, but if thou receyue any, publish it broad.

Requite benefits.

Giue to the needy, yet not so, that thou neede thy selfe.

Giue at the first asking: for it is not freely giuen that is often craued. Seneca.

Giue no vayne and vnmeet gifts, as armour to women, bookes to plow-men, or nets to a Student.

Let thy gifts be such, as he to whom thou giuest doth delight in.

Giue liberally for thy profit. Solon.

Sée that thy gifts be according to thine abilitie: for if they be too big, thou shalt be thought a waster: and againe, if they be too small, thou shalt be thought a niggard.

Succour them that perish, yet not so, that thou thy selfe perish thereby.

Boast not of thy good deedes, lest thine euill be also laid to thy charge. Socrates.

Remember them which haue done thée good, and forget not their benefits.

Benefits ought to be as well borne in minde, as receyued with the hand. Hée is vnthankfull which acknowledgeth not the good that is done vnto him, and he is more vnthankfull that to his power requiteth it not, but hee is most vnthankfull that forgetteth it vtterly. Seneca.

One gift well giuen, recouereth many losses.

The remembrance of benefits ought neuer to waxe old.

A small thing giuen willingly is more acceptable then that which is grudgingly giuen, be it of neuer so great price.

A gift grudgingly giuen of a niggard, is called a barly loafe, which although it be bitter, is néedfull to be receiued of the hungry.

The will of the giuer, and not the value of the gift is to be regarded.

He is worthy to be deceiued, which while he bestoweth a benefit, thinketh of the receyuing of another.

Diogenes. To be worthy of a benefit, is more then to haue giuen a benefit.

The summe of all.

In giuing, these things must be considered,
What thing, to whom, where, and wherefore it should be:
First, the good and needy ought to be remembred,
And they, or else God, shall againe requite thee.
But see thou be mindfull of thine abilitie,
Then, if to giue, thou shalt be disposed,
Giue not to receiue, lest thou be deceyued.

Of Pouertie and Neede. Chap. V.

Philip. POuertie is a vertue learned without a teacher.

No man is poore, but hee that thinketh himselfe poore.

He is mighty, which hauing riches is poore, but he is more mighty, which being poore, is rich.

No riches are to be compared to a contented minde.

Protegeus. In all things the meane is best: and to liue warily is a great treasure: and to liue wastfully causeth pouertie.

He is not to be thought poore, whom his little that he hath sufficeth.

Not he that hath little, but he that desireth much is poore.

I

Socrates. A man were better liue poorely, being assured of the blisse of heauen, then to be in doubt thereof possessing all worldly riches.

As

As that man which hath nothing, is counted but poore and miserable: so is he also counted most miserable and poore, that is not contented with that which he hath. Cicero.

Wicked and couetous men, because their wealth towards them is but vncertaine and subiect to many mishaps, are not onely neuer contented with their present portion, but through their greedy desire still coueting to haue, their state onely is very poore, and of all others noted most miserable.

There is no fault in pouerty, but their mindes that so thinke are faulty.

To know how to vse Pouerty well, is great blessednesse.

Pouerty with security, is better then riches with feare.

Pouerty with ioy and gladnesse is an honest thing. Seneca.

Be satisfied with little, for it will encrease and multiply.

It is better to suffer great necessity, then to borrow of him whom a man may not trust.

More miserable is the pouerty of the minde then of the body. Aristotle.

He is not to be counted poore that hath in youth purchased good disciplines, and honest friends; he is in most wretched estate of beggery, that is not endued with any good quality or gift of knowledge. Diogenes.

Pouerty letteth not a man to exercise mercifull acts.

If thou fauourest the poore that can doe but little, thou shalt be fauoured of God that can doe much.

He that rebuketh the poore because of his pouerty, rebuketh the maker of the poore.

Mar. Aur. Ye may thinke that the Father that dyeth, and leaueth his sonne poore and wise, he leaueth him too much: and he that leaueth his sonne rich and foolish, I thinke he hath left him nothing.

It is better to be a poore man beléeuing in God, then to be rich putting doubts in him.

The miserable lacke of the poore man, and the superfluous riches of the rich man causeth discord among the people.

Socrates. Haue compassion vpon poore men, and God shall reward thée with great riches.

Mar. Aur. When a man is plagued with pouerty and sicknesse (both ioyned in one) and hath no succour nor easement, there ariseth in him an intollerable griefe, a fire not able to be quenched, a sorrow without remedy, a tempest full of wrackes, and a burning flame both of soule and body.

Pouerty is euill, but riches is worse.

If thou desirest to be quietly minded, thou must eyther be a poore man indéed, or else like a poore man.

Plato. A néedy old man is a miserable thing.

Seneca. If thou wilt liue after nature, thou shalt neuer be rich.

The state of pouerty is specially to be redressed by the grace and fauour of God, we alwayes endeuouring our selues by all honest meanes to the helping thereof, and not by corrupt coueting of other mens goods, for thereafter will then follow at hand, the wicked effects of thefts, of periuries, of robberies, extortions, and so forth, to the further kindling of Gods wrath.

At the end honour is giuen to a young person, poore

poore and vertuous, rather then to an old person rich and vicious.

The rich may haue power to be more esteemed with poore people, and accompanied with rich and couetous: but the vertuous poore person shall be better esteemed, and lesse hated. Mar. Aur.

The summe of all.

Pouerty with pleasure or paine doth appeare
In all estates, by sundry condition:
Pouerty with ioy, is more blessed and deare
Before God, then riches without exception;
Wretched pouerty is of beastly affection,
And those sort of men that are poore and vertuous,
Are more worthy honour then the rich and vicious.

THE

THE FIFT BOOKE:

Cap. I.

What mentall Powers or Vertues are.

BEcause the soule of man is the most precious thing belonging to men, the Image of God, and also immortall, it is necessary to shew by what power and meane in vs our soules may attaine euerlasting blisse, that is, continuall abiding in the loue and presence of God: for that is the end, that all our soules naturally doe seeke for.

This blessednesse it attaineth through mentall vertues, that is to say, of certaine powers of our mindes, whereby we discerne what is good, and so labor to enforce our affections to follow the same, contrary to the lust of the fraile body, which alwayes leadeth vs to euill and naughtines. Which mentall powers, what they be, how they are attayned, maintayned and lost, and how they ought to be applyed (according to the mindes of the best Philosophers shall be shewed, and in their appointed places shall be knowne from other vertues, by the title of mentall vertues: which duely

to

to learne and follow I beséech God giue vs all his grace: without which all teaching and learning in this behalfe, is but méere vanitie.

Of Vertue. Cap. II.

Vertue is no other thing, but a disposition and exterior act of the minde, agréeable to reason, and the moderation of nature. Alex. Seu.

Vertue is a strong castle, and can neuer be won: it is a riuer that néedeth no rowing, a Sea that moueth not, a fire that quencheth not, a treasure that neuer hath an end, an army neuer ouercome, a burden that neuer wearyeth, a spie that euer returneth, a signe that neuer deceiueth, a plaine way that neuer faileth, a sirrop that forthwith healeth, and a renowne that neuer perisheth. Mar. Aur.

Vertue in all workes is chiefely and aboue all things to be praised, as the head fountaine and most precious iewell of all manner of riches.

Onely vertue attaineth the euerlasting blessednesse. Aristotle.

Vertue principally aboue all things, purchaseth to man beneuolence, friendship, and loue. Socrates.

Vertue is shut vp from no man, but is ready for all that desire her. She receiueth all men gladly: she calleth all men, both kings seruants, and banished men: shée requireth neyther house, nor substance, but is contented with the naked man. Seneca.

The way of vertue is hard at the beginning, but after thou hast crept vnto the top, remayne there for sure quietnesse. Hesiodus.

The trace of vertue is as good in good things with them that be good, as the vice and dishonesty of euill folkes is in euill things. Mar. Aur.

It

Plato. There can nothing be amended or rightly corrected, but by that which surmounteth it, and is better then it: as vice by vertue, falshood by truth, wrong by iustice, folly by wisedome, ignorance by learning, and such like.

Vertue alone performeth the euerlasting felicitie.

Hermes. It is better to suffer shame for vertuous dealing, then to win honour for vicious liuing.

Mar. Aur. To attaine vertues we haue good desire, but to attaine vices we put to all our workes.

Socrates. Few persons take heed or haue knowledge, wher vertue is to be learned.

Diogenes. The lesse time that a man hath to liue, the more earnestly is the study of vertue to be proceeded in.

Pithagor. To vse vertue is perfect blessednesse.

Seneca. Prudence is the guide of all other vertues.

Socrates. Sow good works, and thou shalt reap the flowers of ioy and gladnesse.

So liue with men as if God saw thee.

Plato. Apply thy selfe so now in vertue, that in time to come thou maiest therefore be praised.

Socrates. Though vertue come not at the first, yet by diligent seeking it may be found out.

Plato. Hee that is vertuous and of godly behauiour, is like vnto God: but he that is contrary, is vtterly vnlike him.

Mar. Aur. It is not possible for any vertuous man (if he be vertuous) that hee vnlawfully take any tast in any other mans goods.

Refraine from vice, for vertue is a precious garment.

Apply thy minde to vertue, and thou shalt be saued.

Be vertuous and liberall, so shalt thou eyther

stop

stop the slandrous mouth, or else the eares of them that shall heare him.

Slæpe not before thou hast considered how thou hast bestowed the day past: if thou hast well done, thanke God: if otherwise, repent and aske him forgiuenesse. Pithagor.

Ensue the vertues of thy godly ancestours. Plato.

The chiefe vertue to young men is, not eagerly to attempt any thing. Socrates.

To a vertuous and well-disposed man, euery day is high and holy. Diogenes.

Nothing can corrupt a minde wholly dedicate to vertue. Aristippus.

The high vertues among all noble vertuous people, consisteth not onely to suffer the passions of the body, but also to dissemble them of the soule. Mar. Aur.

Trauaile and take paynes to spend thy life in the trade of vertue: the payne is but short, but thy vertues shall euer endure. If contrarily, thou shalt haue pleasure to do that which is euil, thy pleasure abateth, but the euill tarrieth still. Musonius.

Vertue verely excædeth all things: for if liberty, substance, health and liuing, our countrey, parents and children do well, it happeneth by vertue, she doth aduance all, and hath all things vnder her gouernment. And in whom great plenty of vertue is found, no good thing is at any time daintie. Plautus.

Vertuous men feare more two dayes of prosperitie, then two hundred dayes of aduerse Fortune. Mar. Aur.

Vertue by aduersitie is best tryed. Legmon.

That person is not worthy to liue, that will not study to liue vertuously. Diogenes.

With

Mar.Aur. With vertue God sustaineth vs, and with the order of Iustice the people are well gouerned and ruled.

Diogenes. Vertue is praised of many: but there is no man that effectually followeth it.

Men will put themselues to paynes for the attaining of all things saue vertue and honesty.

Mar.Aur. In all voluntary things a man may be vertuous, but in naturall things, I confesse euery man to be weake.

Hermes. Like as the eye cannot see at once both aboue and beneath, no more may the wit apply both vertue and vice together.

Socrates. Like as in a paire of tables, nothing can be wel written, before the blots and blurs be wiped out: so vertue and noblenesse cannot be séene in a man except he first put away his vices.

Pyrrhus Rex. To a vertuous man, it is but a small reward to be Lord ouer all the earth: and it is but a small chastisement to take a vicious mans life from him.

Diogenes. Vertuous and well disposed persons haue honestie, and shamefastnesse in all places.

Plato. Like as a precious stone in a golden ring: so shineth an heart that is setled in vertuousnesse.

Mar.Aur. Young vertuous persons are bound to honour auncient wise men.

Hermes. Like as men choose good ground to labour and to sow, so should they choose also vertuous and honest men to be their seruants.

Plutarch. It is a great vertue to flye those things our selues, which we reproued in others.

Thales. Without vertue man is but in the number of beasts.

In vertue may bee nothing counterfayte: but

but therein is the onely Image of vertue called Simplicity.

He that liueth vertuously in this life, his Spirit shall haue rest with God. Mar.Aur.

The summe of all.

Vertue in all workes is greatly to be praysed,
As the head fountaine and iewell most precious.
By Vertue friendship and loue is purchased:
Vertue is a garment most comely and curious,
To obtaine Vertue therefore be studious:
For he that loueth vice and doth Vertue detest,
May well be compared to a loathsome beast:

Of Wisedome: a mentall Vertue. Chap. III.

Sapience is the science of things diuine and humane, which considereth the causes of euery thing, by reason whereof that which is diuine shée followeth, and that which is humane shée estéemeth very light. Tullius.

Sapience is the foundation and róote of all noble and laudable things: by her we may winne the good ende, and kéepe vs from euerlasting paine. Aristotle.

Wisedome is the knowledge of diuine things, and is the head of all other Sciences.

True Wisedome teacheth vs as well to doe, as to speake.

It sufficeth not a louer of wisedome to reproue the vices of others by words, but it is necessary he doe himselfe that which he requireth others to doe. Mar. Aur.

Of all the gifts of God, Wisedome is the most excellent Plato.

excellent: shee giueth goodnesse to the good, and forgiueth the wicked their wickednesse: she ordereth the minde: shee directeth the life, and ruleth the workes thereof, teaching what ought to bee done, and what to be left vndone, without which no man can be safe

Wisdome is life, and ignorance is death, wherefore the wiseman liueth, because he vnderstandeth what he doth: but the ignorant is dead, because he doth he knoweth not what.

The haters of wisdome, are louers of death.

Wisdome is the defence of the soule, and the mirrour of reason: and therefore blessed is hee that trauaileth to get her, for shee is the ground and root of all noble deeds: by her wee obtaine the chiefe good, that is, euerlasting felicity.

Wisdome and iustice are honourable both to God and Man.

Hermes. Of all the good gifts of God, wisdome is most pure, she giueth goodnesse to good people she pardoneth the wicked, she maketh the poore rich, and the rich honourable: and such as vnfainedly embrace her she maketh like vnto God.

Prudence is the guide of all other good vertues.

Wisdome garnisheth riches and shadoweth pouertie.

To men of low degree wisdome is an honour, and foolishnesse is a shame to men of high degree.

As we see oftentimes vnder a bare and torne coat Wisdome lyeth hid: so likewise vnder rich vestures and ornaments folly greatly and hurtfully lurketh.

Pithagor. Wisdome at the beginning seemeth a great wonder.

Wis-

Wisdome throughly learned will neuer bee forgotten.

Wisdome is like a thing fallen into the water, which no man can find except he search at the bottome.

It is not possible for him to obtaine wisdome and knowledge, that is in bondage to a woman.

Wisdome most commonly is found in him that is good and vertuous. Boetius.

That man is vnhappy wheresoeuer hee come, that hath a wit, and will not learne Wisdome. Socrates.

Wisdome causeth a man to be honoured. Alex. Seu:

A quiet man ioyneth his Wisdome with simplenesse.

By Wisdome is marked and substantially discerned the words, acts, and demeanour of all men, betweene whom happeneth to bee entercourse or familiarity, whereby is ingendred a fauour or disposition of loue.

Wisdome causeth a man to know his Creator. Hermes.

He that desireth Wisdome, desireth the most high and diuine estate. Solon.

Hee that findeth Wisdome findeth life here in this life, and in the World to come.

He that seeketh Wisdome the right way findeth her, but many erre, because they seeke her not duly, and blame her without cause.

Science is had by diligence, but Wisdome and discretion commeth from God. Aristotle.

The feare of God is the beginning of Wisdome. Socrates.

Honour Wisdome, and deny it not to them that would learne it: and shew it not vnto them that despise it. Pithagor.

All such persons as are to bee approued very Hesiodus:

 vile

vile and nothing at all profitable, which being of themselues void of vnderstanding and wisedome, will stubbornly disobey such as gladly would giue vnto them both sage and wise counsaile.

Aristippus. The report of wisedome and vertue, is good in a Tyrants opinion, so long as he thinketh that nothing which is spoken or done, be repugnant against his affections: for he accounteth vainely, (iudging as a sicke man) nothing to be good that agreeth not with the scent or tast of his owne lothsome appetite.

Plato. Wisedome is a tree that springeth from the heart, and beareth fruit in the tongue.

Without study of Wisedome the mind is sicke.

Early rising and much watching are profitable to keepe a man in health, and to encrease his Wisedome.

Plato. Wisedome in the heart of a foole, is like a flying thing that cannot long continue in one place.

A man of perfect Wisedome cannot die: and a man of good vnderstanding cannot be poore.

Archelaus. It is a speciall point of Wisedome to know to what purpose the time best serueth.

Seneca. Power and might is in young men: but Wisedome and Prudence is in the aged.

Wisedome maketh men to despise death, and ought therefore of all men to be imbraced, as the best remedy against the feare of death.

As the Plow rooteth out from the earth all brambles and thistles: euen so Wisedome rooteth out all vices from the minde.

Plato. Like as an hand is no part of a man, except it can doe the office of an hand: so is Wisedome no part of a wise man, except it be occupyed as it should be.

Like as the eye without light can neyther see it selfe nor iudge of any thing else: so the soule that lacketh Wisdome is brute, and knoweth nothing.

As health conserueth the body, euen so Wisedome conserueth the soule. Socrates.

Like as the sicke man which asketh counsaile, and is taught of the Physitian, is neuer the nearer health except he take the medicine: so hee that is instructed in Wisedome & vertue, and followeth not the same, is neuer the better therefore, but loseth the health of his body, and blessednesse of his soule. Seneca.

Like as an Adamant, by a secret and hid power draweth iron vnto it: euen so Wisedome by a secret meane draweth vnto it the hearts of men. Plutarch.

As hee which in the game place runneth swiftest, and continueth still his pace, obtayneth the crowne for his labour: so all that diligently learne and earnestly follow Wisedome and vertue, shall be crowned with euerlasting glory. Seneca.

Among wise men, hee is wisest that knoweth much, and sheweth to know but little.

Upon perfect and true Wisdome, waiteth continually two hand-maidens, that is to say: Humility and Sobernesse.

A wise man is knowne by two poynts: he will not lightly be angry for wrong that is done vnto him, nor is proud when he is praised.

A perfect wise man mortifieth his worldly desires: by meanes whereof he subdueth both his soule and body. Seneca.

There is none happy but the godly wise man: No man is rightly happy, except hee be both wise and good: for perfect and true felicitie is not without Wisedome and goodnesse.

Plato. Contrariwise, they which be ignorant, and of euill disposition, be vnhappy: for where ignorance and sin is, there infelicity and misery most plainly appeareth.

He is wise that acknowledgeth his ignorance, and he is ignorant that knoweth not himselfe.

It is not possible for him to be wise, that desireth not to be good.

It is better to be wise and not to séeme so, then to séeme wise and not to be so: yet men for the most part desire the contrary.

Isocrates. A wise man vnderstandeth both the things that are aboue him, & those also that are beneath him, he knoweth the things that are aboue him, by the benefit which he receiueth thereby, and things beneath him, by the vse that he hath of them.

Aristotle. A wise man is knowne by thrée points: in making his enemy his friend, the rude learned, and in reforming the euill disposed vnto goodnesse.

Wise men for the truths sake ought to contrary one another, that by their contention the truth may the better be knowne.

A young man cannot be perfectly wise, for wisdome requireth experience, which for lack of time yong men cannot haue.

A wise man ought to repute his errour great, and his goodnesse small.

He shall be wise that kéepeth wise men company.

It is a shame for a wise man to say, I thought not so much.

It is a point of Wisedome to cut away all occasions which might hinder the doing of honest profitable things.

No man can refraine from doing amisse, but a wise man by one perill will auoid another.

He

He is a wise man that doth good to his friends, but he is more then a man, that doth good to his enemies. Hermes.

He that forbeareth to speake, although hee can doe it both wisely and eloquently, because neither in the time, nor in the hearers, he findeth opportunity, so that no fault may succeede of his speech, he therefore is vulgarly called a wise person.

A wise man cannot be slandered of any thing.

A wise man meriteth more punishment for a light deede done openly, then a secret murtherer. Mar.Aur.

A wise man ought to thinke that while hee liueth in this world, hee holdeth his felicity but at aduenture, and his aduersity for a naturall patrimony.

The mother of extreame mischiefe, is worldly wisedome. Plato.

Who so hath lands and goods enough, shall soone haue the name of a wise man. Cicero.

Nothing can happen better to a wise man, then mediocritie of substance. Tullius.

Desire not to be wise in words, but in workes: for Wisedome of speech wasteth with the world, but workes wrought by Wisedome increase vnto the world to come. Aristotle.

The summe of all.

Wisedome the most high and diuine estate,
The roote of all noble and laudable things,
The great gift of God, most sweet and delicate,
The tree of all pleasure that in the heart springs,
Whose deare and dainty fruit the tongue forth brings;
And they that to wisedome themselues would apply,
Must diligently haunt wise mens company.

Of Learning and Knowledge, two Mentall Vertues. Cap. IIII.

Plato. PLato affirmeth that there is set in the soule of man, comming into the world, certain spices, or as it were seedes of things, and rulers of Socrates. Arts or Sciences. Wherefore Socrates in his booke of Sciences resembled himselfe to a midwife, saying: in teaching yong men, he did put into them no science, but rather brought forth that which already was in them: like as the midwife brought not in the childe, but being conceiued did help to bring it forth. And like as in Hounds is a power or disposition to hunt, in horses & greyhounds an aptnesse to run swiftly: so in the soules of men is ingenerate a limbe of Science, which with the mixture of a terrestiall substance, is darkened. But where there is a perfect master prepared in time, the brightnesse of the Science appeareth cleare, like as the power and aptnes of the beasts before rehearsed appeareth not to the uttermost, except it be by exercise prouoked, and that sloth and dulnesse, being plucked from them by industry, bee induced to the continuall act, which (as Plato affirmeth) is proued also in the Master and the scholler.

Socrates. Euen so the aforesaid Socrates in Platoes booke of Sapience, saith to one Theages: Neuer man learned of me any thing, although by my companie hee became wiser, I onely exhorting, and the good spirit inspiring.

Learning and knowledge is the onely good thing of the world, and ignorance the onely euill thing.

Learning

Learning is no other thing, but the aggregation of many mens sentences and acts, to the augmentation of Knowledge. Alex. Seu.

A Person void of Learning, and sufficient utterance, differeth nothing from a stone. Aristippus

Who so laboureth to aduance the minde with good and laudable qualities, and with vertuous and honest disciplines, shall be assured of much the better friends. Diogenes.

Those men that doe most excell in Learning and eloquence, and doe in such things more then other men, they should be most renowned, most worthily praysed, and duely preferred. Æneas. Siluius.

Learne such things while thou art a childe, as may profit thee when thou art a man. Plato.

Endeauour thy selfe in thy youth to learne, although it be painfull: for it is lesse paine for a man to learne in his youth, then in his age to be ignorant.

It becommeth a man from his youth to be shamefast in filthy things, and to be studious in those that are honest. Hermes.

He is to be commended, which to his good bringing vp, ioyneth vertue, wisedome, and Learning.

Be sober and chaste among young folke, that they may learne of thee, and among old folke, that thou mayest learne of them. Plato.

Giue good eare to the aged, for hee can teach thee of the life to come.

Forget not to giue thankes to him that instructeth thee in learning.

When thou art weary of study, sport thy selfe with reading of good stories.

Where can a man be better accompanyed then with wise men, or else reading among bookes? Mar. Aur.

Learne to honour vertue, to reioyce in temperance, and to giue honour to sobriety, lowlinesse, or meeknesse.

Endeauour thy selfe to doe so well that others may enuy thee therefore.

Tullius. We must take good heed and beware with diligence, that we in our calling doe nothing rashly, aduenterously, fondly, negligently, & vnaduisedly, for we be not to this end ingendred of nature, that we should seeme to be created for the effects of vanitie, or lightly to spend our time in pastime and playing, in iesting, wantonnesse, and iollity, but we be rather created and borne to sagenesse, & to the exercise of more graue and profitable studies.

Playing and honest passing the time is lawfully to be permitted and vsed, but yet in such wise to be vsed, that our naturall sleeping, or other necessary means of resting be not neglected: and that at such time, as we haue sufficiently ended (in our estate and calling) all such graue and earnest causes as needfully we haue to doe.

Tullius. Hee that in certaine pleasures of this life hath some delight, must very warily keepe a measure, lest he want in time the inioying of the same.

If thou desirest to be good, endeuour thy selfe to learne to know and to follow the truth: for hee that is ignorant therein, and will not learne, cannot be good.

In whom doctrine hath been found, ioyned with vertue, there vertue seemeth pure and excellent.

Learne by other mens vices, how filthy thine owne are.

He is sufficiently well learned that knowes how to doe well, and hee hath power enough that can refraine from doing euill.

What

What difference is betweene a man presuming to be a man not being learned, and a beast. Mar. Aur.

Better it is to be a begger, then a man without Learning. Aristippus

They are in a wrong opinion, that suppose learning to bee nothing auaileable to the gouernance of a Common-weale. Phil. Rex.

No small vtility groweth to a Common-wealth by the Sapience of a learned Prince, Ruler, or Gouernour. Aristotle.

The most Learning and Knowledge that wee haue, is the least part of that we be ignorant of. Mar. Aur.

He that knoweth not that he ought to know, is a bruit beast among men, he that knowes no more then he hath need of, is a man among bruit beasts, and he that knoweth all that may be knowne, is a God among men. Pithagor.

Esteeme him as much that teacheth thee one word of wisdome, as if hee gaue thee abundance of Gold.

Keepe company with them that may make thee better. Xenoph.

Be apt to learne wisdome, & diligent to teach it.

Search for the cause of euery thing.

Labour not for a great number of Bookes, but for the goodnesse of them. Seneca.

Let it not grieue thee to take paines, to goe to learne of a cunning man, for it were a great shame for young men not to trauaile a little by Land to increase their knowledge, sith Merchants do saile farre by Sea to augment their riches.

An opinion without Learning cannot be good.

The vnlearned must beware that they presume not to iudge of matters which they vnderstand not without some authoricall direction.

Lear-

Learning consisteth not in the greatnesse, but in the goodnesse.

Aristippus Learne diligently, the goodnesse that is taught thee, for it is as great a shame for a man not to learne the good doctrine that is taught him, as to refuse a gift offered him of his friend.

Learning is Studies sister.

Learning maketh young men sober, comforteth the old men, is riches to the poore, and garnisheth the rich.

Socrates. Of all things the least quantity is to be borne, saue of Learning and Knowledge: of which the more that a man hath, the better may he beare it.

To lacke Knowledge is a very euill thing, to disdaine to learne, is worse; but to withstand and repugne the truth against them which teach the truth, is worst and furthest from all grace.

Socrates. Intelligence is King both of heauen, and also of earth.

It is not possible for one man to know all things, yet should each man labour to know as much as he might.

Isocrates. It is no shame for a man to learne that he knoweth not, of what age soeuer he be.

Know thy selfe.

Macrob. He that knoweth himselfe well, esteemeth but little of himselfe: he considereth from whence he came, and whereunto he must, hee regardeth not the vaine pleasures of this brittle life, but extolleth the Law of God, and seekes to liue in his feare.

Hee that knoweth not himselfe, is ignorant of God, willfull in wickednesse, vnprofitable, and vtterly gracelesse.

Demosth. Sicknesse, pouerty, and aduersity, are meanes requisite

requisite (as by the rod of God) to ouerthrow, chastice, and keepe low the power of the proud flesh: whereby a man shall the better know himselfe.

The Knowledge of the law of God worketh a man to know himselfe, and is the onely right way to eternall saluation.

Cunning continueth, when Fortune flitteth. Alex. Seu.

To vnlearne euill, is the best Learning.

Me thinks that great vexation & trouble should be in the minde of him that dwelleth with a wise man, and can learne nothing of him. Hermes.

The godly being giuen to the studies of learning and wisedome, doe chiefly bestow their wisedome, prudence, and vnderstanding to mens commodities. Tullius.

The vnderstanding and knowledge of vaine men are but beast-like to those that are possessed with the heauenly spirit, which is secret and hid: and whereas they speake and vtter their knowledge, all others ought to be still. Mar. Aur.

Hearing in a man is a great help to knowledge. Aristotle.

Much babling is a signe of small knowledge. Pithagor.

Knowledge seemeth to be a thing indifferent both to good and euill. Aristippus

Knowledge is better in youth then in age.

In a short while we learn much euill, but in a long season we cannot learne any goodnesse. Mar. Aur.

The more we exalt & raise our selues with Learning and Knowledge, the more low do we put the flesh with miseries.

Both sleep and labor are enemies to Learning. Plato.

To learn better is a good punishment for ignorance.

Learne to liue wel by teaching of righteousnesse.

The vertue of learning. Learning and knowledge is sought for of good men, and lodged euen in their breasts, to this end onely, that they may thereby know sin, and eschew the same, and know vertue and attaine vnto it: for if it be not applyed hereunto of them that haue it, she leaueth in them her whole duty vndone.

Alex.Sen. In vaine is that long trauaile in study and learning, where actual experience doth not shew forth her fruits.

Socrates. Like as a field, although it be fertile, can bring forth no good fruit except it be first tilled: so the minde, although it be apt of it selfe, cannot without learning bring forth any goodnesse.

Seneca. As we behold our selues in other folks eyes, so should we learne by other mens report, what doth become vs, and what doth not.

Like as in meates the wholesomenesse is as much to be required as the pleasantnesse: so in hearing and reading authors, wee ought to desire as well the goodnesse as the eloquence.

Plato. Like as Bees out of flowers sucke forth the sweetest: so should men out of Sciences learne the best.

As a captaine is a director of a whole hoast: so Reason ioyned with Knowledge is the guide of life.

The summe of all.

In mans soule there is set at his first entrance
Into this short life of care and misery,
Certaine hid seedes of pure and liuely substance,
Rulers of Sciences, as Plato *doth testifie:*
Whereby at all times we may the more worthily
As men among men through Science and Learning,
Differ from beasts in wise mens company:
Else as beasts among men be regarded nothing.

Of

Of Feare. Cap. V.

Feare is a vertue that groweth of an vndoubted beliefe in God, and it hath in it such force, that it maketh courage to flye, and maketh a man to abstaine from sinne and wickednesse. Anachar.

No man can be iust, without the feare of God. Socrates.

If thou wilt desire truely to know what is the feare of God, thou must vnderstand it to be, both to desire deuout things, and also to liue deuoutly and holily. The Feare of God is also to be vnderstood to be the well of life, springing vp into euerlasting life, whereby are washed onely the repentant sinners, and such as are not filthily spotted. Mar.Cels. *What the Feare of God is.*

Feare dependeth on loue, and without loue it is soone had in contempt.

Feare God aboue all things, for that is righteous and profitable, and so order thy selfe that thy thoughts and words be alwayes of him: for the speaking and thinking of God surmounteth so much all other words and thoughts, as God himselfe surmounteth all other creatures: and therefore men ought to loue, feare, & obey him, though they should be constrained to the contrary. Socrates.

If thou knowest not what is sinne, nor what is vertue, by the Feare and loue of God thou shalt know both.

Thinke vpon the reward of sinne, and feare to offend. Consider how full of griefe and misery, how short and transitory this present life is, and the vaine pleasures thereof: how on euery side thine enemies compasse thee, and that death lyeth in wait against thee, and euery where catcheth thee sodainely and vnawares. Plato.

Feare

Pithagoras Feare the great vengeance of God, as much as thou maist: consider his might and puissance: and that shall keepe thee from sinne, and when thou thinkest of his mercy, remember also his righteousnesse.

Feare not threatning, neyther be ouercome with sweet words and faire promises: for with these twaine, the godly (of the wicked) are sharpely assailed in this world.

Socrates. By the feare of God we attaine help of the holy Ghost, which shall open to vs the gates of saluation, whereunto our soules shall enter, with them that shall obtaine euerlasting life.

Hermes. He that feareth God as he ought, shall neuer fall into the pathes that leade men into euill.

Socrates. The feare of God is the beginning of wisdome: and the want of Gods feare is the very ground and foundation of all foolishnesse, sinfulnesse, and abhomination.

When the Feare of God is once gone from a man, there remaineth then nothing else but lightnesse of life, extreame rashnesse, forgetfulnesse of God, and running head-long into all kinde of sin and mischiefe.

A man that feareth God, serueth God, prayeth faithfully vnto God, and distributeth liberally to the poore.

Propertius Hee that rightly feareth God, and esteemeth well the excellencie of his maiestie from his heart, cannot forget such precepts as hee receyued of God, but will alwayes thinke vpon the obseruance of them.

The feare of God doth not onely withdraw the hand & other parts of the body from committing euil, but also it helpeth to the clensing of the mind

and withdraweth the consent thereof to euill.

Nothing is sweeter then the feare of God.

There is no strength of Empire so great, which suppressed by feare can long continue. Tullius.

He ought to feare many, whom many doe feare. Aristippus

Whom many men doe feare, they doe hate, and euery man whom he hateth, he desireth may perish. Ennius.

They that desire to be feared, needs must they dread them of whom they be feared. Tullius.

There is nothing so sure which standeth not in danger of his inferiour.

He that is not inuironed with charity, is attended with terror.

The summe of all.

Without the feare of God, no man can be iust;
Nor yet rightly rule his corrupt nature:
Feare strongly mortifieth all filthy lust,
Feare findeth entrance into a life most pure,
Which Feare upon loue dependeth all sure:
Or else feare without Loue, encreaseth hatred:
And whom men doe feare, they wish were perished.

Of Death not to be feared. Chap. VI.

Death is the dissolution of the body. Hermes.

Death is none other thing but the parting of the soule from the body. Aristotle.

What thing is Death but a trap-doore wherein the tent is closed, in the which are folded all the miseries of this life. Mar. Aur.

Death doth looke for thee euery houre. Basil.

As soone as thou art borne to possesse the earth, death issueth out of his sepulchre to finde thee.

As

As thou knowest not when or where death will meete thee, so thou must remember that alwayes and in euery place he seeketh for thee.

It behoueth a man so to vse himselfe, that hee looke for death euery houre: and to be alwayes in a readinesse for the comming of death.

August. There is nothing that more calleth a man backe from sinne, then the remembrance of death.

Blacke ougly Death maketh all subiect to the rigor of his Law.

Death deadly woundeth without dread or dalliance.

Experience plainly teacheth, and all ages approueth, that Gods plagues threatneth, sicknesse calleth, old age warneth, death sodainely taketh, and the earth finally deuoureth.

The life of man is like water poured out of a bucket, which the earth quickly sucketh vp, and appeareth not againe.

Pithagor. Death is a thing that cannot be eschewed, wherfore it ought to be lesse feared.

Socrates. Death is common to all persons, though to some one way, and to some another.

Mar.Aur. An euill death putteth great doubt of a good life: and a good death excuseth an euill life.

It were better for a man to dye, and loose this life, to attaine much wealth, then to escape, and to liue in misery.

A worshipfull death, is better then a miserable life.

Death is not to be feared of them that be good.

The carnall and wicked worldly men, who haue their felicity in this life, and are ouerwhelmed with the vanities of this world, they immoderately feare Death, and they tremble and shrinke in

their

their bodies, when they heare of death: whose wicked hearts and mindes are so giuen ouer, to imbrace and hold fast the fickle pleasures of this life, that they doe vtterly forget, or rather appeare doubtfull of the euerlasting world to come.

Though the bodily death, by diuers means and for diuers causes be vnto men very tedious and bitter: yet the death thereof, for the testimony of Gods truth is vnto the godly most easie, most ioyfull, swéete and delectable: because hée seeth (through the eye of faith) the present performance of Gods heauenly promises.

Death is life to him that looketh to haue ioy after it. Aristotle.

Death of the euill, is the suertie of good.

Life iudgeth vndirectly of death.

Praise no man before death, for death is the discouerer of all his workes. Isocrates.

Death is the finisher of all tribulation & sorrow. Seneca.

By that same way that life goeth, death commeth. Mar. Aur.

If we liue to dye, then we dye to liue. Mar. Aur.

Death despiseth all riches, and glory, and coucheth both rich and poore folke together. Boëtius.

Death riddeth the body out of paines. Diogenes.

As the beginning of our creation commeth of God: so it is méete that after death our soule returne to him againe. Aristotle.

To men occupied about diuine things, life seemeth a thing of no reputation. Plato.

The most profitable thing for the world is the death of couetous and euill people.

Death is the rest of all couetous people. Solon.

Like as age followeth youth: euen so death followeth age. Horace.

Mar. Aur. Short is our life, and shortly death commaundeth vs to close our eyes, and to follow the course of death.

Plutarch. After winter the spring time followeth, but after age youth neuer commeth againe.

The end of sicknesse is death, and the end of darkenesse is light.

Mar. Aur. When the life passeth, there is no prudence in a prudent, nor vertue in a vertuous, nor Lordship in a Lord, that can take away the feare of the spirit, nor paine of the flesh.

Plato. Hee which feareth to haue paynes after Death, ought in his life time to auoid the cause, which is his owne wickednesse.

A rash and wicked eye that delighteth to behold vanitie, may well be called the window of Death, for it is the deadly minister of the hearts concupiscence, & fore-runner of filthy facts, thefts, robberies, and such like.

Socrates. None need to feare death, saue those which haue committed so much iniquitie, as after death deserueth damnation.

It is a happy mans lot to dye before hee deserueth death.

Hee is in a miserable state that wisheth to dye.

Thou must needes dye, but not so oft as thou wouldest.

Plato. For vnrighteousnesse and other mischieuous deedes, the soule after death is sore punished.

Death is sweet to them that liue in sorrow.

Plato. Take not so much thought to liue long, as to liue well.

Hermes. Dispise bodily death, and it shall be life to the soule: follow truth and thou shalt be saued.

Wisedome maketh men to despise death, and

ought

ought therefore of all men to be embraced, as the best remedy against the feare of death.

It appertaineth to men that be valiant, rather to despise death, then to hate life.

Death and sleepe be cosin-germanes. Qui.Cur.

This is to be alwayes noted, that when thou goest out of thine house, thou art not certaine to returne into thine house againe, and going into thine house, thou art not sure thence to goe out againe: likewise when thou goest to thy bed, thou art not sure to rise from thence againe. Seneca.

Liue and hope, as if thou shouldest die immediately. Plinius.

One day deemeth another, but the last day giueth iudgement of all that is passed. Homer.

Death ought rather to be desired, then despised: for it changeth vs from this world of vncleanenesse and shame, to the pure World of worship: from this transitory life, to life euerlasting: from this world of folly and vanities, to the world of wisedome, reason, and truth: and from this world of trauell and paine, to the world of rest and consolation.

O how happy were it for the vnhappy man (if forgetfulnesse deceiue him not) to remember the state of this life, how short it is, how full of misery, vanity, and woe, an approued exile, and hath nothing in it permanent? It is a continuall conflict, strife, and warre, a wandring wildernesse, and a vayle of wretchednesse, wherein we are continually compassed with most terrible, fierce, and fearefull enemies, to the deadly wounding, slaying, and ouerthrowing of body and soule into hell. O (these mischiefes considered) why should man then haue such desire to dwell in this wretched World, and Mar.Aur.

to liue in such a loathsome and laborious life? to tarry in such wretchednesse, and to remaine in such a perillous state? were not death much rather to be desired? were not the houre of death much better then the continuance of such a life? for to the godly, death is the most happy messenger and quick dispatcher of all such displeasures, the end of all trouble and sorrow, the bed of all rest, the doore of good desires, the gate of gladnes, the port of paradise, the hauen of heauen, the entrance to felicity, and harbour from all misery, and the beginning of all blessednesse. Therefore the day of deaths happy visitation is not to be contemned or feared, but rather to be highly celebrated with ioyfulnesse, mirth, and melody. Farre off therefore be it, that wee should eyther at the hearing, or presence of death, haue feare in vs and trembling, that such a friend should not bee welcome vnto vs, that the foulenesse of his face should feare vs from his good conditions: that the bitternesse and hardnesse of his rough huske, should hinder vs from the sweet taste of such a comfortable kernell: yea, farre off be it, that the feare of deaths discommodities, should hinder vs, or plucke vs backe from the ioyfull embracing of so many and innumerable commodities which he daily bringeth, for the most quiet state of the godly, and not to heare, see, and feele this: woe be to those deafe eares, blind eyes, and hard hearts, whereby men wickedly feare, and flie from that which (with most ioyfull desire) they should wish and imbrace. Consider therefore thy selfe, feare to offend the presence of God, and feare not the day and houre of death, but abide with patience thine appointed turne, and thanke thy maker for thy change.

We

We saile with great trauell through the great Mar. Aur.
and dangerous perils of this short life, and sodainly at one houre we are commanded to take land, and discharge vs of our flesh, and to take the earth for a Sepulchre.

In these our dayes of misery, wee reade many things, we heare, we see, we desire, we doe attaine, we possesse, suffer, and doe rest much, and sodainly we are called by death: and of all these things we shall beare nothing away, because all they and we are nothing.

All the trauels of the world are weighty, but the Mar. Aur.
trauels of death are weightiest.

All be perillous, but that is most perillous.

All be great, but that is the greatest.

All things at the last haue an end by death, saue onely death, whose end is vnknowne.

Then (if we be good) sith wee shall change this weary life and company of men, for the sweetnesse and ioy of God: and the doubts of fortune, for this sure life: and this great and continuall feare, for perpetuall peace: and this euill and naughty corrupt life, for great renowne and glory: we ought to thinke verily this should be no euill, but a change most blessed and happy.

Oh what blessednesse is it to haue death due for our sinnes, diuerted into a demonstration and testification of Gods truth?

When our last houre is come, necessity carrieth Phocion.
vs hence, though we be not willing: but if we bee willing, then haue we with God, both ioy, and euerlasting reward.

Doubtlesse, so onely shall the soule of man most happily at the last by death depart from the body, as shee hath aforehand, through true knowledge,

diligently recorded and practised death: and hath also long time before (by despising of things temporall, and by contemplation and loue of things spirituall) vsed her selfe to be as it were in a manner absent, or a-part from the body.

The summe of all.

Death is the dissoluer of each mortall body,
Driueth all againe to their first matter, Dust;
Which while we liue should put vs in memory
From whence we came, and hence to what we must:
Fearefull to the euill, but ioyfull to the iust,
Who after this life, through death transitory,
For deathlesse life ioyned with ioy doe trust,
Whose life by death is led to greater glory.

Of Liberty. Chap. VIII.

Diogenes. THe best thing in this present life, is liberty: Liberty be it neuer so poore, is to be preferred before all delights and pleasures where liberty is not.

Cicero. He is to be counted free and at liberty, which is voide of all lust and concupiscence.

Liberty is a power giuen vnto man, whereby he may liue, as he himselfe shall thinke good. And he liueth properly, as he lusteth to himselfe, which followeth, in conuersation, those onely things which are good and honest, who inioyeth freely his office, who hath a fore-sight how to liue well, who obeyeth not the Law for feare of punishment, but for truths sake and equity: and with whom there is nothing more effectuous, then the good successe of his owne aduise and iudgement.

So

So pleasant a thing to man is the state of libertie, that life is to be aduentured for the happie recouerie thereof.

To a man that is once brought vp with freedome and Libertie, there is nothing vnto him more grieuous and miserable then to be restrained of the same.

Death truely is to be preferred before seruile slauerie and bondage.

That is most truely seruitude, when a man without moderation or stay of his appetite, doth follow ouermuch his owne lust and pleasure: which to ouercome is more commendable and praise-worthie, then winning of many, both rich and great Cities. Diogenes. What Seruitude is.

Hee is subiect to a seruile state, and bondage, which cannot refraine from his owne affections. Cicero. Plato.

Hee that is a good man and a wise, looseth not libertie at any time: no, not so long as breath in him endureth.

Of our selues we haue no Libertie, nor ability to doe the will of God, but are subiect to sinne, and shut vp vnder sinne. Augustine.

In very much libertie it is hard to be moderated, or to put a bridle to wanton affections. Aristotle.

Hee that hath Libertie to doe more then is necessarie, will oftentimes doe more then is tending to honesty. Macrobius.

Too much Libertie turneth into bondage. Seneca.

Hope is bondage, but mistrust is Liberty. Thales.

The couetous person, the ambitious, the lecherous, with such other giuen to vice, cannot be free and at Libertie. Diogenes.

A tyrant neuer tasteth of true friendship, nor of perfect Libertie.

Alex.Seu. Slaues and bond-men, haue only this liberty, to vse a proud countenance, because they be shameslesse: and noble men be alwayes knowne by their gentlenesse.

Seneca. They be out of libertie that doe not labour in their owne businesse, that sleepe at an other mans winck, and set their feete where another man steppeth

Mar.Aur. Where there is corruption of customes, their liberties should be broken.

Terence. Surely of ouermuch licence happeneth great pestilence.

Alex.Seu. All things desire libertie, and man-kinde most specially.

Cicero. It is better for a man to keepe his owne libertie, then to take libertie from another man.

Will constrained, seeketh euer opportunitie to slip off the choller.

Nothing is in the perfect state of ioy, if libertie be away.

The summe of all.

Although honour, health, riches, and dignitie,
Be daintie pleasures that nature doth imbrace,
Yet Libertie as Writers doe testifie,
Is the best thing that a man can purchase:
The poore mans libertie doth plainely deface
The rich in prison, or bond-slaue to riches,
Whose liues are wasted in most wretched distresses,

Of

Of Goodnesse. Cap. VIII.

That thing is to be called good, which includeth in it selfe a dignitie that sauoureth of God & heauen, so that those things are onely worthy the name of Goodnesse, which hath a perpetuitie and stedfastnesse of godly substance. Plato.

As God himselfe is all Goodnesse, so hee loueth all things that are good, which is Righteousnesse and Vertue: and hateth the contrary, Vice and Wickednesse.

Those persons verely may be called good which doe so behaue themselues, and in such wise do liue, that their faith, suertie, charitie, and liberality be sufficiently proued: and that there be not in them any couetousnesse, wilfulnesse, or foole-hardinesse, and that in them be great stability and constancy. Tullius.

It is not onely sufficient for a person to be good, but it is necessary that he put from him all things that are reputed euill. Mar. Aur.

It is good right, that they which be good men, and doe well, receiue the honour which they bee worthy to haue: and to them which be good, and already aduanced to honor, they giue such courage, that they endeuour themselues with all their power to increase that opinion of goodnesse, whereby they were brought to aduancement, which needs must be to the honour and benefit of those, by whom they were so promoted. Plato.

Many yeeres of a mans life are not to be reckoned, but rather the good and godly works that he hath done.

Those be a curious kinde of men that will seeke to know another mans life, and behauiour, and be

be slow to seeke the amendment of their owne liues.

Hermes. Hee may be called good, that other men fare the better for his goodnesse.

Iuan.varius. He is to be counted a good man among them that are good, whom neuer man saw to doe any euill works, nor heard him speak any euill words, nor doe any thing but it was to the comfort of the needy, and profitable to the common-wealth.

Socrates. Thou canst not be perfectly good, if thou hatest thine enemie; what shalt thou then be if thou hatest thy friend?

Let him that is a good man be a louer of all good men, because they be good, and for the goodnesse that is in them, let him haue pleasure in their familiaritie and company: for God shall thereby be praised, and hee himselfe well commended, ioyfully comforted, and blessedly rewarded.

Plato. There is no greater delectation and comfort to him that is good, then to be seene in the company of good men.

Plato. Like as a man passing through the Citie and seeking where hee may finde a good Carpenter, or a good Smith, hearkeneth where the most hewing is, or beating with hammers, and there goeth in, supposing to finde that which hee looketh for: euen so, if thou wilt haue a good man, go and looke him out where thou hearest sicknes sharpely raigneth, or where iniustice gouerneth, will ruleth, or great power oppresseth, there shalt thou surely finde him that thine heart desireth.

Plato. Aduersitie is sent of God vnto good men, not vniustly nor cruelly, but for a good consideration and louingly, as the doing of a good Father, which with an incomparable charitie desireth the

aduancement

aduancement of his sonne to perpetuall honour and dignity, by such manner of excesse as most aptly tryeth his vertue.

Who doubteth but that they are to be accounted good men, which in aduersity be patient, and dealeth vprightly both in word and deede with all men. Boetius.

The greatest goodnesse of all goodnesse is, when tyrants are put vnder by vertues acquired, or to finde remedy against accustomed vices, with good inclinations. Mar. Aur.

If thou intendest to doe any good, tarry not till to morrow: for thou knowest not what may chance thee this night. Pithagor.

The goods of the soule, are the principal goods.

Nothing is to be counted good, that may be taken away. Pithagor.

Friendship is the chiefest good thing in a City or Countrey. Aristotle.

Good men reioyce, that not onely they, but all others be cleare of such mischiefes as be put vpon them. Socrates.

Men ought to doe well to good people, and to chastise the wicked by rigor. Aristotle.

In good things behold the mercies of God: and apply them aptly to thy selfe. And in all euill things and plagues behold his iudgements, through the which thou mayest learne and feare to offend him.

Doe not what thou wouldest, but what thou shouldest.

There is nothing so well done of them that be good, but forth-with it shall be counterfayted of them that be euill. Mar. Aur.

The tongue is both good and euill to a man.

The

Pithagor. The hearts of good people are the Castle of their secrets.

Socrates. He that doth good, is better then the good which he doth: and he that doth euill, is worse then the euill that hee doth.

Legmon. A good thing the further and the more largely or appertly it is knowne, the further the vertue thereof spreadeth and rooteth it selfe in mens hearts and remembrance.

If thou doest good to the euill, it shall happen to thee, as it doth to them that feede another mans dog, which barketh as well at his feeder, as at an other stranger.

Mar. Aur. If good men be diligent to seeke others that be good, no lesse ought they to hide themselues from them that be euill: for a godly man with one finger hath power ouer all them that be vertuous, but to withstand one euill person, he hath neede of hands, feet, and friends.

A good rich man may seldome be found.

He that is mighty, is not by and by good, but hee that is good, is immediately mighty.

It is the part of a good honest man to forget dishonest things, which to remember is a point of euill.

Plutarch. It is better for a man to amend himselfe by following the good example of his predecessours, then to make his successours waxe worse by following his vnthrifty vicious liuing.

Cicero. The greatest fault in a man that is good, is to approue euil rather then good, and the greatest euill in an euill man, is to condemne good for euill.

Mar. Aur. The euill man is alwayes desired for his wickednesse to be dead: but the good meriteth alwayes to haue his death bewayled.

The

The goodnesse that commeth of an ignorant man, is like hearbs growing vpon a dunghill. Hermes.

That man seemeth good that is meeke and gentle of condition, soft in words, and restfull in person, and gracious in his conuersation. Mar.Aur.

Vertuous and well-beloued persons, loue honesty and shamefastnesse at all times, and in all places. Diogenes.

There is nothing so good, nor so well beloued, but course of time causeth vs to leaue it, to dispraise and abhorre it, and finally to be weary of it.

Good men be called to ioy, and euill men bee drawne to paine.

The summe of all.

All goodnesse is giuen vs from God aboue,
The author of vertue, grace, and good gouernance,
Whose loue and liuely light should euer moue
Mankinde, by good life, his glory to aduance:
The goodnesse of God is of long continuance.
And those that be wise men and learned will say,
Nothing is good, that may be taken away.

Of Praise and Dispraise. Chap. IX.

APply thy selfe so now in vertue, that in time to come thou mayest therefore be praysed. Plato.

It is meere wickednesse, to seeke prayse by counterfayted vertue. Diogenes.

Challenge not to thy selfe the Prayse of other mens inuentions.

In all thy doings seeke chiefly the Prayse of God.

When

Chrisost. When God is blessed, and when thankes and prayses be giuen vnto him of men, then the more plentifull blessings are giuen of him, euen for their sakes by whom hee is blessed: for hée that blesseth God, maketh him debtor of a greater blessing.

Mar.Aur. He is greatly to be praysed that leadeth an vncorrupt life, that loueth and feareth God, that is friendly to his friend, fauourable to his enemy, temperate in his words, and restfull in his person.

Prayse nothing that is not commendable, nor dispraise ought that is prayse worthy.

Prayse honest and good things.

Prayse not the vnworthy, because of his vaine riches.

Prayse a man for that which may neither be giuen him, or taken from him, which is not his faire house, nor his goodly garments, nor his great houshold, but his vertue, wit, and perfect reason.

Prayse little, but disprayse lesse.

Hee that to his noble linage addeth vertue and good conditions, is highly to be praysed.

Anachar. The good workes of old and ancient persons are to be praysed, rather then their white hayres: for honour and prayse ought to be giuen for the good life, and not for the white head.

If thou wilt prayse any man because hee is a Gentleman, prayse his Parents also. If thou wilt prayse him for his riches, that appertaineth to fortune. If thou prayse him for his strength, remember that sicknesse will make him weake. If thou prayse him for his swiftnesse of foote, remember that age will take it away. If for his beauty, it will soone also vanish away: but if thou wilt praise him for his manners, wisedome, and learning, that

is

is his owne, and neyther commeth by heritage, neyther altereth with fortune, nor is changed by age, but is alwayes one with him.

Doe not such things thy selfe, as thou wouldest dispraise in another. Pithagor.

He that praiseth himselfe, & dispraiseth others, is not worthy praise. Protogeus.

In the multitude of men, there are few to be praised, and many to be dispraysed. Mar. Aur.

Nothing disprayseth a man so much as his owne praysing, specially when he boasteth of his owne good deedes.

To be praysed of euill men, is as euill as to be praised for euill doing.

If a man praise thee, remember to be thine owne Judge. Cato.

Wee must beware wee open not our eares to such as praise vs falsely, nor suffer our selues to be flattered. Tullius.

None be in so much danger of Flatterers as the Prince, noble men, and such as be in authoritie.

The cluster of flatterers walke in the Court. Ouid.

If it were as painefull a thing for men to praise honest things as it is to doe them, then should they be as little praysed as followed.

If thou wilt disprayse him whom thou hatest, shew not that thou art his enemy.

It is a poynt of flattery, to prayse a man to his face. Seneca.

Unmeasurable laud and praise is to be reproued. Diogenes.

All things that are good, hath euer the preheminence in praise and comparison.

It is sufficient to praise and exalt a childe, seeing his honest towardnesse, disposition or aptnes well proued by such things as be taught him.

Pride

Pride is cause of hatred, and sloath of Dispraise.

Aristotle. As they which giue willingly seeme to haue but little themselues: euen so they which praise other folks slenderly, seeme to desire to be praysed themselues.

Plutarch. Like as the famished for lacke of other meate, are faine sometime to eate their owne flesh: so many that are vaine-glorious are forced to prayse themselues because no man will else.

Hermes. As the shadow followeth the body, so praise followeth vertue. And as the shadow goeth sometimes before, and sometimes behind, so doth praise also to vertue: but the later that it commeth, the greater it is, and the more of value.

Isocrates. Praise no man before death, for death is the discouerer of all his works. Life iudgeth vndirectly of death.

The summe of all.

So vertuously endeauour thy selfe to liue,
That men euen worthily thy life may commend:
Counterfaite not vertue for men will it repriue,
And praise thee for thy profit, if rightly thou intend.
Both Praise and Dispraise on our liuing doth depend.
And as after the body there followeth a shadow,
Euen so after Vertue, praise doth also follow.

THE

THE SIXT BOOKE:

Of the ſeauen cardinall Vertues, following in their order, againſt the ſeauen capitall Vices; commonly called the ſeauen deadly ſinnes.

Cap. I.

Of Humilitie and Gentleneſſe.

HUmilitie for her excellencie ſhould be the ſiſter of true nobilitie.

God hath moſt reſpect vnto them that with humbleneſſe of heart, caſt themſelues lowly before the preſence of his maieſtie.

Like as the lowlineſſe of heart maketh a man highly in fauour with God: euen ſo meekeneſſe of words maketh him to ſincke into the hearts of men. Propertius.

The vertue of humilitie encourageth to attaine truely the law of God: and maketh apt and méete veſſels to receiue the ſpirit of God.

Nature giueth vnto age eſtimation and authoritie: but méekeneſſe of heart is the glory both of youth and age, and giueth vnto them both dignitie and honour. Pontanus.

That man is worthily counted happy, which the highter that fortune hath aduanced him in ſubſtance and dignitie: ſo much the more lowly he valleth his courage. Seneca.

Gregory. He that doth gather vertues together (for estimation and comelinesse) without the vertue of humilitie, doth as he that openly beareth fine pouder in a rough and boysterous winde.

Alex.Seu. Gentlenesse and affabilitie are worthy vertues; that causeth men to be heartely and deerely beloued.

Nothing surely more entirely and fastly ioyneth the hearts of subiects to their prince or soueraigne then mercie, affability, and gentlenesse.

Cicero. Among many vertues belonging vnto Princes, none is so proper vnto them, or so honourable and princely, as timely to helpe suppliants, to comfort the afflicted, to encourage them, and to deliuer men from danger in their distresse.

Nothing breedeth so great deformitie in a Prince, as to ioyne vnto his high estate and authoritie, the noysome bitternesse of his hard and euill tempered nature.

They doe seeme indeed well to instruct and aduertise vs, which giue this admonishment vnto vs: that is to say, the higher we be in authoritie, so much the more gentle and lowly we should behaue our selues: for nothing is more seemely or commendable to a Prince or a noble man, then vertue, gentlenesse, meekenesse, and humility.

Cruelty and gentlenesse be two contraries: the one is of all men hated, and the other beloued: for cruelty is in an enemie mercilesse vnto the mild nature of man. Men are not in any thing more like vnto God, then in gentlenesse and humility, which most playnely consisteth, in doing good one to another.

Liue gently with thine vnderlings, as thou wouldest thy betters should liue with thee, and doe

to

to all men as thou wouldest be done by. Seneca.

Worship gentlenesse, and hate cruelty.

If thou wilt correct any man, doe it rather with gentlenesse, then with violent extremity. Use measure in all things.

Thinke not thy selfe to be that which thou art not: nor desire to seeme greater then thou art in deede.

Be gentle and louing to euery body, flatter none, be familiar with few, be indifferent and equall towards euery man, be slow to wrath, and swift to mercy and pitty.

Auarice is the thing, that taketh away the name of gentlenesse. Aristotle.

The gentle and lowly person, cannot be hated. Alex. Seu.

The gentleman gently intreated, is content to doe all things, but the vile natured man familiarly vsed, grudgeth at all things.

Giue place to thy betters, and to thy elders. Be not high minded. Please euery body. Be seruiceable to euery body. Doe not that to another, which thou thy selfe hatest. Get by perswasion, and not by violence. Hate violence. Be gentle in thy behauiour, and familiar in communication.

It belongeth to gentlenesse to salute gladly them that we meete: and to familiarity, to talke with them gently and friendly.

It seemeth to be vncomely and great vngentlenesse, a man to be vnthankefull.

It is due to render deserued thankes.

Humanity and gentlenesse will rather of a friend hope the best, then fore-thinke the worst.

If thou desire that thy friends loue may continue, be courteous and gentle towards him, both

in spéech be and also in manners: forbeare him in his anger, reproue him gently in his errour, and comfort him in his aduersity.

Like as pride slayeth loue, prouoketh disdaine, kindleth malice, confoundeth iustice, and subuerteth weales publike, euen so gentlenesse, affability or humblenesse, doe stirre vp affection, augment beneuolence, increase charity, support equity, and preserue most surely Countries and Cities.

The summe of all.

Humblenesse and affability are two worthy vertues,
That most happily purchase friendship and fauour;
Yea, euen Princes, and Rulers, that these vertues doe vse,
Cause subiects to obey them, and giue them due honour.
Hate cruelty, be lowly, and of gentle behauiour:
For as Pride slayeth loue, and ingendreth all wickednesse.
So Loue liuely flourisheth by the meanes of humblenesse.

Of Loue and Charity: Two mentall Vertues. Cap. II.

Constant loue is a principall vertue.

Hermes. Without loue no vertue may be perfect.

Plato. He that lacketh loue, ought not to be regarded.

Seneca. It is not possible to doe any thing well without loue.

Propertius. True loue is that which is not idle, but worketh to serue him whom he loueth.

Socrates. Loue all men, and be in subiection to all lawes, but aboue all things loue and obey God.

The greatest argument of godly loue, is to

loue that which God willeth: and not to loue that which God loueth not.

The true louer of God (which is properly the charitable person) is vnder no rule, but he is Lord aboue all inuentions, all precepts, and all commandements, that God hath giuen to man: For charity hath no bond. Alex. Seu.

He erreth in mine opinion, that preferreth feare before loue: without the which (witnesse Socrates) nothing either with God or with man, may long indure or abide. Socrates.

We are bound to loue, maintaine, and preserue, the common attonement and fellowship of all mankinde. Tullius.

The nature of fauour and grace, is farthest off of all things from selfe-loue, seeking nothing lesse then her owne commodity, but rather respecting the commodity of others.

None of vs loueth God, that enforceth to will any thing contrary to Gods will. He perfectly loueth not God, that doth any thing without God. He perfectly loueth not God, that thinketh any thing besides God. The perfect loue of God, cannot stand with any care or study for this life. The perfect loue of God abideth not the coupling with any other loue. The perfect loue of God knoweth none affection to kindred, it knoweth no difference betweene poore and rich, it knoweth not what meaneth mine and thine, it cannot diuide a foe from a friend: for hee that truly and perfectly loueth God, must loue God alone, nothing besides God, nor with God, but loue all indifferently in God, and for God. Pacuuius.

There are two kindes of loue, the one naturall, and the other heauenly.

The good louer loueth his soule better then his body.

The euill louer loueth his body, & not his soule.

Pithagoras A man of feeble courage annoyeth himselfe lightly with that which he loueth.

Homer. To be louing to him that hurteth vs, is the most acceptable thing in the sight of God that a man may doe. Thou shalt be beloued of God, if thou follow him in this point: In desiring to doe good to all men, and to hurt no body.

Mar.Aur. There is true loue, where be two bodies separate, and but one heart together.

Loue is payed with loue.

Pithagor. Small substance increaseth where concord raigneth: by discord, great things are scattered, and come to naught.

Of loue mixed with mockery, followeth the fruit of infamy.

There be fiue wayes noted of louing one another, of the which number one way is praysed, three be vtterly dispraysed, & one neither praysed, nor dispraysed. First a man may loue his neighbour for Gods sake, as euery good vertuous man loueth euery man. Secondly, a man may loue his neighbour for naturall affection, because he is his son, his brother, or kinsman. Thirdly, he may loue for vaine-glory, as if hee looked of his neighbour to be worshipped, or aduanced to honour. Fourthly, a man may loue for couetousnesse, as when hee cherisheth and flattereth a rich man for his goods, or when he maketh much of them that haue done him pleasures, or may doe. Fifely, and lastly, he may loue for his sensuall lust & appetite, as when he loueth for delicate fare, or else when his minde foolishly runneth and doteth vpon women,

women. The first way to loue his neighbour for the loue that hee beareth to God, is onely worthy to be praised. The second way, naturally deserueth neyther praise nor dispraise. The third, the fourth, and the fift, to loue for glory, aduantage, or pleasure, all thrée be vtterly naught.

Likenesse of manners maketh stedfast & perfect.

Of all things, the newest is best, saue of loue and friendship: which the elder that it waxeth, is euer the better. Seneca.

Too much selfe-loue is cause of all euill.

Repentance is the end of filthy loue.

Lewd loue is the businesse of loyterers.

Loue cannot be mingled with feare.

There is nothing so dark, but that loue espieth.

Loue leaueth no danger vnattempted.

It is not possible for a seruant to be diligent that loueth not his maister.

Hee that hath a whole and cleare heart, without inforcing, vttereth louing words: hée that hath an euill heart, alwayes ouercommeth others with words of malice. Mar. Aur.

That person that is entirely beloued, causeth euer great griefe at his death.

The loue of a foole is more noysome then pleasant. Socrates.

As one bird loueth another, and one beast another, and one wise man another: so one foole loueth another. Mar. Aur.

Loue peace, maintaine concord, be mercifull to the penitent, despise not thine vnderling.

Haunt not too much thy friends houses, for that engendreth no great loue: nor be not long from thence, for that engendreth hate, but vse a meane in all things. Aristippus

Loue betwéene neighbours suffereth to be mitigated with water: but it is requisite that the loue of the Prince and the people be perfect and pure.

Aristotle. It is better for a man to loue good-fellowship then money.

There is no perfect loue, where is no equalitie betwéene louers.

Mar. Aur. Loue in young bloud, in the spring time and flowrishing youth, it is a poyson that forthwith spreadeth into euery veyne: it is an hearbe that by and by entreth the entrals: a swounding that incontinently mortifieth all the members: and a pestilence that assaileth the hart, and finally, it maketh an end of all vertues.

Plato. As in euery place Iuie findeth somewhat to cleaue to, so loue is very seldome without a subiect.

Mar. Aur. The great voyce outward, is a signe of little loue inward: and the great inward loue kéepeth silence outward.

The old lecherous louer is a Léeke, with a white head and a gréene taile.

Hermes. Like as the fire wasteth the fire-brand, so doth scornefulnesse wast loue betwéene friends.

Better are the stripes of him that faithfully loueth, then the deceitfull kisses of him that hateth.

This is the iust ordinance of God, that he that loueth shall haue an end, and it that is beloued shal take an end, and the time that we are in shall also end: then it is reason that the loue wherewith we doe loue should end likewise.

Hermes. What charitie is. Charitie is a good & gracious effect of the soule, whereby mans heart hath no fancy to estéeme, value, or ponder any thing in this wide world beside

beside or before the care and study to know God.

God, as hee himselfe is all Charitie and Loue, and the onely beginning of all goodnesse, so there floweth freely from him, as from the onely fountaine of his grace into the heart of man (the instrument of all grace) all good motions to worke well, and that freely, louingly, and of good-will, by the power and freedome of his spirit, without respecting of merit thereby, or iustification, but reuerently (with all ioyfulnesse) tendering and seeking the only glory of him, by whom (through grace) hee is so freely and mercifully iustified, made righteous, and saued.

Charitie is the childe of Faith. Chrisost.

Good workes make not a man iustified or righteous: but a man beeing once iustified, doth good workes. Augustin.

No deserts of men can haue place before the grace of God.

Charitie is not like one vertue, but is such a thing, that by many degrees of diuers vertues it must be gotten, as the finall conclusion of all labour and trauaile in vertue.

All Charitie is Loue, but it is not true that all Loue is Charitie.

Charitie maketh men to forsake sinne, and imbrace vertue.

Charitie is the whole perfection of a good man.

Charitie maketh a man absolute and perfect in vertues. Plato.

The filthy effects of bribery, hindereth greatly the worke of Charitie.

As couetousnesse, bribery, and extortion, are neuer contented, but needy: so charitable liberalitie is euermore blessed with plenty.

By

By our Charitie with God, wee learne what is our duetie towards man.

August. The two wings wherewith a man flyeth vnto God be these: if thou forgiuest him that hath offended thee, and dost helpe him that hath néede of thee.

How can Charitie to man stand, when Charitie to God (which is obedience to his will) is ouerthrowne?

Sixe things here following are specially to be noted, that in what man soeuer any of them doe raign, there abideth not in him any spark of Gods Charitie: First, looke vpon the vnmercifull and cursed man, that being voyd of pitty cannot forgiue, but still boyleth in his appetite to be auenged. Secondly, looke vpon the enuious stomacke, how he without rest fretteth in coueting the sight of his hurt whom hée so cruelly spighteth. Thirdly, looke vpon the insatiable Glutton (without godly regard) hee beastly prouideth his belly chéere. Fourthly, looke vpon the filthy Lecher, how busie hee is to compasse his vngratious thoughts. Fiftly, looke vpon the wretched Couetous man, how without reason and good order, hée continually scrapeth, and beateth his braine to gather gaines. Finally, looke vpon the Ambitious and hautie hearted fellow, how busily hée bestirreth him to get promotion and worship. These kinde of men, through their vaine and corrupt fantasies (not possessed with the grace and Charitie of God) be no lesse gréedy to satisfie these their vnsatiable desires, then the hungry and thirstie bodies (through naturall necessitie) séeke to be refreshed.

Whosoeuer féeleth in his heart any power or title

title of hatred or enuy, for any manner of cause against any man, that person may be well assured that he is not in Charity with God.

Charity is a word much vsed with euery man and woman, but not so well perceiued, as it is commonly spoken.

Like as fire is an instrument, without which few workes can be finished, so without Charity nothing may be well done, and honestly. Plutarch.

Like as God, and the Children of God are alwayes knowne to be all one in Charity, mercy, pitty, patience, long-suffering, wishing welfare, health, and life to euery man: so the Diuell, and the children of the Diuell are knowne to be alwayes one, by their enuy, spight, and malignity, by their cruelty, tyranny, impatiency, swift reuengement, oppression, impouerishing, and spoyling, hinderers of health, and very murtherers.

The summe of all.

In this life, of Loue there are two kindes,
That draweth men to ioy and paine:
On filthy Loue some set their mindes,
And godly Loue some men retaine,
The wicked doe count such Loue but vaine:
But Gods heauenly Loue and Charity,
Purchaseth th' euerlasting felicity.

Of Patience: a mentall Vertue. Cap. III.

Patience is a noble vertue, appertaining as well to inward as to exteriour gouernance, and is the vanquisher of iniuries, the sure defence against all the effects and passions of the soule, retaining alwayes glad semblance in aduersity and dolor.

How to obtaine Patience. The meanes to obtaine Patience, is by two things principally: a direct and vpright conscience, a true and constant opinion in the estimation of goodnesse, which seldome commeth onely of nature, except it be wonderfull excellent, but by the diligent study of very Philosophy (not that which is sophisticate, and consisteth in sophismes) nature is thereto prepared and holpen.

Socrates. Patience and good beliefe in God, maketh a man victorious.

He is perfectly patient, which in his fury can subdue his owne affections.

Ambrose. Better is hee that contemneth iniury, then hee that sorroweth: for he that contemneth it as hee nothing felt it, passeth not of it: but hee that is sorrowfull, is therewith tormented, as though hee felt it.

Epictetus. Sustaine, abstaine: sustaine, and beare aduersity, and abstaine from all euill and filthy pleasures and pastimes.

Mar. Aur. It is oftentimes seene that it cannot faile in a man that can suffer and hath patience, to haue vertue and force.

He is worthy to be called couragious, strong, and stout, who doth not onely with Patience suffer iniuries, rebukes, and displeasures done vnto him,

him, but also doth good against those euills.

One of the vertues that a wise man ought to haue, (wherein he shall be knowne as wise) is that he can suffer well: for a man that can suffer well, was euer wise and well mannered.

Hee that is patient and sober, shall neuer repent him.

Be patient in tribulation, and giue no man cause to speake euill of thee. Hermes.

Let not thy heart faile thee, although Fortune turneth her face a while from thee: but patiently beare the time: for merry euen-tides oftentimes follow carefull mornings.

Receiue patiently the words of correction, although they seeme grieuous. Hermes.

In suffering afflictions, Patience is made strong.

Patience and perseuerance are two proper notes: whereby Gods children are truly knowne from hypocrites, counterfaites, and dissemblers.

By patience wee are rendred vnto God, and approoued of among men.

Humility, Patience, and faire speech, are the pacifiers of wrath and anger.

The trauailes that come of necessity, ought with good courage to be endured. Mar Aur.

Be constant and patient in aduersity, and in prosperity wary and lowly.

The best way for a man to be auenged, is to condemne iniury and rebuke, and to liue with such honesty and good behauiour, that the doer shall at the last be thereof ashamed, or at the least lose the fruit of his malice, that is to say, shall not reioyce and haue glory of thy hinderance and damage. Mar.Aur.

Euen

Euen as yron, except it be often scoured, will soone corrupt and waxe rusty: so except the sinfull heart of man, and his flesh, be often scoured with the whetstone of aduersity, they will soone corrupt, and ouergrow with the rust of all filthinesse and sinne.

The summe of all.

Patience is a Vertue both noble and necessary,
Appertaining to the inward and exterior gouernance:
Patience is a vanquisher of approued iniury;
A sure rocke of defence against all disturbance.
This Vertue therefore to obtaine, giue diligent attendance.
By two things thou shalt learne it, to thy comfort in distresse,
An vpright conscience, and constant esteeming of goodnesse.

Of Diligence, Agility, or Quicknesse. Cap. IIII.

Seneca. Diligence quickly dispatcheth all things.

Aristotle. Hee that diligently attendeth to his businesse, can neuer repent him, but bringeth all his workes to a perfect and good conclusion.

Diligence and carefulnesse are the keyes of certainty.

Hermes. Diligent purueyance is great surety.

Cicero. There is nothing so fearefull vnto wise and circumspect men, but by diligence it may be foreseene, and happily brought to passe: neither is there any euill, but that it must readily fall vpon those which be vndiligent, carelesse, and sluggish.

Cicero. God which is immortall, doth (as it were) sell all things vnto vs for our labour and trauaile.

They which will come to an happy estate, must diligently labour in this world.

A thousand euils do afflict daily that man, which hath to himselfe an idle and an unprofitable carkeise. Salust.

There was neuer any man that obtayned renowne by his carelesse sluggishnesse.

Diligent labour preuayleth mightely: yea, it ouercommeth all things. Virgil.

Those studies which séeme laborsome in youthfull yéeres, are made right pleasant rests unto olde age.

By the deceitfull poyson of sloath, vertue béeing ouercome, it yéeldeth to the breach of confusion, and falleth on a sodaine to utter decay.

We know that there is nothing so easie but it will séeme hard, if it be not with chearefulnesse taken in hand. Terence.

Nothing unto man is so hard, but by diligence it may easily be found out.

If by diligence thou shalt bring any noble thing to passe: thy labor shall soone be ouer-past and gone, but thy glory shall still remayne: and if at pleasure thou accomplish any vile act, the remembrance doubtlesse of the villany shall still remaine, euen when thy pleasure is farre past and gone. Virgil.

The waking eye, and well occupied hand, attaineth of right unto many great things.

There is nothing so good to make a Horse fat as the eye of his Maister, neyther is there ought better to make Land fertile, then the steps of the owner, that is to say, the Maisters diligence. Diogenes.

By danger, dread, and doubtfulnesse, diligence is greatly hindered. Demosth.

It oftentimes happeneth, that they which be slacke and undiligent in doing their duties at the beginning, after that they haue béene admonished thereof Alex.Seu.

thereof, eyther by their friends, or by the goodnesse of their owne proper wits, they haue béene industrious and very diligent. Contrariwise, others which at the first haue béene quicke, with a maruailous dexteritie and promptnesse, they haue afterwards by little and little relented: yea, and hauing gathered together (as diuers haue) good estimation and abundance of substance, haue withdrawne themselues from painefull affaires, and at the last, be to no man, but onely to themselues, profitable.

Pittachus. Nothing shall cause a man more diligently to do his dutie, then to thinke what he would require of him that is inferiour to him.

Musonius. Hée that is diligent shall enioy the profit of his labour and diligence.

The summe of all.

Diligence is a quicknesse and liuelinesse of minde,
Whereby all things are finished most aptly:
Diligence doth alwayes this commoditie finde,
It neuer repenteth but endeth most gladly.
Carefull diligence is the key of certaintie,
And if with diligence men doe their businesse,
What reward shall follow the end will expresse.

Of Liberalitie. Cap. V.

Aristotle. Liberalitie is as well a measure in giuing as in taking of money and goods.

Liberalitie is not in the multitude or quantitie of that which is giuen, but in the habit or fashion of the giuer.

It is Liberalitie to giue according to a mans abilitie.

That

That is not to be approued Liberality, wherein is any mixture of auarice or rapine, for it is not properly liberality to exact vniustly, or by violence or craft to take goods from particular persons & distribute them to a multitude: or to take from many vniustly, and enrich therewith one person or a few: for the true precept concerning benefits or rewards is, to take good heede that he contend not against equity, nor that he vphold any iniury. Tullius.

There be two fountaines which doe approue liberality, that is, a sure iudgement and an honest fauour. Valerius Max.

He onely is liberall, which distributeth accor=ding to his substance, and where it is expedient. Aristotle.

Liberality taketh the name of the substance of the person from whence it proceedeth. For it resteth not in the qualitie or quantitie of things that be giuen, but in the naturall disposition of the giuer.

Wonderfully is the loue of the multitude stir=red with the fame and opinion of liberality, boun=tifulnesse, iustice, and faithfulnesse, and of all those vertues which appertaine to the mildnesse of man=ners, and gentlenesse. Tullius.

It should séeme that as man being the most pre=tious and goodly creature of all others vpon the whole earth, & so in large manner wonderfully en=dewed with diuine grace from the high God a=boue, should in such wise most earnestly regard his estate and creation, that not only (as a Lord ouer them) to haue and inioy the pleasures of them (for his sufficient and néedfull purpose) but also most louingly with all diligence to sée to the reliefe and comfort of those that by creation are like vn=to himselfe. Theophr.

Aristotle. Liberalitie in a Noble-man, is to be commended, although somewhat it exceed the termes of measure. And if it be well and duely employed, it requireth perpetuall honour to the giuer, and much fruit and singular commoditie thereby encreaseth. For where vertuous and honest men be aduanced and well rewarded, it stirreth the courages of them that haue any sparke of vertue, to encrease therein with all their force and endeauour: Wherefore next to the helping and releiuing of a communaltie, the most part of liberalitie is to be employed on men of vertue and good qualities: wherein is to be required a good election and iudgement, that for hope of reward or fauour (vnder the cloake of vertue) be not hid the most mortall poyson of flattery. Liberalitie which is vpon flatterers employed, is not onely perished, but also spilled and deuoured.

Seneca. He is liberall that delighteth more in good renowne then in money.

Socrates. A liberall man cannot be enuious.

He that is liberall cannot liue amisse.

Giue liberally for thy profit.

As liberality maketh friends of enemies: so pride maketh enemies of friends.

They that be liberall, doe with-hold or hide nothing from them whom they loue: whereby loue increaseth, and friendship also is made perpetuall and stable.

Hermes. He that is liberall neglecteth not his goods, nor giueth it to all men, but vseth it so, as he may continually help others, and giueth when, and where, and on whom it ought best to be imployed.

Tullius. Liberalitie and beneficence be of such affinitie, that the one may neuer from the other be separate, for

for the employment of money is not liberality, if it be not for a good end or purpose. Beneficence is neuer taken but in the better part, and is taken out of vertue, where liberality commeth out of the coffer.

Liberality causeth men to be greatly maruailed at. Alex.Seu.

A liberall heart is cause of beneuolence, although sometime perchance power lacketh. Tullius.

That same liberality that standeth in trauell and diligence, is both most honest, and also spreadeth farthest, and is able to profit most.

It is the greatest part of Godlinesse, to knowledge the liberality of Gods goodnesse towards vs: and to giue onely prayses vnto him, from whence all things are yeelded to our reliefes. Pacuuius.

The summe of all.

Liberality is a certaine measure,
That springeth of fauour, friendship, and amity;
In giuing or receiuing land or treasure,
After a mans substance or ability:
But chiefly in comforting the poore and needy,
For that is liberality in very deede,
To helpe the poore miserable in time of neede.

Of Temperance and Moderation.

Cap. VI.

Temperance is a noble vertue, and chiefly appertaineth to the honourable estate of mankinde, whereby the Princely gouernour, Reason, (which raigneth as a King in man) is knowne to beare sway in man: whereby is happily tempered all his doings, and thereby differeth from the effect of beasts. Photion.

Temperance is enemy to lust, and lust is a wayting seruant vnto bodily pleasure.

Boëtius. Temperance calleth a man backe from all grosse affects and carnall appetites, and letteth him not excéede neither in foolish reioycing, nor in vngodly sorrowing.

Cicero. Temperance is the pacifier of all tumults.

Isocrates. Grosse affections and lusts, are either vtterly to be refused, or else with moderation to be vsed.

Plutarch. He is to be called a temperate and moderate person, which not onely hath power ouer his wanton and corrupt affects, but so endeauours also himselfe, that in his Countrey he is chargeable to no man, to no man cruell or grieuous, neither to any man dangerous.

For hee is tempered with the light of the heauenly grace, he is of nature familiar and gentle: he is easie to men that will come and speake with him: whose house is vnlocked, not shut, but open to all men, where euery man, as it were in tempests and stormes, may repaire for their relieuement and succour.

Anaxag. Youth vntemperate and full of carnall affections, quickly turneth the body into age, to be full of infirmities, foule and féeble.

Cicero. When the vnbrideled carkasse or fraile flesh of man is not well tempered or discréetly ruled, but ouermuch cherished, set at liberty, and pampered, then is the soule the lesse regarded or looked vpon, but abideth in most deformed state and miserable. And the more delicately the body is handled, the more stubbornely it wrastleth against the minde, and doth cast it off, euen as a Horse too well cherished, vseth oft to cast his rider. The heauy burthen of the body sore oppresseth the minde.

He

Hee cannot commend temperance, which thinketh that the chiefe good thing consisteth in pleasure, for temperance is thereto enemy.

As temperance doth mitigate all grosse appetites, and causeth them to be obedient to reason, and doth preserue the iudgement of the minde, so temperance is thereto an enemy, for it greatly troubleth and inflameth much the minde. Cicero.

If thou wouldest consider the excellency of mans nature, and the dignity thereof, thou shouldest well perceiue how foule and dishonest a thing it is to be enclined vnto Lechery, immoderate eating and drinking, and to liue loosely and wantonly: and contrarily, how honest, faire, and commendable a thing it is, to liue continently, temperately, sadly, and soberly. Tullius.

He is worthy to be called a temperate and moderate person, which firmely gouerneth and bridleth (through reason) the vice of sensuality, and all other grosse affections of the minde. Thucid.

The summe of all.

Of all noble vertues that God giueth to man,
And (whereby as reasonable) he is knowne from beasts;
Temperance is of force, apprehend it who can,
To bridle grosse effects, which the wise detests:
It preserueth excesse at banquets, and at feasts,
It offereth also to a contented minde,
To take with thankfulnesse such as it doth finde.

Of Chastity. Cap. VII.

Propertius CHastity, purity of life, continency, or refusing the corrupt pleasures of the flesh, and of this world, are precious in the sight of God, and doe possesse such as keepe their bodies cleane and undefiled, and in life refraine from all euill.

Chastity is the beauty of mans life.

Chastity and purity of life consisteth either in sincere virginity, or in faithfull matrimony.

Chrisost. Hom. de inuent. cru. The first degree of Chastity is pure virginity, and the second faithfull matrimony.

Abstinency and Continency are two forcible vertues against Auarice and Lechery, two capitall vices: which being refrained by a noble man that liueth at liberty and without controulement, procureth unto him (besides the fauour of God) immortall glory: and that City or Realme hath long prosperity, whose Gouernors are not acquainted with these vices: For as Valerius maximus saith, Val. max. wheresoeuer this feruent pestilence of mankinde hath entry, iniury raigneth, reproach and infamy spread and deuoure the name of Nobility.

Thesilius. That thou maist auoid filthy loue, a dissolute and libidinous life, with other kinde of filthinesse, embrace that loue which God alloweth, and keepe chastity and purity of life, which consisteth in sincere virginity, or in the faithfull state of matrimony.

Apuleius. A chaste heart (which is onely seene and approued of God) is most precious and blessed in his sight, and therefore deserueth of all men so farre forth to be well iudged or condemned, as the words uttered from the mouth, the manner

of

of outward gesture, the vsage in eating & drinking, and the order of apparell, seemeth to be honest, modest, temperate, and seemely.

A wise man when hee is once stirred vp to the vnnaturall desire of wanton and vncleane things, hee will by and by charge himselfe with the loathsome state of filthinesse, and will flye (to his power) euen from the very secret and inward consent of them, and much rather from the committed fact.

It must needes be a poynt of great continencie and integritie (if it be possible for any man) not to be caught with the intisements of vayne beautie, comelinesse of body, outward and gay glory, nor with the vaine pleasures of the World, but to be restrayned by the respect of iustice, equitie, cleanenesse and chastitie: yea, and with the bridle of the feare of God, not to consent to corrupt concupiscence, which doth in that sort deceyue them (specially all carnall men) and blindeth right iudgement in them. Musonius.

Some men there be whom bodily lust tickleth not at all, such men ought not by and by to ascribe that vnto vertue, which is an indifferent thing, for not to lacke bodily lust, but to ouercome, it is the office of vertue. Socrates.

Neyther suffer thy hands to worke, nor thy tongue to speake, nor thine eares to heare, that which is filthy and euill.

Beware of the baytes of wanton women, which are laid out to catch men, for they are great hinderance to him that desireth wisedome. Socrates.

Fly from filthinesse of life.

At thy Table let all things be pure, chaste, and holy, euen as hee is holy whose gifts thou shalt there haue in hand.

Cassidorus There be sixe things that preserueth Chastitie, sobernesse in diet, labor, sharpenesse of thinner apparell, brideling the senses, that is to say, the fiue wits: also, little communication, and that with honesty, and eschewing opportunity of the person, the place, and the time.

August. Where necessitie is ioyned, or layd vnto chastitie, there authority is giuen to lechery, for neyther is shée chaste, which by feare is compelled, neither is shée honest, which with néed is obtayned.

Bernard. Chastity without charity, is a Lampe without Oyle: take the Oyle away, and the Lampe giueth no light: take away charity, then chastity pleaseth not at all.

Pontanus. That man whose minde is wholly dedicated to the vse of vertue and purity of life, and despiseth the vanities of this short life, most certainely preuayleth, and obtayneth saluation in the end.

The summe of all.

Because flesh is fraile and procureth filthinesse,
And worketh with woe the soules deformitie,
It behoueth in time to eschew such wickednesse,
And willingly to imbrace the vse of Chastitie,
Handle not, heare not, nor speake that is filthy,
Detest from the heart Women light and wanton,
For many by their baits are caught to destruction.

THE SEAVENTH BOOKE.

Cap. I.

An Admonition to auoid all kinde of Vices.

The causes of all inconueniences and hurts that may happen to man, are his owne vices: which bringeth him into the hatred both of God and man, yea, and of himselfe also at the length. Wherefore the Philosophers aboue all things haue euer abhorred them, and by all meanes indeuoured to quench and destroy them, both in themselues and in all others. And although there be sundry sorts of vices, some naturall, some vnnaturall, and some against nature: I thinke it not néedfull to distinguish them, but because they are all euill, I therefore endeuour to make them all abhorred. Wherefore I haue in this Bóoke gathered the sayings of the Philosophers concerning the vilenesse and corruption of the most part of them: shewing what detriment and hurt commeth through them, which I wish that all men would diligently note, lest not béeing warned by other mens harmes, they do (through their owne) teach others to beware.

Of

Of Vice, Sinne and Wickednesse. Cap. II.

LIke as Vertue is a garment most comely and precious, whereby the soule is garnished, to the glory of the most high God: so Vice and Wickednesse is filthy, abhominable, and vncomely: which corrupteth and destroyeth the soule, contrary to the will of God.

Mar. Aur. Cursed is the man that knoweth not to be a man, but maketh himselfe lesse then a man by his Vice.

Anaxag. The life of that man is wicked, that many bewaileth: and in whose death euery man reioyceth.

Protegeus. As there is nothing vpon the earth better then good creatures: so there is nothing worse then vicious and wicked men.

Aristotle. They that be daily inclined and vtterly disposed to vice and wickednesse, shall not at any time increase in riches, nor profit in any science.

All such as for the multitude of their sinnes & wickednesse are hopelesse, and such as haue committed thefts and slaughters, with such other like wickednesses: the iustice of God, and their owne deserts damne themselues vnto euerlasting death, from the which they shall neuer be deliuered.

If thou hast wickedly sinned, repent thee speedily, and tarry not till to morrow.

Plato. Woe be to that wicked and sinnefull man that hath not power to turne from the filthy workes of fleshly and vayne pleasures, which hinder him from the blessed estate, and keepe backe his soule from the presence of God.

Mar. Aur. It is meere wickednesse to change or alter good

good lawes to awake strife, and raise noyses, to abate noblenesse, to exalt the unworthy, to banish innocents, and honour theeues, to loue flatterers, and disptaise them that be vertuous, to embrace delights, and tread vertue vnder foote, to weepe for them that be euill, and laugh them to scorne that be good: and finally, they are all wicked that take lightnesse for their mother, and Vertue for their stepmother.

It is very wickednesse to seeke praise by counterfaited Vertue.

Sin, and seeke wickednesse, where thou knowest God is not. Hermes.

An euill man is neither his owne friend, nor yet any other mans.

It is great corruption vnto the people, to haue a vicious and corrupt Ruler. Aristotle.

Beware of sin as the serpent of the soule, which spoyleth vs of all our ornaments and seemely apparell in Gods sight.

Neither suffer thy hands to worke, nor thy tongue to speak, nor thine eare to heare that which is euill or wicked.

If thou dost not intend to doe good, yet at the least refraine from doing euill.

Flye and eschew thine owne vices, and be not curious to search out other mens. Plato.

Thinke all things may be suffered saue filthinesse and vice.

As wee are set in diuers pleasures by our vice, so wee fall hourely into diuers miseries, and are noted, to our great infamy. Mar. Aur.

Nothing is euill but that which is coupled with some vice and wickednesse. Diogenes.

He that is rooted in sinne, will not be corrected.

The

Plutarch. The euill which vicious persons doe in the company of a Prince are reputed his.

Use not familiaritie with any vicious person.

Hermes. Without comparison he is worse that fauoureth euill, then he that committeth the euill: for the one procéedeth of weakenesse, and the other of malice.

Rulers and men in authoritie sinne excéedingly, that giue others license to sinne.

It is hard for a man hauing license to sinne, to kéepe himselfe there-from.

Anachar. Sinne plucketh the soule from God, whose Image the soule should beare.

Plato. Through sinne and wickednesse kingdomes are altered and changed.

Iuuenal. Through sin Princes are remoued from their royall state and dignity.

What sin is. Sinne is an act straying from the order of the end unto which it should be directed, contrary to the rule either of nature, or of reason, or of the euerlasting Law.

Ambrose. Sin is the breach of Gods Law, and the disobedience of the heauenly Commandements.

Augustine. Sin is either that which is spoken, committed, or couered, contrary to the euerlasting Law.

Sinne (like an euill trée) hath many branches, as the loue of our selues, the loue of pleasure, of whoredome, drunkennesse, and gluttony, the loue of glory, honor, ambition, and such other vices: and upon this wicked rabble and such like, crafty Concupiscence waiteth as a seruant at inches, applying each of them the obiects of their kinde. And if it be not obeyed, there must also néeds be suffered the rule and gouernment of sin: for experience often teacheth that in this respect the malice of concupiscence is great, and therefore not to be spoken. *Concupiscence.*

There

There be three things that cause vs to sinne: first, foolishly to flatter our selues, and thinke that God seeth not our sinnes: secondly, to perswade our selues that God careth not for our sins: thirdly, because we waigh not Gods iustice, but respect him onely to be mercifull, and will of purpose be more sinfull. *The occasion of sinne.*

Hee that is in seruitude to sinne, the strength thereof and the power of Sathan is such, that no vertue or strength of man, no nor the strength of any celestiall spirits can doe any good, or helpe to make him free: for it is onely the power of the heauenly and most mighty Spirit of God, that freely purgeth the hearts of men, and freeth them from the bondage of sinne and Sathan. *The seruitude of sin.*

The wickednesse of mans life maketh the spirit of God dull in the heart of man, that is, not to worke in him according to his diuine nature.

If a man would rightly vnderstand the high Maiesty and puissant state of the great and terrible God: would he not thinke that when he hideth himselfe in darknesse, and doth the deeds of darkenesse, that he should be neuerthelesse manifest vnto him in all his doing, who is able to perceiue the secret of the heart? *A good meane to forsake sin.*

Where sin by authority is duely punished, there the country & people are most happy and blessed.

Cities are well gouerned when the wicked be punished.

The feeble are defended from the mighty, and the true from the vntrue, by the vertue of Iustice: who also rooteth out the wicked from among the good.

Hee is a vicious person that intendeth onely his owne profit.

Xenoph. If thou intendest any thing whereof may grow any goodnesse, deuise to proceed with all diligence: but if by thy workes may chance that which is euill, then be as swift to conquer thine owne will.

Plato. Thou canst not alwayes keepe thy sinne and wickednesse vnspyed, though for a season it be secret and hid: for Truth, the true daughter of God and of Time, hath sworne to detect sinne and vice.

Mar. Aur. They that be euill, be alwayes doubly euill, because they beare armour defensiue to defend their owne euils, and armour offensiue to assayle the good manners of others.

They liue very badly that alwayes begin to liue, forasmuch as their many beginnings doe make their owne euils still vnperfect.

Hermes. It is better to suffer death, then by compulsion to doe that which is euill.

There is but one way to goodnesse, but the wayes to euill are innumerable.

To be much inquisitiue about others offences, is a signe of an euill disposition.

Mar. Aur. The greatest euill of all euils is when a man forgetteth that he is a man, putting reason vnder foote, straying his hand against Vertue, and letting Vice rule the bridle.

What doth it profit thee to haue an expert tongue, a quicke memory, a cleare vnderstanding, great science, profound eloquence, or a sweet stile, if with these graces thou hast a wicked will.

Socrates. Rulers by vsing vitiousnesse destroy not onely themselues, but all others besides, that are vnder their gouernance.

Plato. Hee is no good Gouernour that commandeth others to auoide Vices, and will not leaue them himselfe.

Vertues

Vertues cannot be séene in a man, except he first put away his vices. Hermes.

As some poysons are so contrary by nature that one cureth another, so it is likewise of deceits and vices. Seneca.

Hee which giueth riches or glory to a wicked man, giueth Wine to him that hath a Feauer. Plutarch.

If they be miserable which haue cruell Maisters, although they may go from them: how much are they more miserable that serue their Vices as their Masters, from whom they cannot flye? Virgil.

A thousand euils doe follow wickednesse, but specially that most wretched torment and vexation of a guilty conscience.

Sinne accuseth to eternall death.

An hundred tongues and mouthes as many,
Although I had with eloquence high:
And though my voyce all Iron were
In strength, yet could I not declare
The vice of men, nor yet can tell
What paines therefore they suffer in hell.

As the hearts of the wicked are altogether hardened and impenitent, so they heape vp displeasure vnto themselues against the day of Wrath, and the terrible appearing of the iust iudgement of God.

The match to kindle against vs the fierce fire of Gods wrath, is our sinnes.

The fault committed is of our selues, but God is blamelesse. Cato.

He is a foole that committeth sinne: hée is wise that repenteth him of his sin, but he is to be counted most wise that flyeth from the fact of sinne.

Euery sinne is conceyued first in the heart, and afterward finished in word or fact. Arnobius.

The

The heart of man is defiled and uncleane: and all the sinnes committed by men procéede from thence, as from a fountaine of all euill and mischiefe.

Plato. As in euery Pomegranate there is some graine rotten: so there is no man but hath some euill condition.

Socrates. As a man appeareth more in a mist then in cléere weather, so appeareth his vice more when hée is angry, then when he is at quiet.

Hermes. As to the good their goodnesse is a reward: so to the wicked their wickednesse is a punishment.

Plato. Like as the fire which féedeth vpon corrupt things, despiseth the swéet and pure hearbes: so wickednes doth follow the wicked, dispraising all goodnesse.

Socrates. Like as one branch of a trée, being set on fire, kindleth all the rest: so one vicious fellow destroyeth a whole company.

Hermes. As men for their bodily health do abstaine from euill meates: so ought they to abstaine from sinne for the saluation of their soules.

The summe of all.

As the soule which by vertue is chiefly garnished
Doth shew and set forth Gods eternall glory:
So the soule that with Vice is replenished,
Forgetteth God and sinneth most wickedly,
Embrace then Vertue, for Vice is most filthy,
And Vertue at no time in man can shine cleare,
While Vice and Wickednesse in him shall appeare.

Of

Of Ignorance, and Errour. Cap. III.

Ignorance is a madnesse of the Soule, which while it laboureth to attayne the truth, is confounded in the knowledge of it selfe. Plato.

Great is the hurt that hath chanced by ignorance.

They which be ignorant and of euill disposition be vnhappy: For where ignorance and sinne is, there infelicitie and miserie most plainely appeareth. Plato.

To be ignorant of Gods true seruice, is not to be commended: but to be rather vtterly blamed and punished by the hand of God.

As the light of godly knowledge encreaseth vertue, and worketh a godly life: so the darknesse of ignorance hindereth Vertue, and increaseth a wicked life.

There is nothing worse then to liue beastly and out of honest order: and the greatest and most euident cause and token thereof is, the sin of ignorance, which is an vtter enemie and contrary to the vertue of knowledge. Plato.

The ignorance of knowledge that is in brute beastes, maketh plainly the difference betwéene men and men: for so much differeth man from the dull and brutish beast, as he sheweth himselfe by knowledge to bée cléerely vnspotted of ignorance. Plato.

Hée is properly to be tearmed brutish, that is grosse and dull of sense, and lacketh the capacitie of knowledge: and finally, brutishnesse is very ignorance. Aristippus

As ignorance maketh a man beast-like, and

keepeth him low, and in the state of beggery and misery: so knowledge putteth away beastlinesse, it rayseth a man vp, and setteth him in the seate of dignitie.

Plato. What ignorance is. The vertue of Gods truth is an instruction of them that be ignorant, for the minde of man is not so bright by the light of Nature that it can by the owne sharpenesse know the things that be of God, and necessary to be knowne for the saluation of man: wherefore it behoueth him to haue a more godly light, whereby hee may haue the true light, and thereby be truely taught: that is to say, by the light of the spirit of God, in the vnderstanding of the Word of God.

An ignorant man may be knowne by three poynts: hee cannot rule himselfe, because hee lacketh reason: hee cannot resist his Lusts, because hee lacketh wit, neyther can hee doe what hee would, because he is in bondage to a woman.

There is none so ignorant, as hee that trusteth most to his owne wit: none so vncertaine as hee that most trusteth fortune: nor any so much out of quiet as he that is combred with an vnruly brawling wife.

The boldnesse of the ignorant, ingendreth all euils.

Through lacke of wit, springeth much harme: by meanes of ignorance much good is left vndone.

Socrates. The ignorant in their banquets vse minstrelsie to cheere them, but the learned with their voyces delight one another.

Hee that is ignorant in the truth, and led about with opinions, must needes erre.

It is a great shame for an olde man to be ignorant.

It is a shame to be ignorant in that which euery man ought to know. Socrates.

He is an ignorant foole, that is gouerned by womens counsell.

He that doubteth and merualleth, seemeth to be ignorant.

It is better to be ignorant in vile things, then to know them. Pithagor.

Hee that knoweth not how much hee seeketh, doth not know when to finde that which hee lacketh. Socrates.

That which is well done is done wittingly: but that which is euill done is done ignorantly.

Ignorance in a Prince is a stroke of pestilence, it slayeth diuers, and infecteth all persons, and vnpeopleth the Realme, chaseth away friends, and giueth heart to enemies of strange Nations, that were before in dread, and finally, damageth his person, and slandereth euery one. Mar. Aur.

Idlenesse ingendreth ignorance, and ignorance ingendreth errour. Plato.

Of small errours not let at the beginning, springeth great and mightie mischiefes.

The beginning of errour is to thinke those things to please God, which pleaseth our selues: and those things to displease God, whereat our selues be displeased. Augustin.

Those things be very delectable and pleasant vnto vs: which doe eyther like our eyes. with their outward curiositie, glistering and gaynesse, or our eares with some speciall pleasantnesse: and therefore we doe also think that they doe in like manner please the diuine senses

of the most heauenly God.

Mar.Cels. It is an old saying, that the multitude of them which doe erre, and their agréement in that errour, cannot make the errour allowable.

Custome without truth is but an old errour.

Cyprian. He is as well out of the way, which doth commit an errour, seduced by the iudgement or inticement of another body, as hée that is seduced of himselfe.

It is most right that they which doe refuse the gift of the knowledge of God, should be againe refused, and haue it taken farre from them: and be ouerwhelmed to the uttermost, with the curse of ignorance and errours.

An errour is not ouercome with violence but truth.

Errour at the end is knowne to be euill, and truth thereby is much the better knowne.

He that erreth before he know the truth, ought the sooner to be forgiuen.

Mar.Aur. The understanding which is dusked in errours, and depraued in malice, cannot be healed by medicines, nor redressed by reason, nor holpe by counsell.

The summe of all.

Ignorance of the soule is very madnesse,
Which while it laboureth the truth to attaine,
Is confounded and wrapped in heauinesse,
Through selfe-knowledge, and feeblenesse of braine;
Yea, it is also most euident and plaine,
That as ignorance is bred by idlenesse,
Euen so is errour by ignorance doubtlesse.

Of

Of Foolishnesse. Cap. IIII.

There is no greater enemy to Man-kinde, then folly. Pithagoras

To be ouercome with affections, is a plaine euident token of foolishnesse.

Among the foolish hee is most foole, that knoweth but little, and sheweth himselfe to know much.

A foole cannot be knowne among fooles, nor a wise man among sage folke. Mar. Aur.

It is a foolishnesse to trust much to dreames.

Fond and foolish dreames deceyue them that put their trust in them.

They be grosse and foolish Physitions, which take any counsell at the patients dreames.

When God will send dreames and visions, they chance to wise men in the day time.

It is a lamentable and miserable thing, a wise man to be vnder the rule and gouernance of a foole. Hermes.

Miserable is the state or change of the wealthy or poore Woman, that in stead of a wise man and godly, she fasten vpon a foole to gouerne her person, her goods, and family. Legmon.

It is a foolish madnesse to thinke that rich men be happy.

It is better to be wise and poore, then to be foolish and a great Lord.

It is a shame to make the disciples of fooles, maisters of Princes.

Seeke not the gouernance of a foole, for he cannot peyse nor conceyue what doth him good, no more then a Horse or any other brute Beast, which Portegeus.

which taketh no heede whether it be charged and burthened with gold or grauell.

Instruction in a foole increaseth more folly.

It is foolishnesse for a man to boast himselfe of such feates as other creatures by nature can doe better then he.

Tullius. It is the propertie of a foole to seeke out other mans faults, and forget his owne.

Mar.Aur. Among wise men the foole is made bright, and among fooles wise men doe shine.

Chilon. A foole that from base pouertie is raised vp to riches and worldly prosperitie, is of all men most forgetfull and vnfriendly to his friend.

Protogeus The more Riches a foole hath, a verter foole he is.

It is a great folly for a man to muse much vpon such things, as doe passe his vnderstanding.

Isocrates. Giue not too light credence to a mans wordes, nor laugh thou them to scorne: for the one is the property of a foole, and the other the condition of a mad man.

Diogenes. A well-fauoured and fayre person that is a foole, is like a fayre house and an euill hoast harboured therein.

Mar.Aur. There is nothing so assured, but the recouerance thereof ought to be feared if a foole haue the guiding thereof.

Many times of wise young men commeth olde fooles, and of young fooles customably commeth wise old men.

It is no general rule that all persons shall alwayes be young and light, nor that olde persons should be alwayes wise.

This is most true, that if the young men be borne with folly, the olde man liueth and dieth

without

without couetousnesse.

Trust not a foole in his foolishnesse. Protogeus

They that be prudent, though they be demanded, say little, but foolish folk will speake too much, without the asking of any question.

The beasts are more profitable to labour the earth, then the foolish persons be to serue in the Common-wealth. Mar. Aur.

Like as raine cannot profit the corne that is sowne vpon drye stones: so neyther teaching nor study may profit a foole to learne wisedome. Seneca.

The summe of all.

There is to mankind no greater enemie
And that more hindereth his estimation,
Then the loathsome burthen of beastly folly,
Which plainly appeareth in each condition,
Fooles are ouerthrowne with their light affection.
And as corne vpon stones is sowne in vaine,
Euen so are good counsailes to a foolish braine.

Of Wine and Drunkennesse. Cap. V.

The wine bringeth forth three grapes; the first of pleasure, the second of drunkennesse, the third of sorrow. Anarcharsis.

Like as with water malt is made sweet: euen so a sorrowfull heart is made merry with Wine. Hermes.

Wine inordinately taken, troubleth mans reason, maketh dull the vnderstanding, enfeebleth remembrance, worketh it forgetfulnesse, poureth in errours, and bringeth forth sluggishnesse. Boetius.

A small quantitie of wine is sufficient for a wise and learned man, yea for any man, for therewith

when he sléepeth, he shall not be troubled, nor féele any paine.

As too much wine weakeneth the sinewes in a man: so it also killeth the memorie.

Isocrates. Wine vnmeasurably taken, is an enemy to the soule.

Much wine and Wisedome may not agrée, for they be two contraries.

Wine giuen out of time may be anoyance.

By Wine beautie fadeth, and age is defaced,
Wine maketh forgotten, that late was imbraced.

Wine and wrath drowneth both the reason and senses.

Galen de sanitate tuenda. lib.5. Of too much drinking procéedeth dropsies, wherewith the body, and oftentimes the visage is swolne and defaced: beastly fury, wherewith the mindes be perished: and of all other most odious is swine drunkennesse, wherewith both the body and soule is deformed, and the figure of man is as it were by inchantment transformed into an ougly and loathsome image.

It is not to be permitted, that perfect and pure Wine without alay of water, should in any wise be giuen to children: for as much as it hindereth the body, and maketh it moyster or whotter then is conuenient.

Also it filleth the head with fume, in them specially, which be like, as children of hot and moist temperance.

Diogenes. To take excesse of drinke is euery where abhominable.

Excesse bibbing and drinking, pricketh fast forwards to lecherie.

Demosth. To drinke wel, is a propertie méet for a spunge, but not for a man.

Drunkennesse

Drunkennes is an abhominable vice in a teacher.

A drunkard is unprofitable for any kinde of good seruice. Plato.

Drunkennesse undoeth him that delighteth therein.

Wrath maketh a man a beast, but Drunkennesse maketh him worse.

Drunkennesse maketh a man unruly.

Drunkennesse ought to be eschewed of all men, but especially of Rulers, Watchmen, and Officers. Plato.

Like as when Wine spurgeth, it breaketh the Vessels, and that which is in the bottome commeth up to the brim: so Drunkennesse discouereth the secrets of the heart. Plutarch.

The best meanes to keepe a man sober, is to behold, see and remember the filthy beastlinesse of Drunkards. Anachar.

The summe of all.

The Vine freshly flourisheth, and yeeldeth by kinde
Three sundry grapes, and of contrary condition:
Of pleasure, of drunkennesse, and sorrow, thus we finde
By daily experience: through our grose affection,
Wine inordinately taken troubleth mans reason,
And the filthinesse of Drunkards if thou see and remember
Shall sufficiently admonish thee to keepe thee sober.

Of Lying and blaspheming. Cap. VI.

Lying is a sickenesse of the soule, which cannot be cured but by shame or reason.

Lying is a monstreus and wicked euill, that filthily defileth and prophaneth the tongue of

of man: which (of God) is otherwise consecrated, euen to the truth, and the vtterance of his prayse.

Solon. By lying the truth is broken, God grieuously offended, our owne state and our neighbours also much impayred, all which take harme, when in lying we will séeme to please others.

By lying, faith and credit, (which we cannot lacke) is greatly weakened, and sometimes taken away.

Cicero. Hee is not to be credited, which hath once violated his oath: yea, although he sweare by all the Gods.

It is not good to credit them which will lye for aduantage.

It is not the propertie of a good man to lye for profits sake.

He that is accustomably affected to lying, shutteth out himselfe from the company and presence of God, and most horribly ioyneth himselfe to the diuell, yéelding himselfe to his bitter bondage and power.

Hee that lyeth (bearing the countenance of an honest man) by his outward countenance of honesty sooner deceyueth and seduceth then many others appearing to the contrary.

Propertius Hée horribly lyeth and flattereth, that corruptly reporteth a knowne wicked man to be happy and blessed.

Seneca. There is no difference betwéene a great teller of tydings and a Lyer.

Let him be of like credit with thee that is a Lyer, as one that is full of words.

Hermes. Beware of lyers and flatterers, and if thou be in authority punish them.

Fly the company of a Lyer: but if thou must

néeds

néedes kéepe company with him, beware that in any case thou beleeue him not.

There is no goodnesse in a lyer. Plato.

Hee that dare make a lye vnto his Father, or Terence. séeke meanes to deceyue him, such a one much more dareth be bolde to doe the like vnto another.

Beléeue him not that telleth thée a lye by another body, for he will in like manner make a lye of thée vnto another man.

He ought not to lye that taketh vpon him to instruct others.

It is lawfull for a gouernour for the maintenance of his estate, and safe-gard of his people to lye, but not for a subiect to lye in any cause.

The reward of a lyer is, not to be beléeued when Solon. he speaketh truth.

A common lyer, not to be double in his tale, néedeth a good memory. Pithagor.

A boaster is much more to be despised then a Lyer.

A wicked soule is knowne by that it delighteth in lyes and blasphemie.

If at any time thou takest vpon thée to sweare, sée that thou swearest not (by the will of the Diuell) falsely and vntruely, or vainely and triflingly through the common manner of accursed custome, whereby the vengeance of God shall fall infinitely vpon thée, to confound thée héere in this life, and after that to be condemned for euer with the Diuell, and that with all his malignant members: but in swearing, sweare lawfully: for oaths lawfully taken and in due time, are not refused of Kings, Princes, Judges, Rulers, nor of Magistrates themselues: for common Lawes by

that

that meanes are or ought to be euermore truely obserued, and kept vnviolate. By lawfull oathes iustice is with indifferency ministred, innocent persons, Orphants, Widdowes, and poore men are defended from cruell Murtherers, from oppressours, from the periured, from lyers, from out-facers, shamelesse persons, and theeues, that they suffer no iniury by them, nor take any harme at their hands. By lawfull othes likewise mutuall societie, amitie and good order is continually kept in all Communalties, as in Cities, Boroughs, Townes and Villages. And againe, by lawfull oathes, the truth of malefactours is searched out, wrongfull dealers the more sharply punished, and the sustayners of wrong are iustly restored to their right: Wherefore to sweare lawfully thou mayest be bold, it is no euill thing, for it bringeth therewith to thy reioycing, many godly, good, and necessary commodities: whereas on the contrary, by thy false swearing, lying, and custome in blasphemy, heapes of incommodities shall daily fall vpon thee, to confound thée.

The summe of all.

The soule with lying is often infected,
As with a pestilence and hurtfull maladie:
The soule in that state is knowne to be wicked,
Whereof shame, or reason, is th'onely remedy,
And as great tellers of newes are seldome credited,
So lyers and boasters are alwayes dispised.

Of

Of Flatterie. Cap. VIII.

Flattery is a pestilent and noysome vice. Diogenes.

The Flatterer diligently applyeth the time. Æneas.

To flatter, glose, or lye, requireth glorious and painted words, whereas truth desireth a simple and plaine vtterance, and no glosing nor fainting at all. Plato.

Of slanderers and flatterers take heede if ye will, Diogenes.
For neyther tame nor wilde beasts can bite so ill:
For of wilde beasts, slander is the most bitter:
And of the tame most biteth a Flatterer.
For a man much better it is among Rauens Theophr.
To fall and be taken, then among Flatterers:
For Rauens but of flesh dead bodies doe depriue,
But Flatterers deuoure men while they be aliue.

Like as a Camelion hath all colors saue white, so hath a flatterer all poynts saue honestie. Hermes.

As a Looking-glasse representeth euery thing that is set against it, euen so doth a Flatterer. Aristotle.

Like as the shadow followeth a man continually where euer he goe: euen so a flatterer applyeth himselfe to whatsoeuer a man doth. Plutarch.

Know thy selfe, so shall no Flatterer beguile thée. Socrates.

Within thy selfe behold well thy selfe, and to know what thou art giue no credence vnto another. Seneca.

Flatter not, nor be thou flattered.

The familiar companion which is alwayes alike pleasant, and gapeth for thanks, and neuer biteth, is of a wise man to be suspected. Plutarch

They

They that haue good wits may soone perceyue and finde out flatterers, by considering diligently their owne qualities and naturall inclination: for the company or communication of a person familiar, which is alwayes pleasant & without sharpenesse, inclining to inordinate fauour and affection, is alwaies to be misliked.

As wormes doe soonest bréed in soft and swéete wood, so the most gentle and noble wits inclined to honour, replenished with many honest and curteous manners, doe soonest admit flatterers, and be by them abused.

Socrates. Those men are most worthy to suffer shamefull death, that with false adulation doe corrupt, and adulterate the gentle and vertuous nature of a Noble man.

Hée that flattereth, both slayeth his owne soule, and also séeketh to destroy the good renowne of his Maister.

A godly Prince or Gouernour, like the father of a Country, by his excellent wisedome, and the rule of iustice, wil prouide that all false flatterers, false accusers, and their abbettours may be so punished that they and all other persons of like inclination, may be afraid to abuse the clemency and gentle natures of such vertuous and gracious gouernours.

Flattery from friendship is hard to be disseuered: for as much as in euery motion and effect of the minde they be naturally mingled together.

Mar.Aur. The Mothes and soft wormes fret the cloath: and the canker worme pierceth the bone, and flattering men beguile all the World.

Let no man by flattery perswade thée to doe any

any euill, nor to beleeue otherwise of thy selfe then thou art indeede.

Neither flatter nor chide thy wife before strangers. Socrates.

Neither slander nor flatter, nor be thou a seeker out of other mens matters: set thine owne workes alwayes before thine eyes, but cast out other mens behinde thy backe.

The summe of all.

Flattery from friendship is hardly disseuered,
Being mutually knit with the effects of the minde:
Busie-bodies and pick-thankes are not to be trusted,
As wise men their subtiltie will quickely out finde,
Nobles by flattery oft are made blinde:
And as wormes in soft wood doe breede most gladly,
So gentle and noble wits, are soone hurt by flattery.

THE

THE EIGHT BOOKE:

Of seauen capitall Vices; commonly called the seauen deadly sinnes.

Cap. I.

Of Pride and Arrogancie.

Cleobulus

PRide, Statelinesse, Loftinesse of minde, or arrogancie (an euill effect, grounded by the Deuill in the heart of Man) is an ougly and loathsome Monster in the sight of God: a vice most odious vnreuerent, hateful, hurtful, and to be vtterly abhorred both of God and of good men.

Pride is the onely ground or chiefe cause of all variance, hatred, and mischiefe.

Polion.

What wicked euill can be committed vpon the earth at any time, eyther against God or good men, which the proud heart of man attempteth not?

Among the proud men of this world, emulation, hatred, contention, and auarice, is alwaies common.

The Almightie and righteous God, as he resisteth mightily & iustly the contemptuous, hauty, and proud: so hee detesteth and vtterly abhorreth the whole broode of priuie michers, secret vnderminers,

vnderminers, hypocrites, and double dealers: specially all those, which (vnder the pretence of amitie, and with the onely outward face of godlinesse, doe long cloake their malice) that with the continuance of time, they may accomplish their mischieuous purposes.

There must be vsed among men of a lowly and milde behauiour, a decent reuerence one towards another (as becommeth good and humble men) not onely vnto those of the higher sort, but also to all the rest of meaner degrées: for otherwise, it should not onely be a signe of great arrogancie and pride, but also a plaine cause of iudgement, that such a one sheweth himselfe to be altogether not onely lawlesse, but also shamelesse and without honest regard, what euer men doe thinke of him. Tullius.

If thou wilt be beloued both of God and good men, thou maist not be proud of the good gifts of God: whether of wisedome, policie, beautie, comelinesse, strength, authoritie, or riches: for it is one God that is onely wise, politique, puissant, amiable, wealthy, and full of all felicitie. Phosilides.

Be not elated nor proudly puffed vp against thine inferiour or poore neighbour, swell not in pride against him: but looke on him with the spirit of humilitie, gladly embracing him, be gentle vnto him, frame fauourably thy good countenance toward him, speake friendly vnto him, and benefit him (by all meanes) if thou maist happily helpe him. Plotinus.

Abuse not thy state, hate pride, desire to be cleanly and not gorgeous in thine apparell. Montas.

And howsoeuer God thy Maker hath formed thee, thinke well with thankfulnesse of his workemanship, and deforme not thy selfe like a Monster.

A man should be kept in such apparrell, that should not be too neate, neyther too filthy, but such as may auoid an vnseemely, rude, and beastly negligence.

Alex. Seu. Pride should not be followed of young men, it should vtterly be disdained of old men, and finally of all men it should be contemned.

As God vnto the godly is most sweet, gentle, and lowly, euen so to the wicked, proud and sinfull hee is very sower, sharpe, and rough, specially appearing and felt of them in the terrible day of death, damnation and vengeance.

The summe of all.

Pride is a vice most monstrous and hurtfull,
And th'onely ground of all mischiefe and discord,
Pride woundeth with strife the hautie and disdainfull,
Pride breaketh the band of amitie and concord,
O humble thy selfe then, and feare the Lord,
Be alwayes gentle to thy friend or brother,
Weare comely apparrell, and care for none other.

Of Enuy. Cap. II.

Pithagor. Enuie and slander are two brethren, which are euermore lincked together for a mischiefe.

Experience hath taught that Enuy hath beene the destroyer of many.

Seneca. What is there that Enuy hath not defamed, or malice left vndefiled? truely no good thing.

Debate, deceit, contention, and Enuie are the fruits of euill thoughts.

The greatest poyson of Enuy spreadeth against

against those whom Fortune doth rayse most high.

It is better to be a fellow with many in loue, then to be a King with hatred and Enuy. Mar.Aur.

Enuy is blinde, and can doe nothing but dispra yse vertue. Tit.Liu.

Cursed Enuy prepareth Poyson secretly for them that be in rest among diuers pleasures. Mar.Aur.

The abundance of wel-fare and felicitie, hath caused cursed Enuy to be in many.

Unhappy is the state of enuious and malicious people. Plato.

Shame of himselfe is the end of indignation. Aristotle.

Enuie is so enuious, that to them that of her are most denyed & set farthest off, shee giueth most cruell strokes with her féete. Mar.Aur.

If any man say euill of thée, and enuyeth thée, see not thereby, and thou shalt disappoynt him of his purpose. Diogenes.

As rust consumeth iron, so doth enuy the hearts of the enuious.

Enuious men are tormentours vnto them-selues. Alex. Seu.

Be not enuious at an euill mans prosperitie, for surely his end shall not be good.

Whereas no light is, there is no shadow, and whereas no wealth is, there is no Enuy. Plutarch.

Cursed is that wealth which euery man doth enuy.

Hard is the remedy against Enuy.

Read all that can be read, and imagine all that can be imagined, demand all that can be demanded, and thou shalt find none other remedy against cursed Enuy, but to banish from vs all prosperitie, and to sit with aduerse fortune. Mar.Aur.

All the World is full of enuy.

Tullius. It is a scabbe of the World, to be enuious at vertue.

Enuy groweth vp among vertues.

Pacuuius. Those are to be hated which in their acts be fooles, and in their words be Philosophers.

Seneca. Malice drinketh the more part of his owne venim. The poysons which Serpents continually doe keepe without any harme, they spew out to others destruction: But the malicious contrariwise hurteth no man so much as themselues.

Hermes. Like as griefe is the disease of the body, so is malice a sicknesse of the soule.

Hée is most wicked that is malicious against friends.

Plato. Priuie hatred is worse then malice.

As a sparke of fire, or the snuffe of a candle negligently left in a house, may set a whole Towne a fire: so of priuy malice and discord commeth open destruction of people.

Hée is vnhappy, that continueth in malice.

Hée is not perfectly good, that hateth his enemy: what is he then that hateth his friend?

Diuersitie of opinions causeth great strife and hatred.

Aristotle. Walke not in the way of hatred.

Men vehemently hate them that haue a proud and hautie countenance, be they neuer so high in estate or degrée.

Malicious words discouereth the euill of the heart.

The way to suppresse Malice, is not with stoutnesse to suppresse it with malice: but with méekenesse, gentlenesse, long-suffering, and patience.

The

The grudge, hatred, and malice of them that be euill, iustifieth the iustice and sentence of them that be good. Mar. Aur.

Nothing is more wretched then to hate: by the which affect the diuels be most miserable.

They are worthily hatefull, who haue a certaine peculiar malice to hurt.

Hastinesse causeth repentance, and frowardnesse causeth hinderance.

Hee is able to vanquish his enemie, that is reasonable in his demaund. Pithagor.

Threaten no body, for that is vnmanlike.

When thine enemy doth threaten thee, trust not his flattering and fayre dissembling face: for serpents neuer sting so deadly, as when they bite without any hissing.

Hee that seeketh the fellowship of his enemies, seeketh his owne destruction.

Take not thy enemy for thy friend, nor thy friend for thine enemy.

The iniury of a friend, is more grieuous then the iniury of an enemy, Socrates.

Better is an open enemy, then a friendly foe. Boetius.

The summe of all.

Enuie and slander are two mischieuous vices,
And knit still in vaine to a wicked end,
To defame or kill they are full of deuises,
They regard none estate be he foe or friend,
Enuy all impayreth, and doth nothing amend:
Dignity, wealth, and worldly felicity,
Doth cause cruell Enuy to be in many.

Of Wrath. Cap. III.

WRath or Irefulnesse is a Vice most ougly, and furthest from all Humanitie: for who beholding a Man by fury changed into a horrible figure: his face enforced with rancour, his mouth foule and imbossed, his eyes wide staring and sparkling like fire, not speaking, but as a wild Bull roaring and braying out despightfull and venemous words, forgetting his estate and condition, if he be learned, yea, and forgetting all reason, who (I say) will not haue such a passion in extreame detestation?

Aristotle. Anger is an heauinesse & vexation of the minde, desiring to be auenged.

Anger is the worker of enmitie and hatred.

Hermes. Wrath commeth of feeblenesse of courage, and lacke of wit.

To the wrathfull, anger approacheth.

Women are sooner angry then men, the sicke sooner then the healthy, and old folk are sooner moued then the young.

Plato. Time appeaseth anger.

If anger be but a little deferred, the force thereof greatly asswageth: but if it be suffered to abide and continue, it increaseth vnto the greater mischiefe.

He that is inclined vnto his owne will, is neare vnto the wrath of God.

Hermes. Wrath and reuengement taketh from man the mercy of God, and destroyeth and quencheth the grace that God hath giuen him.

If thou hast not so much power as to refrayne thine ire and wrath, yet dissemble it, and keepe it secret

secret, and so by little and little forget it.

Forget thine anger lightly, and desire not to be reuenged.

As fire being kindled but with a small sparke worketh oft times great hurt and damage, because that the naturall fiercenesse of it cannot easily nor soone be quenched: so when the raging sparkes of anger, hatred, and enuy, doe set on fire the heart of man, they oftentimes prouoke more mischiefe then possibly before was thought, & stirreth forwards such great and horrible offences, as cannot afterwards be reformed, and therefore with the greater griefe lamented, and euen so most iustly bewailed all the dayes of their liues. And herof we may truely say, that the Well and head-spring of manslaughter, is anger, Wrath, hatred, enuy, malice, and such like.

In words multiplyed, man-slaughter is often committed: that is, when we vtter the poyson of our harts with such piercing and cankered words or spéeches, whereby is easily perceyued and felt from vs the most bitter venim of death: wée also commit hainous murther when we doe railingly burst out against any man into slanderous and contentious words: whereby he may lose his estimation and credit, and procure through the like, to take away his good name or fame.

Eschew anger, though not for wisedomes sake, yet for bodily healths sake.

It is a very prophane and an horrible thing for a man to be furious and angry.

Hée best keepeth himselfe from anger, that alwaies doth remember that God looketh vpon him. Isocrates.

Nothing is so detestable, or to be feared, as wrath and cruell malignity.

In correcting wrath is principally to bee forbidden: for hee that punisheth while hee is angry, shall neuer keepe that meane which is betweene too much and too little.

Be not hasty, angry, and wrathfull, for they be the conditions of a foole. Neyther reproue a man in his wrath, for then thou canst not rule him.

Wrath leadeth shame in a lease.

It is a great thing to see a wise man angry.

It is a foolishnes, or rather madnesse, for a man to be angry for that which cannot be amended: or to desire the thing which may not to be attained.

Hee hath great rest that can refraine himselfe from anger.

Seneca. Forgetfulnesse is a valiant kinde of reuengement.

Quietnesse is sure, but rashnesse is dangerous.

Wrath and hastinesse are very euill counsailours.

Plato. Like as greene wood which is long in kindeling is hotter then the dry when it is fired:

Euen so he that is seldome and long or he be angry, is harder to be pacified then he that is soone vexed.

The summe of all.

Iresidnesse, or wrath, is a most cruell vice,
Accursed of good men, hatefull and ougly,
Repugning peace, that sweet vertue of price,
Which knitteth both God and man in amitie.
It is contrary also to humanitie,
And as the godly and wise doe detest it,
So the wicked and foolish doe imbrace it.

Of

Of Sloath and Idlenesse. Cap. IIII.

SLoath is a vice reproachfull, hurtful, & filthy, Legmon.
very hatefull in Gods sight, and noysome in a Common-wealth.

Sloathfulnesse, vncleannesse, sicknesse, dulnesse of wit, forgetfulnesse, idlenesse, lightnesse of life, deceitfulnesse, wicked destinie, impietie, periury, and beggery, all these hang together in vnitie, to the destruction of the wicked and the sloathfull foolish body.

Sloath purchaseth dispraise, shame, and bitter defiance of all.

Wee haue oftentimes seene, and haue heard of Mar. Aur.
credible persons, that cursed Sloath and Idlenes is one speciall thing which offendeth God, slandereth the world, peruerteth the Common-wealth, endamageth the person himselfe, destroyeth them that be good, and bringeth to naught them that be euill.

Idlenesse, that is, the ceasing from necessary What Idlenesse is.
occupations or studies, is the sinke which receyueth all the stinking channell of vice, which being once brim-full, sodainly runneth ouer through the Citie or Country, and with the pestiferous ayre infecteth and poysoneth a great multitude before it may be stopped or cleansed. And the people beeing Alex. Seu.
once corrupted with this pestilence, shall with great difficultie and long continuance of time be deliuered, and yet notwithstanding a great part of them shall perish, before it be well brought to passe.

Aboue all things flye Idlenesse, which is a thing like a cankering rustinesse both to the body

and

and to the soule, and as an eating consumption, it wasteth and bringeth to naught both vertue and strength.

Anachar. Idlenesse is called the graue of liuing men. It is a thing wherin life dyeth. And thereby the soule of man is twice buryed in him, once in his body, and next in his sloath.

Plato. A man that passeth this life without profit (as one vnworthy to liue) ought to haue the rest of his life taken from him.

Mar. Aur. The filth of secret chambers, the stinch of the pumps in ships, nor the ordures of Cities doe not corrupt and infect the ayre so much, as idle folke doe the people.

Idlenesse, sloathfulnesse, vaine curiositie, and nicenesse, are companions of vnthriftinesse.

Idle people in a common-weale, are like Drones among Bées.

There is nothing so reproachfull and cruell in a Common-wealth, as vagabonds and idle people: for they gnaw and deuoure (a great deformitie) the beautifull state of the common-wealth, and altogether spoyle it, and vse no meanes to increase it.

Antonius. The idle sort of men in a Common-wealth trauell rather to set or sow abroad the thistles, thornes, and wilde wéedes of mans wit, then the wholesome fruits of honestie, Truth, and of Godlinesse.

It is the affect of wicked people to apply their mindes vnto idlenesse, belly-cheare, pride, gluttony and tyranny.

We may daily see, that through Sloath and Idlenesse diuers valiant, strong, and goodly men do fal, some to beggery, some to filthy liuing, some

ſome to picking or ſtealing, and ſome to murthering, which afterward being iuſtly brought to great calamitie and miſery, through the breach of good and godly lawes, doe impute a great part thereof to their Parents, Tutors or Gouernors, who ſo idlely and wantonly did bring them vp in the dayes of their youth. Where on the contrary, if they had béene educated and duely brought vp in ſome literature, honeſt occupation, or miſtery, they ſhould (béeing Rulers of their owne family) haue profited as well themſelues, as diuers other perſons, to the commodity and ornament of the publike weale.

Much eaſe, and default of competent labour, maketh the heate of the body féeble, which ſhould reſolue and make thin that which ought naturally to be purged. Galenus.

The ſumme of all.

Sloath and Idleneſſe are hurtfull and filthy,
And folly defaceth the whole common-wealth:
They both purchaſe ſhame, contempt and beggery,
Enforcing moſt wickedly looſe life and ſtealth,
Vncleanneſſe, ſickneſſe, and want of health,
Neglect of God and eke wicked destinie,
All which worketh with both to end moſt wretchedly.

Of Money, and Couetouſneſſe. Cap. V.

MOney is the bleſſing and good gift of God, whom filthy auarice often abuſeth. Sulpitius.

Inordinate deſire of wealth and authoritie is the firſt matter whereby ſpringeth all euill: For couetous deſire and appetite ſubuerteth Saluſt.

credence,

credence, honestie, good name, and all other vertues.

Tullius. To take any thing from another man, and one man to increase his wealth with another mans detriment, is more repugnant to nature then death, povertie, paine, or any other thing that may happen eyther to the body or other worldly goodnesse.

Alex. Seu. It is very seldome seene that where honour increaseth, avarice abateth.

Mar. Aur. If covetous people were as covetous of their owne honour, as they are of other mens goods, the little moth or worme that eateth the gownes or cloathes of such covetous people, should not eate the rest of their lives, nor the canker of infamie destroy their good name and fame at their deaths.

Diogenes. Where covetousnesse of money is, there raigneth all mischiefe.

Cicero. Sometimes to despise money, is found great and singular advantage.

Tullius. The matter goeth not well, when the same that should be wrought by vertue, is attempted by money.

O thou hunger of Gold and Silver, what is it that thou dost not compell the hearts of men to buy and sell?

The stinking Ravens, and greedy Harpies of this world, have in their gathering together neyther meane, nor bottome, nor end, nor any shame at all.

The wicked avaricious man maketh no account eyther of his name or office, but flyeth on greedily after the smell of gayne, as the hungry Ravens after stinking carrion: and to attaine his purpose, hee will undermine all men, he is trusty to no man, but lyeth in waite for every mans

goods deceitfully, craftily counterfaiting and dissembling, and taketh hold of any occasion to bring his purpose to passe, whether it be for holy things or prophane.

Couetousnesse, or the loue of Riches, is euermore a vice onely among the wicked too too familiarly and commonly vsed: but the contempt and despising of Riches béeing a vertue most excellent and singular before God, is onely in the children of God, who depend onely vpon his fatherly prouidence as their onely sufficiencie, and haue no further care of the rest, except therby they may (as the instruments of his grace,) shew forth his onely praise and glory.

Couetousnesse is such a poysoned euill, and of such force where it is rooted in the heart of man, that it worketh in him not onely a carelesnesse of Gods holy will, but an vtter contempt of God himselfe: for whosoeuer with that affection is sick and intangled, and is carefull in his minde of worldly businesses, as of money and filthy lucre, that man is turned from God.

The soule is lost that delighteth in Couetousnesse. Plato.

Refraine from couetousnesse, and thine estate shall prosper.

Couet not thy friends riches, lest thou be deceyued, and therefore hated. Socrates.

To couet is an affection of the minde, by which man endeauoureth (by all meanes) to draw vnto his owne vse that which best liketh him.

Let no couetous man haue rule ouer thee, nor yéeld thy selfe subiect to Couetousnesse: for the couetous man will defraud thee of thy goods, and Couetousnesse will defraud thée of thy selfe. Aristotle.

Mortifie

Fortifie thy soule with good works, & flye from couetousnesse.

Tullius. The chiefe poynt in all administration of matters and Common-weale offices is, that euen the least suspition of Couetousnesse be vtterly auoyded.

Mar. Aur. Oftentimes auarice séeketh out the auaricious, and sometimes the auaricious séeke auarice.

Tholon. The refuses of a niggard, be better then the larges of a prodigall spender.

Ambrose. The Chariot of auarice is carryed vpon foure wheeles of vices, which are, faynt courage, vngentlenesse, contempt of GOD, and forgetfulnesse of Death. And the two horses that drawe it, are Rapine and Niggardship. To them both is but one carter, Desire to haue. The Carter dryueth with a whip hauing two cords, Appetite to get, and Dread to forgoe.

Stoici. Couetous-men lacke the thing that they haue.

Great indigence or lack commeth not of pouertie but of great plentie: for hée that hath much will néede much.

Mar. Aur. Great is the couetousnesse which the shame of the world doth not reproue, nor the feare of death stop, nor reason appoynt.

Tullius. There is no fouler vice then Couetousnesse: specially in Princes & rulers in the common-wealth.

It is against nature, that with the spoyle of others, we increase our owne riches, substance, and wealth.

It is not onely dishonest, but also most wicked and shamefull to make a gayne of the Common-wealth.

We ought to be fully perswaded, that though wee could hide it from God and man, yet nothing

couetously,

couetously, nothing vniustly, nor nothing wickedly to be done.

An auaritious old man is like a monster. Seneca.

A couetous man cannot learne truth. Hermes.

Couetousnesse cannot be satisfied with abundance: for the more that a man hath, the more hee still desireth. Pithagor.

Couetousnesse is an vnsatiable thing, specially when men desire to fil the vessell that already runneth ouer. Alex. Mag.

Hee hath neede but of a little, that measureth abundance by natures onely necessitie, and not by superfluitie of ambitious desire. Plato.

It is better to haue a man without money, then money without a man.

To delight in money, is a dangerous pleasure.

As a touch-stone tries gold, so gold tries men.

Money is the cause of sedition and euill will.

He that hordeth vp money, taketh paynes for other folke. Plato.

It is better to loue good fellowship then money.

Seruice is a recompence for money.

Hee that for seruice or trauaile giueth money, is well requited, and nothing is due vnto him: for money is no better then seruice. Plautus.

A couetous person will sooner haue a wife that is rich and foule, then one that is poore and faire. Mar. Aur.

It is no maruaile though hee be good which is not couetous, but it were a wonder to see a couetous man good. Plato.

If wealth & authoritie be committed vnto thee, thou hast a double charge, that is to say, to rule and releeue.

Couetousnesse taketh away the name of gentlenesse, the which liberality purchaseth.

Seruants

Diogenes. Seruants serue their bodily maisters, but euill men serue their bodily lusts.

No men (in wordes) doe more cry out vpon Auarice, then those that be auaritious and couetous persons.

He that is a niggard vnto himselfe, must néedes be niggardish vnto others.

Plutarch. Like as a member vexed with an itch, hath alwayes néed of clawing: so the couetousnesse of the minde can neuer be satisfied.

Horace. To the auaritious is no suffisance: for couetousnesse encreaseth as fast as his substance.

Aristotle. Like as a dogge deuoureth by and by whatsoeuer he can catch, and gapeth continually for more: so if it chance the couetous man to obtayne any thing, he setteth little by it, desiring alwayes to obtaine more.

Mar. Aur. Couetousnesse oftentimes beguileth the belly.

Solon. Our liues doe end before Couetousnesse leaueth vs.

Seneca. Death is the rest of all couetous people,
For couetous people to dye is the best,
For the longer they liue, the lesse is their rest:
For life them leadeth their substance to double,
Where death them dischargeth of endlesse trouble.

The summe of all.

Inordinate desire of wealth and authoritie
Is the very roote of all mischiefe and wickednesse,
It subdueth loue, credence, good name, and honestie:
Yea, and lost is that soule that delighteth in couetousnesse:
Fortifie then thy soule with the trade of godlinesse,
And couet not to spare, but right honestly spend,
For most wretched are niggards vnto their liues end.

Of

Of Gluttonie. Cap. VI.

Gluttony is a vice very ougly, monstrous, and filthy: and more fit for rauening birds or brute Beasts, then for reasonable men. Propertius

Dame Gluttony, Auarice and Lechery, are thrée euill mistresses to serue: they alwayes immoderately desire, and are neuer sufficiently contented. Chilon.

When the belly is filled and full fraught, then are the prickings and prouocations to Lechery sone stirred vp. Gregory.

He is not onely to be counted a Glutton that eateth gréedily, and deuoureth much in quantity of meates and drinks, at certaine ordinary times and meales aboue other men: but hee specially, that delighteth daily and hourely to fare deliciously, pampering his carrion carkeise continually, satisfying the pleasures therof, setting his felicity on his belly, and making thereof his God. Legmon.

As meats and drinks are the good gifts of God, and to be thankfully taken of men for their naturall vse and sustentation: so if we behold simply the onely good affect of nature (which must haue her well ordred and due course of nourishment) it séeketh not hurtfull excesse, but barely sufficient to the contentment of it selfe. Legmon.

O what a monstrous sight is it to behold the furnished Table of some vnsatiable and rich glutton, & how with varietie of the most daintie iunkets, costly and delicate dishes, it is throughly beset and couered? And as he himselfe is therin monstrously affected, such monstrous companions commonly will he haue about him: who weighing his inclination, will extoll him in his grosse worke Porregeus.

T of

of wickednesse, and feede his humour with vaine talking, foolish iesting, and now and then some shew of scurrilitie to make good digesting.

When the belly with excesse
 Is puffed vp and pampered,
Then vertuous demeanor
 Is nothing at all remembred.

August. Not the vse of meate, but the inordinate desire thereof ought to be blamed.

The summe of all.

Of all cursed crimes and sleights satanicall,
That poysoneth mans heart to his decay,
None more cruelly catcheth and maketh thrall,
Then wretched Gluttony where she beareth sway:
The Gluttons greedy gut standeth at no stay,
But is pampered vp continually,
Through eating and drinking deliciously.

Of Lust and Lecherie. Cap. VII.

Plato. Lust is a Lordly and disobedient thing.

Lust burneth grieuously whom she findeth idle.

Pithagor. Enforce thy selfe to refraine thine euill lusts, and follow the good: for the good mortifieth and destroyeth the euill.

Diogenes. Fly lecherous lusts, as thou wouldest a furious Lord.

Refraine thy lusts.

God loueth them that be disobedient to their bodily lusts.

Hee that vanquisheth his lusts, is a great conquerour.

Dishonour,

Dishonour, shame, euill end, and damnation wait vpon lust, lechery, and all other like vices. Aristotle.

He that hath bound himselfe to follow his fleshly Lusts, is more bound then any bond-slaue or captiue.

Bodily lusts and pleasures, and all carnall affections that corruptly raigne in the heart of man, are but beastly and earthly, and nothing worthy therefore to be matched with the excellencie that otherwise is in Man, and therefore they ought to be vtterly abhorred, dispised and set at naught of man.

There is no sinne that sooner inuadeth vs, neyther sharper assayleth or vexeth vs, nor extendeth larger, nor draweth moe vnto their vtter destruction, then the filthy lusts of the body: It bringeth with it innumerable inconueniences: first, it plucketh from a man his good name and fame, a possession exceeding precious: for the rumour of no vice stincketh more carrionly, then the name of lechery. It also consumeth his patrimony, it killeth at once both the strength and beauty of the body, it decayeth and greatly hurteth health, it ingendreth diseases innumerable, and them filthy, it disfigureth the flower of youth long before the day, it hasteth, and accelerateth, rejected and euill fauoured age, it taketh away the strength and quicknesse of the wit, it dulleth the sight of the minde, and graffeth in man (as it were) a beastly minde, it draweth him at once from all honest studies and pastimes, and plungeth him altogether in the puddle or myre of filthinesse, be he neuer so excellent, that once he shall not haue any minde to thinke of any thing but that which is sluggish, vile & filthy. It also taketh away the vse of reason, which is the

natiue propertie of man: it maketh a young man peeuish and slanderous, and age odious, wretched, and filthy.

Pithagor. The wrath and lusts of lecherous people, alter their bodies, and maketh many to runne starke madde.

To set forth at large, or to stir vp the stinking and filthy puddle of the most monstrous manners of wanton persons and Lechers, it would quickly (with the loathsome sound thereof,) turne vp the stomacks of the honest and chast hearts, through the very hatefull and villanous sound thereof.

Men that be carefuly affected (and béeing as it were in a transe) perceyue not the seruitude of sinne, whereunto they be subiect, that it tendeth to euerlasting perdition, that they be the slaues of the Diuell, and that their reward shall be eternall death.

Philotas. Offenders, when they cannot sleepe through the vnquietnesse of their trouble and wretched conscience, are wont to be vexed with rages, not onely when their mischiefe is intended, but also when it is ended.

Plato. Like as they who doe follow the concupiscence and pleasant Lusts of the flesh, be alwayes vnstable: so the followers also and louers of such be euer vnconstant, as well in their opinions, as also in their acts.

In most wretched state is that man whose hart is inclined and full fixed to the filthy lusts of Lechery, losing the swéet fruits of prayse, and winning a wicked end.

Lactan. Of prosperitie oft procéedeth luxuriousnesse, and so from thence it goeth vnto other horrible sins and heapes of wickednesse.

Harlots

Harlots being foule of nature, deceiue men with their painted faces: and vnder faire, white, and ruddy colours, they hide their shamelesse and filthy visages. Hermes

Vnseemely gesture of the body, lightnesse of countenance, nicenesse in apparrell, vncleane speech, and the example of wicked doing, encourageth and corruptly stirreth vp the concupiscence of the heart to lightnesse of life and wantonnesse.

Lechery soone ouercommeth that man that is giuen to idlenesse.

All men by nature are naturally giuen to feele the boyling and raging fumes of fickle and fraile flesh.

Whoredome is a poysened serpent, to be vtterly detested and eschewed, namely for this cause, that it swelleth full of certaine poysoned and filthy affects, peculiar hatreds and malices, to the great preiudice and hurt, not onely of others, but also of the person himselfe, whom it cruelly holdeth captiue.

There be some will be so Lordly and valiant in vertues, and so high-minded, that they will needes make vs beleeue, that they liuing in the flesh, and being of flesh, onely feele not the flesh.

If by Lechery thou art tempted, or by lust stirred to filthinesse, set before thee the minde of death, put before thine eyes the day and end of this life: call to thy remembrance the terrible doome of the high God, forget not the torments of euerlasting fire, and the horrible paines of hel.

To conclude, who so will with valiant and lusty courage take vpon him manfully to fight against all the whole host of his vices (of the which we heare there be seuen counted as chief captains)

must of necessitie prouide for themselues two speciall meanes, that is to say, Prayer or praying continually, without stop, vnto heauen: and knowledge, otherwise called godly learning, which naturally is skillfull to fence and to arme the minde with wholesome precepts and honest opinions, and putteth man in remembrance of vertue, which is the light of Gods gracious countenance shining vpon him: so that neyther of these two (as things inseparable) can be one without another.

The summe of all.

Filthy lusts and Lechery are most disobedient euils,
Which with violence burneth, when it fastneth on idlenesse:
The stinking loathsome Lechers, with their idle pretenced wils,
Looseth the fruits of prayse, and winneth the end of wickednesse.
Shame, euill end, and damnation followeth their filthinesse:
Fly from whoredome, loue cleannesse, and leaue to liue wantonly,
And seeke the prayse of temperance, sobernesse, and chastitie.

THE

THE NINTH BOOKE:

Cap. I.

And first, why it is here placed.

BEcause the conscience of Man is not ignorant of the state of righteousnesse: but possesseth in it selfe, through the light of grace, the true knowledge of Gods holy law, whereby man should be moued by them to doe alwaies well, & feare to offend at any time: which Conscience also béeing the true booke of Records, a true testimonie or witnesse of mans whole life & conuersation, both in Gods sight, and euen so felt in himselfe, and what occasion of heauenly ioyfulnesse it worketh in the mindes of the godly: and contrariwise, vnsufferable torments by infinit occasions and accusations, to the condemnation of the vngodly, I thought it not amisse immediately to note somwhat therof vnto you, after this long discourse of the soule deformed, and of sin that hedious Monster, (whereby the terrible plagues of Gods vengeance fall daily vpon the earth, to the destruction of kingdomes and nations, and whereby an innumerable company of men are drawne to the Diuel) that men well considering therof, may

more aptly follow good counsaile, not to abuse nor striue against his owne conscience, but beeing at vtter defiance with sinne, which fouly defileth the conscience, hee may through the abundance of Gods grace, embrace betime true repentance, apprehend the great mercy of God, through a liuely faith, and haue continuall accesse by prayer, to the throne of his Maiestie for the daily increase of his grace: all which foure Chapters, following in their order prescribed, are the onely contents of this ninth Booke: beseeching almightie God to grant vnto the godly Reader grace, both aptly to consider the thing that he readeth, and also to follow it.

Of Mans Conscience. Cap. I I.

Antisth. The conscience of man is (in himselfe) a secret knowledge, a priuie opener, testimonie, or witnesse, an accuser, an inward troubler or tormentor, it is also a satisfier or ioyfull quieter of the minde of man in all his doings.

Cleobilus. A mans Conscience (of it selfe) greatly conuinceth and giueth testimony of the truth vnto the iudgement of God.

The conscience of man is not voide of the knowledge of Gods lawes, and of his iudgements: because he should be moued by them, and therefore feare to offend.

Phosilides. It is better to trust in a good and quiet conscience in all our honest & godly doing (in the sight and presence of God) then to trust in the satisfying of our selues in the vaine pleasures of this world, or the wicked motions and pleasures of the flesh, with the terrour of a wicked conscience.

A

A mans conscience may be quiet for a season, by the trust that hee hath in the constitutions and vaine holy deuises, of men: but when the perseuerance of Gods terrible iudgements, and the prick of sinne doe rise in our hearts, then such gracelesse and vaine trust is vtterly ouerblown, and vanisheth away to nought.

Where the conscience is drowned with worldly pompe and riches, there wisedome is turned to great foolishnesse.

The loue of this vaine and wicked world maketh men to doe many things contrary to the Law of their conscience: for in them that loue the world, is there little regard of God, neither doth his loue abide in them. Zeno.

Where the conscience of man is disquieted, and feeleth iustly in it selfe the condemnation of God, there wanteth no store of miseries (both of body and minde) vnspeakeable and innumerable. Aristides.

He that frameth himselfe outwardly to doe that which his conscience reproueth inwardly, cannot please God.

Feare to doe that whereby the conscience should be wounded, for the conscience is sooner wounded then we be aware of.

The conscience that is wounded and ouer-burdened with sinne, feeleth euen in this life parcell of hell torments.

The conscience of a man is vnto himselfe as a thousand wickednesses. Socrates.

It is very hard for a man, being accused of crimes committed by him, (through the working of his owne conscience) not to bewray himselfe by his owne confession. Quintilian.

A troubled conscience tormenteth the minde, but

but a quiet conscience is high felicitie, passing all worldly pleasure and dignitie.

Socrates. There is no grieuouser damnation then the doome of mans conscience.

Fearefulnesse and trembling of conscience followeth sinne and wickednesse.

Epictetus. The Diuell, desperation, a wicked end, and eternall damnation, are companions commonly to a wicked conscience.

As a small moate will soone appeare in a cleare glasse, euen so the conscience of godly men (being more cleere then Christall) will quickly accuse them, euen at the least fault they do commit, whereas the wicked and vngodly haue their conscience clogged and corrupted through the custome of sin, that they cannot once see nor perceyue their owne most shamefull and wicked worke, vntill God set the same before them for their vtter destruction, and so their consciences being terribly wounded, and accusing them, they damnably fall into desperation without regard of God, or hope of his mercy.

Polion. We carry nothing away with vs out of this life, but eyther a good or an euill conscience.

Keepe thy conscience pure and vndefiled, and striue not against the rule of it.

If the Diuell, thine owne conscience, or Gods Law doe accuse, vexe, or trouble thee, for any euill conceiued or done, confesse thy fault speedily, defer not the time, dally not with God, be earnestly repentant, trust in his mercy, and hide not thy fault from him, so will he haue mercy vpon thee, and not impute sinne vnto thee.

Xenoph. Discerne discreetly, and practise reuerently those things that are best, that thy conscience may

may be cléere, and others in thy doings not troubled.

To walke ioyfully in the presence of GOD, is to liue (as it were before his eyes) in a godly and vpright conscience, after the manner of honest seruants, who standing in the presence of their master, continually depend vpon their sodaine becke.

The lesse iustice that a godly man findeth at the hands of the vngodly, the more consolation (through patience) shall hée finde in conscience, at the mercifull hand of God. Const.

The summe of all.

In what order soeuer mans life is led,
The conscience accuseth or excuseth plaine;
Otherwise to perswade standeth in no stead,
It preuayleth in witnesse, to ioy or to paine.
Feare God, trust in him, and wickednesse refraine,
Keepe safe thy conscience from feare and trembling,
That true faith and peace may be at thy ending.

Of Repentance. Cap. III.

Repentance signifieth very anguish and vnfayned sorrow, bred in the heart of him that hath grieuously sinned, and endeauoureth to amend, by forsaking his wickednesse, and following godlinesse.

True repentance is to cease from sinne. Ambrose.

True repentance procéedeth of faith, and not of the feare of punishment.

He that truely repenteth him of his euill doings, hee it is that considereth well the old errour of life. Lactan.

Sinne

Iust. Mar. Sinne goeth before Repentance, and after repentance followeth newnesse of life.

God mercifully worketh in all the hearts of the godly these three speciall graces: first, unfainedly to be repentant for their sins: secondly, to haue in themselues an hearty reconciliation: and thirdly, a willing submission and obedience to the will of God in all things.

No man doth repent him of his sinne, but by some warning first of Gods calling: therefore true repentance commeth first by the grace of God: secondly, by the word of Gods calling and warning: and thirdly, by the faith of Gods word.

Augustin. Grace goeth before the merit of Repentance.

God offereth the grace of repentance to all, but unto the wicked it is to no purpose, who although at a sodaine they seeme to repent, yet they doe not continue therein, because they doe not heartily and truely receiue the grace offered of God, but colourably and hypocritically for a season: and therefore it is to them in vaine.

Hermes. Trouble is a preacher sent from God to bring man to the knowledge of his sinne, and to call him to repentance.

Most happy and blessed are those men, which beholding the sharpe iudgements of God upon others, doe the rather in themselues increase in repentance.

Like as the sinners minde that is turned from God, is farre from God, and strange unto him so long as it is giuen to the desire of sinne: so by repentance it is turned unto God, and doth now reuerently feare him, worship and serue him, whom he before despised. If thou offendest, the best remedy is repentance and amendment of life. It is no matter

matter how corrupt the ayre is, so that thy conscience be cleane from sinne.

An accusing conscience is the most secret and terrible thing that can be at the approaching and comming of death. Plotinus.

Thou shalt wash away the spot of sinne with teares, with repentance, with continuall inuocation of Gods mercy, faithfully cleauing, and trusting wholy thereunto. Boetius.

When thou repentest and askest mercy for thy sinne, then thy sins cannot disquiet thée, nor haue power against thée, but when thou art vnrepentant and ceasest to cry for mercy, then thy sinnes rage ouer thée, and cry daily for vengeance against thée.

Sléepe not without repentance for thy sinnes done and past. Plato.

Repentance deserueth pardon. Xenoph.

It is the duety of a good man, and a point of humanity to forgiue, where the party that is forgiuen repenteth, and is ashamed of his fault.

The summe of all.

The short life of man, sinfull and miserable,
Compassed with snares of mortall destruction,
Encurreth Gods vengeance, and state most dammable
Without repentance and faith in him alone:
That is the onely way to depend vpon,
Aske mercy, and sleepe not without repentance,
And with all Sathans sleights be at defiance.

Of

Of Faith and Truth. Cap. IIII.

Tullius. FAith is a constance and truth of things spoken or couenanted.

Faith is the gift of GOD, and breathed by the spirit of God into the heartes of those that be the children of God.

Didimus. Through a liuely, quicke, and fruitfull faith, we Alexander haue our first entrance vnto God: but the Faith that is without good workes, is not a liuely but a dead faith, and therefore now not to be called Faith, no more then a dead man is to be called a man.

A good faith (which onely is planted in the harts of good men) neyther sleepeth nor is idle, but alwayes awaketh when it should be occupied, or busied in good workes.

The works of Faith. These be the workes of Faith: namely, a quiet and good conscience, the loue of God, and hope of things to come, a boldnesse to repaire to the throne of grace, inuocation, adoration, and worship, confession of the truth, obedience, perseuerance, in yeelding vp of the spirit, and to goe immediately vnto God.

The true doctrine of the faith most chiefly shineth and cleerely, by the vse of accustomed and perfect prayer.

The power of true faith worketh constancy in men, and keepeth them in quietnesse, and worketh in them strength and patience in afflictions.

Augustin. Good liuing cannot be separated from true faith which worketh by loue.

All goodnesse, gracious conuersation, health, wealth, libertie, and such like, ought (with a good faith)

faith) to be both looked and asked for, onely at the hand of God, as only at the very author of the same, and of none other: for without him nothing that is good can eyther be giuen or receyued.

As faith that is liuely and quicke stirreth the minde to call (without doubting) vnto God: so incredulity and mistrust maketh a man doubtfull, and plucketh him backe from the calling vpon God. Incredulitie.

Faith must néeds fayle, when the authoritie of Gods truth standeth wauering. August.

The way to encrease Faith, is first to haue Faith.

The increase of true faith in good men is known two wayes: first, by their mutuall loue towards their neighbours: secondly, in all their afflictions and troubles to be patient and quiet.

To beléeue rightly in God, is to direct all our hope vnto God, and with sure trust to depend onely vpon his truth and goodnesse. Anathali. in Gala.

Faith alone hath power to iustifie.

The power of faith in all respects preuayleth mightily, and without faith nothing can happily prosper.

Nothing kéepeth a publike-weale so together as doth faith.

Without faith a publike-weale may not continue: and therefore it followeth (according to the saying of Aristotle) that by what meanes or policie a publike-weale is first constituted, by the same it is preserued. Then seeing Faith is the foundation of Justice (which is the chiefe constitutor and maker of a publike-weale, and by the aforementioned authoritie conseruator of the same:) it may well be concluded, that Faith is both the Aristotle.

originall

originall and principall constitutor and conseruator of the weale publike.

Plato. Whatsoeuer thing cleaueth fast in the minde of man, too surely rooted with a constant and perfect faith: the same vndoubtedly euery man declareth in his manners and conuersation.

Faith, without manners worthy of faith, preuaileth nothing.

Chrisost. Euery man beléeueth as much as he liketh.

Socrates. A faithfull man is better then gold.

Performe thy promise as iustly as thou wouldest pay thy debts: for a man ought to be more faithfull then his oath.

Faith not exercised, waxeth sick, and being vnoccupied, it is assaulted with diuers pleasures.

A fruitlesse and dead faith. That faith which is grounded eyther vpon long customes, or mans counsailes, or the authoritie of Princes, or on great multitudes of people, or on the outward glittering shewes of holinesse, rather then vpon the onely truth of GOD, must néeds be but a very fruitlesse and dead faith, springing out of the barraine soyle of Mans reason: which swimmeth like a fume in the outward parts of mens thoughts, neuer piercing downeward to the bottome of their hearts, through the which inconuenience multitudes of people are so holden captiue, and fast fettered in the chaynes of darknesse and ignorance, that they cannot atteyne to the fréedome of true faith and godlinesse.

Faith in God maketh innumerable strong champions of inuincible stomackes, not onely against death, but also against the most cruell deuises that can be found to make death (if it were possible) more painefull then death.

From faith (if it be perfect and liuely) we come to

to feare, from feare to flying of sinne, and from flying sinne, we take a patient minde to suffer tribulation: whereby wee take hope and trust in God, through the which hope our Soules sit in a sure chaire of a certaine expectation of that which is laid vp in store for vs in heauen.

Faith shineth in danger. Aristotle.

Put thy whole trust and affiance in God, who seeth and knoweth all secrets, and he shall mercifully iudge thee at his comming in the terrible and great day, when he shall giue remuneration to the good for their goodnesse, and euerlasting punishment to the euill for their wickednesse. Hermes.

Truth is the daughter of Time. Aul.Gel.

Truth is the guide of all goodnesse. Hermes.

Forasmuch as GOD is the truth, and that truth is God, hee that departeth from the one, departeth from the other.

Truth is the messenger of God, which euery man ought to worship for the loue of her master. Plato.

Without the true knowledge of Gods Law, which is the rule of all honesty and godlinesse, the truth of God is violently oppressed, and wrongfully defaced and wrested: and the kingdome of lyes highly magnified and established by the armour of mens mastry and gouernance.

They which be euill affected towards the doctrine of truth, haue their mindes so blinde, that they cannot abide the light of the truth. Boëtius.

Mans fickle and shifting flesh (ouerwhelmed with instability and lightnesse) turneth it selfe vnto all fashions, because it will not be brideled or compelled to obey the truth of God in all things. Periander.

Those that slip from the authority and rule of truth, being led by their owne blinde iudgements

(as weake and rude of vnderstanding) are oftentimes trayned out of the way of truth by likely glenings of reason, and so slip into sundry noysome errours, from whence they can neuer (or with much adoe) be brought backe agayne to the right of truth.

A friendly and prudent modestie in vttering cases of truth, being ioyned with a learned godlinesse, is of such force and vertue, that it mightily preuayleth where it shall be vttered: without the which many other good gifts of knowledge shall hardly profit the truth, but rather hinder it.

August. When the truth is reuealed, let custome giue place to the truth, let no man prefer custome before reason and truth, for reason and truth excludeth custome.

Gregory. Custome be it neuer so auncient, and neuer so generally receyued, yet ought it by all meanes to giue place vnto the truth:

Custome without truth is but an old errour.

Cyprian. The seruice of God in truth and vertue, is nothing else but with true Faith and Obedience to depend onely vpon his will reuealed in his word: which procéedeth from the reuerent feare of God, and is the right entrance to true obedience, and to kéepe truely the Law of God.

Plotinus. Vertue sometime at the first séemeth to be very darke, hard, and vnpleasant: although at length it appeareth most bright, amiable, louely, and comfortable.

Offence, hatred, and extreame cruelty commonly follow the profession of the truth.

Hermes. The Truth may be shadowed, but will not be suppressed: it may be blamed, but not shamed.

The righteous and godly, hauing in them the zeale

zeale of constancy, feare not the cruelty of man, but will boldly stand to the truth untill death.

Hee that useth truth, hath moe, and mightier servants then a King. Socrates.

In all things and towards all men use a simple truth, without fraud, deceit, or guile in word or deed.

Loue righteousnesse and truth.

Beare witnesse to the truth, & not to friendship. Hermes.

Honour is the fruit of vertue and truth, and for the truth a man shall be worshipped.

Loue God and truth, so shalt thou saue thy soule.

The greatest fault that can be in a man of honestie, is to spare the truth, and to be variable. Mar. Aur.

Let not thy thoughts depart from the truth.

That man or woman that with-draweth their eares from hearing the truth, cannot possibly apply their hearts to loue any vertue.

The truth shall more draw thee to loue and to follow vertue, then the common example shall entice thee to follow vice, the which no man can loue, no, not the very filthy sinner himselfe.

Beleeue not him that saith he loueth truth, and followeth it not. Seneca.

Reason not with him that will denie the principall truths.

Affirme nothing before thou knowest the truth.

Maintaine truth.

Truth ought to be preferred before friendship and amity.

If thou feele thy selfe more true to thy King then many other, and hast also lesse wages of him then they, yet complaine not, for thine will continue, and so will not theirs. Aristotle.

Be the selfe-same that thou pretendest.

Be not ashamed to heare truth of whomsoeuer it be: for truth is so noble of it selfe, that it maketh them honourable that pronounceth it.

Lactantius Truth is hated of the wicked, they cannot abide it, because they would liue in their wickednesse, without the controulement of it.

A couetous man cannot learne the truth.

Iermes. If men in reasoning, desire as much the truth of the thing it selfe, as they doe the maintenance of their owne opinions, and glory of their wits, there would not breed so much hatred as there doth, nor so many matters laid aside and left vnconcluded.

x.Seu. In all Common-wealths and at all times, about noble Princes and most faithful Gouernors, there be some which for their owne commodity, aduancement, displeasure, or for other corrupt and lewd affection (not hauing before their eyes the iust and terrible doome of God, and their owne consciences) the displeasure of their Prince, nor shame of the World, let not to hinder and darken the manifest and cleere causes of truth, whose beautifull and bright beames (according to their worthinesse) should comfortably, franckly, and with free libertie, spread forth his brightnesse to the glory of God, to the honor of the Prince, and to the great reioycing, comfort, and quietnesse of the Common-wealth.

The Prince ought to feare, and with all prudence and wisedome to fore-see such inconueniences and great dangers, which else would fall vpon him and his people, through the corruption and euill nature of loathsome miching members, that with craft couertly creepeth in fauour, and then by flattery and dissimulation endeauour to abuse his

his honest and gentle nature: whereby is not onely lost or greatly blemished the deere and obedient loue, good name, and immortall praise, due vnto him of his people, (notwithstanding the name of vertue, wisedome, learning, and politike gouernance) but also his whole Realme is brought to much trouble, extreame misery, losse and hinderance: yea, and sometimes hasty and swift confusion. For neuer did there chance greater mischiefe to any Country or Common-wealth, nor neuer were the vertuous natures of good Princes and Rulers sooner corrupted and abused, then when they haue beene either misinstructed and falsely informed by fawning and fleering flatterers, or else when those that were in most fauour and credit about him, dissembling the cleere causes of truth, in stead of equity and iustice, sought to worke their owne most wicked purposes.

The truth alonely among all things is priuilledged, in such wise, that when the time seemeth to haue broken her wings, then as immortall shee sheweth her force. Mar. Aur.

The summe of all.

Faith is a stedfastnesse and truth of things
Spoken or couenanted of God or man:
A right Faith in God with it alway brings
Inuincible power, that mightily can
Withstand the assaults of cruell Satan:
For he that is faithfull and true in each thing,
Hath mightier seruants then Lord or King.

Of godly Prayer and Deuotion: a mentall Vertue. Cap V.

PRayer is a diuine and heauenly affect of the soule, and signifieth the desire (generally) of all things that are of necessity to the sustentation and nourishment both of soule and body: specially from the hand of God, or otherwise from man, as from the speciall instrument of God, that man by man (through him) might be most graciously blessed, releeued, and comforted, to the onely praise of him from whence all blessings procede.

Hermes. Prayer is the chiefest thing that a man may present God withall.

Pithagor. It is a right honourable and blessed thing to serue God, and to sanctifie his Saints.

Perfect deuotion and the knowledge of Gods Law, all men had neede to haue presently with them: for deuotion hath this strength, it doth eleuate the minde unto God: and knowledge doth sustaine and uphold the same, that it may with liuely courage continue, and not fall downe: it also doth incense and kindle it, that it mounteth upward into heauen unto the presence of God: where the sauour of them both together smelleth farre more sweetly before him, then any earthly fumigation, be it neuer so pleasant, doth pleasantly smell in the nose of man.

Men in their deuotion may often be beguiled and falsely seduced, except knowledge doe alwayes assist the same for to sustaine and direct it, which being knit together, strengthen men very much in all their intents: yea, and that very comfortably in all stormes of troubles and temptations, so that it

it is greatly expedient for all men (as nigh as they can) to haue prayer and knowledge annexed together.

It is greatly hurtfull to men, and an offence vnto God, to haue deuotion without true knowledge of God, ſhewed vnto vs in his law, though it be in deuout praying, faſting, charitable relieuing, or otherwiſe in moſt ſtraite order and manner of liuing.

To know truely the will of GOD, is to pray truely, and to liue deuoutly and holily.

Firſt, before thou prayeſt, caſt away from thée (with a repentant heart) all thine iniquitie: and then call vpon God, and he will heare thée, relieue thée, quiet thy conſcience, and moſt ioyfully comfort thée. Plotinus.

True and acceptable prayer vnto God, is to craue any thing at the hand of God anſwerable to his will, hauing our heart lifted vp vnto him during all the time of prayer.

Pray to God at the beginning of thy workes, that thou mayſt bring them to a good concluſion. Xenoph.

Worſhip God with a pure heart: pray vnto him, and he will aduance thée.

When thou wilt faſt, purge thy ſoule from filth, and abſtayne from ſinne, for God is better pleaſed therewith, then with abſtayning from meates. Hermes.

Pray earneſtly for Repentance, and continually make thy faithfull petition and ſupplication to the euerliuing God: call vpon him in the day, and forget him not in the night.

When temptation inuadeth thée or giueth vnto thée a cruell and ſharpe aſſault, then earneſtly, heartily, and faithfully call on God for his helpe, Pithagor.

and that by prayer being continuall, perfect, and pure, thou maist preuaile and obtaine the victory.

Hierome. With reuerent fasting, and abstinence, the bodily passions of man are to be cured: and with Prayer the pestilent infections of the minde are to be healed.

Prayer is a vertue that preuayleth against temptation, and against all cruell assaults of infernall spirits, against the delights of this lingering life, and motions, and the flesh.

Antisthen. The surest way for men to escape the danger of all their enemies, is alwayes to be busily occupyed in deuout praying, and to be continually mindfull of well-doing.

Plato. Thou oughtest daily to pray for the happy estate and prosperitie of thy Prince, and of others that by him are set in authoritie, for of them dependeth the peace and tranquilitie of the Common-wealth.

Vertuous and well disposed men, doe daily pray vnto God for the cleansing of the impurity of the heart, and doe watch it with all diligence that they can, and labour to restraine the corruption thereof, that it burst not out, eyther to the hurt of themselues or others.

Socrates. God hateth the prayers and sacrifices of wicked people.

Put thy trust in God, and pray vnto him, and hee will keepe thee from a wicked wife, for which there is none other remedy.

To be watchfull in Prayer is the certayne and onely meanes to obtaine all our desires, ioyning thereunto an assured faith in God, before whom

Plotinus. we make our prater. Pray that God may giue thee true, hearty, and earnest repentance, and increase

of

of thy faith: for they both (for their excellency) as the speciall gifts of God, are most conuenient for thee: because the word of God (which he himselfe hath spoken) is the truth, and shall iudge in the last day.

When thou enterest into prayer, let thy prayer be to this end, specially that God (as he is mercifull, so he) will mercifully reueale and open more and more to thine heart, the true feeling, knowledge and vnderstanding of his truth, and to giue thee also grace that in thy conuersation thou maist truely expresse the fruits thereof.

Make thy prayer perfect in the sight of God: for prayer is like a ship in the Sea, which if it be good, saueth all therein, but if it be nought, suffereth them to perish.

Pray not to God to giue thee sufficient, for that he will giue to each man vnasked, but pray that thou mayest be contented and satisfied with that which he giueth thee. Plutarch.

Tyrants prayers are necessary.

The summe of all.

Prayer is the most holy and diuine seruice
That man here in earth vnto God may present:
Prayer with repentance is the due and perfect seruice,
That withstandeth the Diuell and his cursed intent.
Pray to God, trust in him, but first be penitent:
For as a sound ship saueth them that be therein,
So Prayer with repentance saueth from drowning in sinne.

THE

THE TENTH BOOKE:

Cap. I.

Of Women.

Diogenes. HEe that seeketh and desireth to haue the fellowship of a Wife, ought to win her with vertuous disposition, honesty, manners, and good behauiour.

Mar.Aur. Naturally in times past, wiues were adorned with these Vertues, to wit, to be shamefast in their countenances, temperate in words, wise of wit, sober in going, meeke in conuersation, pittifull in correction, well regarding their liuing, no company-keepers, stedfast in promise, and constant in loue.

Socrates. Crabbed Wiues are compared to rough stirring horses.

As a shrewde horse must haue a sharpe bridle, so a shrewde Wife should be sharply handled.

Order thy Wife as thou wouldest thy kinsfolke.

Seneca. Giue thy wife no power ouer thee, for if thou suffer her to day to tread vpon thy foote, shee will to morrow tread vpon thy head.

Socrates. Hee that can abide a curst wife, needeth not to feare what company he falleth in.

Mar.Aur. There is not so fierce and perillous an enemy to a man as his wife.

A

A nice wife and a backe doore,
Oft maketh a rich man poore.

The vse of friendship, the comely port and the estimation of an honest man, is not a little impayred by an idle and light wife.

Like as a blocke though it be decked with gold, pearles, and gems, is not to be regarded, except it represent the shape of something: euen so a wife be shée neuer so rich, yet if shée be not obedient to her husband, shée is nothing at all worthy to be regarded. Plato.

Such wiues as would rather haue foolish husbands, whom they might rule, then to be ruled by sober wise men, are like him that would rather lead a blinde man in an vnknowne way, then follow one that can both sée, and also knoweth the way well. Hermes.

Like as no man can tell where a shooe wringeth, but he that weareth it: so no man knoweth a womans disposition, but he that marrieth her. Socrates.

The husband that forsaketh his wife because hée is grieued with her manners, is like him, who because a Bée hath stung him, doth forsake the hony. Hermes.

He that fisheth with poyson, catcheth fish, but euill and corrupted: and so they that endeauour to get them wiues or husbands by deceits and charmes, may lightly get them, but better vngotten. Plato.

Like as they which kéepe Elephants, weare no light coloured garments, nor they which kéepe wilde Buls, weare any Purple, because such colours doe make them fierce: so ought a wife to abstaine from such things as shée knoweth will offend her husband. Plutarch.

They

Aristotle. They which were wont to doe sacrifice vnto Iuno the Goddesse of married women, tooke alwaies the gals out from the beasts which they sacrificed: signifying thereby, that all anger and displeasure ought to be farre from married folkes.

Socrates. The rule for a wife to liue by, is her husband, if he be obedient to publike lawes.

The best way for a man to keepe his wife chast, is not to be iealous, (as many fond fooles are) but to be chaste himselfe, and faithfull vnto her.

Aristotle. There can be no greater honor for an honest wife, then to haue an honest faithful husband, which careth for her and for no woman else, thinking her more chaste and faithfull then any other.

The husband can doe his wife no greater wrong then to seeke the fellowship of another woman.

Mar. Aur. It is but small wit in a man to set by the fantasies of his wife, or to chastise openly, that may be righted betweene them secretly.

Socrates. Wiues must be the more borne with, because they bring forth children.

It were better for a woman to be barren,
Then to bring forth a vile wicked carren.

Mar. Aur. Women be of right tender condition, they will complaine for a small cause, and for lesse will rise vp into great pride.

Portegeus In three points women and fooles are commonly of like condition: they are full of vaine affections, curious and peeuish to please, and very wilfull in foolishnesse.

Tertullian Woman was the first forsaker of Gods Law, the discloser of the forbidden tree, and the gate of the Diuell.

Aristotle. A Woman is a necessary euill.

Women in mischiefe are wiser then men.

Hardly

Hardy is that Woman, that dare giue counsell to a man, but hee is foole-hardy that taketh it of a woman: he is a foole that taketh it, and hee the more foole that asketh it, but he is the most foole that fulfilleth it. Mar. Aur.

Women be more pittifull then men, more enuious then a serpent, more malicious then a tyrant, and more deceitfull then the diuell. Socrates.

It is better to be in company with a serpent, then with a wicked woman. Socrates.

Women by nature are borne malicious. Mar. Aur.

As it is naturall for a woman to despise the thing that is giuen her vnasked: so is it death to her to be denied of that shee doth demand. Mar. Aur.

There is no creature that more desireth honor and worse keepeth it then a woman.

Gay apparelled Women stand forth as baites to catch men that passe by: but they take none but such as will be poore, or else such as be ignorant fooles, which know them not.

Women desire to see and to be seene. Chilon.

A faire whore is a sweet poyson.

He that hunteth much womens company, cannot be strong: nor can hee be rich that delighteth much in wine.

Womens counsaile is weake, and a childes is vnperfect.

We note inconstancy in children, and likewise in women: the one for slendernesse of wit, and the other as a naturall sicknesse. Seneca.

In men we note audacity, but commonly in women timerosity. Alex. Seu.

Women with their lightnesse, and children with their small knowledge, occupy themselues in things present: but wise men doe thinke on that Mar. Aur.

that is past, they ordaine for that which is present, and with great study doe prouide for the time to come.

Pithagor. There are in a womans eyes two kindes of teares, the one of griefe, the other of deceit.

Use no womans company except necessity compell thee.

Pithagor. They that had rather be conuersant amongst women then amongst wise men, are like Swine that had rather lie rooting in durt and draffe, then in cleere and faire water.

With the fairest women brothell houses are peopled.

Mar. Aur. Beauty in womens faces, and folly in their heads, are two wormes, which fret life, and waste goods.

Women that will haue ioy of their daughters, ought to take from them all such occasions and liberty, whereby they should be euill.

The woman that will keepe her selfe from care and her daughter from perill, let her see the time of her daughter alway well spent in some honest and godly exercise.

When the hands are occupied with any good exercise, then the heart is void from many idle and vaine thoughts.

Mar. Aur. Women are so fraile, that with keepers with great paine they can keepe themselues. And for a small occasion they will loose altogether.

Mar. Aur. Women are so extreame in all head-strong extremities, that with a little fauour, they will be exalted and grow into great pride, and for a small vnkindnesse they retaine great hatred.

Women for a little goodnesse looke for a great hire, but for much euill no chastisement.

Take

Take heede to the meate that a iealous woman giueth thee. Senec.

A fierce beast and a perillous enemy to the Common-wealth is a wicked woman: for she is of much power to doe great harme, and is not apt to follow any goodnesse. Mar. Aur.

The with-drawing and keeping of Women close, is a bridle to the tongue of ill men, and the woman that doth otherwise, putteth her good name in danger.

It were better for a woman neuer to be borne then to be defamed. Socrates.

A wicked woman once defamed, thinketh all others to be so likewise, and desiring they should so be, will indeede say that they are, and procure to haue them euill famed: for to the intent shee may couer her owne infamy, shee infameth all others that be good.

All things done wickedly is sinne, and may be amended: but a dishonest woman alwayes is infamed.

A woman of good name feareth no man with an euill tongue.

Women cannot conserue the reputation of their estate and degree, but by keeping their persons in great feare, honesty, and good order.

It were great wickednesse in men to say that all women are euill that be euill spoken of.

Those women that keepe themselues in their houses, well occupyed in their businesse, temperate in their words, faithfull to their Husbands, well ordered in their persons, peaceable with their Neighbours, being honest among their owne families, and shamefast among strangers, such (I say) haue attayned great renowne in their liues, Mar. Aur. Socrates.

and

and left eternall memory of them after their death.

Plutarch. Neither gorgeous apparell, nor excellent beauty, nor plenty of gold or riches, become a woman so well as sobernesse, silence, faithfulnesse, and chastitie.

Women are no lesse apt to learne all ill manner of things then men are.

Sweet sauours and oyles are more meete for women then for men.

Like as a Trumpetter soundeth out his meaning by the voyce of the Trumpet, so should a woman let her husband speake for her.

Hermes. Silence in a woman is a pretious vertue.

The summe of all.

He that gladly seeketh the company of a wise
Ought onely to winne her by vertuous disposition,
To imbrace her for her vertue, and to leade a quiet life,
Refusing much riches with whorish conditions:
Women be commonly of most tender affection,
And better it is with a Serpent to be in company,
Then with a wicked woman for to marry.

Of the Tongue, Detraction, Speech and Silence. Cap. II.

The Tongue is a slippery and nimble instrument, wherby commonly the treasures of the heart are in such wise vnlocked, layed forth, and spread abroad, that not onely thereby friendship is greatly ingendred, earthly Treasures increased, the life quietly stablished, perpetual praise and euerlasting felicitie obtayned, but contrariwise friendship is decayed, worldly riches are dimi-

diminiſhed, the life moſt miſerably waſted, infamy and immortall payne is thereby purchaſed.

The tongue, if it be well vſed, is the moſt precious member of a man, but otherwiſe the moſt deteſtable pernitious euill, and full of peſtiferous poyſon.

It is a moſt plaine and ſure argument, that the heart within is very filthy, and foulely defiled and corrupted, whenſoeuer the tongue is wickedly bent and vttereth vncleane, filthy, and wicked ſpeeches.

Detract not, neyther ſpeake euill of thy Neighbour behinde his backe. Boëtius.

Detraction is, to ſpeake euill of him that heareth not: or it is a lying, malicious, hypocriticall, crafty, pernicious, and hurtfull ſpeech.

Detraction, being a venemous euill, or rancke poyſon of the Diuell, is poured by him into the hearts onely of wicked and malicious men, who naturally in their proud, ouer-lofty, and ſtout courage, wickedly ouer-whelmed with ſelfe-will and folly, ſpare not at any time (in the contempt of all vertue, true Religion, and honeſty, and for the ſatiſfying of their deſpightfull and curſed humors) to blow out with euill-ſauoured and ſtinking breaths, the very ſhamefull and hurtfull blaſts of ſlanderous and euill reports; whereby euen the very godly are of their good name and fame impayred, their eſtimation diſcredited, their friends abated, their wel-fare much hindered, and their ioyes here ſo ſhaken in this life, that as men drowned in dolor and heauineſſe, voyde of worldly ioy, they are driuen with bitter teares to cry daily vnto God for helpe, and to be deliuered of ſuch their curſed detractors.

Such a mischieuous euill commonly is this sin of detraction in the heart of the proud and wilfull foolish man, that there is neyther long familiarity, accustomed fellowship, nor causes of approued friendship, neyther affinity, kindred, or consanguinity, neyther yet any state or degree that can once bridle him or stay him from doing much mischiefe, if hée can, with his most poysoned and venemous tongue.

Like as Rats and Mise eate and gnaw vpon other mens meate: so the Detractor eateth and gnaweth vpon the life and flesh of others.

Back-biting, lying, and slandering, are sworne companions together.

Back-biting hath this peculiar euill, that is, it hurteth a man absent, and so couertly and craftily that the party is not aware of it, but is sodainely vndone (O poore wretch) before hee doth eyther know by whom, how, when, or wherefore hee is vndone.

The first euill of back-biting is, that it eyther hurteth Charitie, or else when it hath otherwise impayred, it giueth vnto it a great wound, and so extinguisheth it commonly altogether.

Back-biting hurteth charitie, when it disseuereth friends asunder, and bringeth them into dissention and hatred, and it is thereby the sorer wounded when it decayeth it, and (if he can) doth also vtterly extinguish it, when it increaseth the fire betwixt them that be already in dissention, inflaming it more and more.

He that is giuen to the vice of back-biting and slandering, is worthily subiect vnto the common hatred of all men, and to be eschewed of all men as a most pestilent plague. And at his entrance into

into any other place, among company, euery mans mouth to be eyther stopped against him, or otherwise opened to hisse him out of the doores.

Whilest the back-biter liueth, all the world curseth him: if he be in danger or doe perish, there is no man sorry for him, and the remembrance of him after he is dead, raigneth, in cursing and banning of him.

He is to be counted vertuous and wise that alwayes disposeth his tongue to speake of God, and godlinesse. Plato.

Speake euer of God, and God will alwayes put good words into thy mouth: for the speaking and thinking of God surmounteth so much all other words and thoughts, as God himselfe surmounteth all other creatures. Socrates.

As our talke of God ought to be most reuerent and holy, with most sweet and faire words: so must also all our deedes before him be most holy, sweete, perfect and good.

Let not thy tongue run before thy wit.

Let thy minde rule thy tongue.

Vse thine eares more then thy tongue.

Moderate thy lusts, thy tongue, and thy belly.

Hee is wise and discreet that can refraine his tongue.

The tongue is the bewrayer of the heart. Pithagor.

There is not a worse thing, then the deceitfull and lying tongue. Socrates.

An euill tongue is sharper then a sword.

Death deliuereth a man from all enemies saue the tongue.

The tongue of a foole is the key of his counsaile, which in a wise man wisedome hath in keeping. Socrates.

The tongue of a wise man is in his heart, but the heart of a foole is in his tongue.

Socrates. The ordering the tongue is a tryall most true
To know if a man his lust can subdue:
For he that cannot rule his tongue as him list,
Hath much lesse power other lusts to resist.

If by wicked Tongues thou art stirred to unrest and griefe, and feelest thy in selfe through thine owne innocency to be by them abused: let this be unto thee against them a neere and speciall remedy, that is, arme thy selfe with patience, with meeknesse and silence, lest through multiplying of words with thine enemy, thou be found amongst wise men to be as euill as he.

Mar.Aur. It is a thing certayne, when one is merry, hee saith more with his tongue, then hee thinketh with his heart: and contrariwise, when one is heavy, the eyes weepe not so much, nor the tongue cannot declare that, which is locked within the heart.

Aristotle. Keepe measure in thy communication, for if thou be too briefe, thou shalt not be well understood: and if thou be too tedious, thou shalt not be well borne in minde. Eyther talke of vertue thy selfe, or giue eare to them that talke thereof.

It is better to heare then to speake.

Thales. Wee ought to heare double as much as wee speake, and therefore nature hath giuen us two eares, and but one tongue.

Socrates. A man hath power ouer his words till they be spoken, but after they be uttered, they haue power ouer him.

A man ought to consider before what hee will speake, and to utter nothing that may afterwards repent him.

He

He that speaketh little, hearkeneth and learneth at the speech of others, but when hee speaketh, others learne of him. Pichagoras

To talke of God is the best communication, and to thinke of him is the best silence.

Talke no euill of God, but search diligently to know what he is. Socrates.

The filth of worldly wisedome is knowne by much speech.

Words without good effect, are like a great water that drowneth much people, and doth it selfe no profit. Plato.

Abstaine from words of ribaldry: for a tongue ouer-liberall nourisheth folly.

They that robbe, speake euill of, or slander the dead, are like furious dogs, which bite and barke at stones.

He that bableth much, declareth himselfe to haue small knowledge.

Cast whisperers and tale-bearers out of thy company.

Let no man say, I would and I cannot withdraw me from vice: It is better said, I may, but I will not follow vertue. Mar. Aur.

Men ought not to vse any talke or communication, but such as should be fruitfull to edifie, as well the hearer as the speaker. Diogenes.

So speake as thy words be not reproued.

An idle word shall not escape vnpunished.

When the vngodly and malicious persons are suffered to speake what they list, without reprofe and punishment, there is nothing more pernicious in the world to make debate, and to breake the bond of that most incomparable vertue of Amity.

Philip. It lyeth in our selues to be well or euill spoken of.

Thesilius. Rude words that are profitable and true, are better then sweete words being full of deceit and flattery.

Diogenes. The habite of the minde is best perceiued by a mans talking.

Hieronie. Deuout conuersation without communication as much as by example it profiteth, by silence it hurteth: for with barking of dogs, and with the staues of shepheards the raging woolues be hindered of their purposes.

Socrates. Silence and speech are both good, vsed in due time, but otherwise are both nought.

Pithagor. Frame thy speech according to thy garments, or fashion thy garments like vnto thy speech.

Giue no man cause to speake euill of thee.

Hermes. Neither suffer thy hands to worke, nor thy tongue to speake, nor thine eares to heare that which is euill.

Socrates. When thou talkest with a stranger, be not too full of communication, till thou know whether hee be better learned then thou, and if thou be better, speake thou the boldlier, else be quiet and learne of him.

Plato. Hastinesse of speech causeth men to erre.

Philotas. It is much more easier for an innocent to finde many words in his speaking, then for a man in his misery to keepe a temperance in his tale.

The holinesse and cleannesse of the mouth, standeth in the vtterance of rightnesse & truth: and the prophanation & defiling thereof, is by lyings and vntruths: for as no cleane stuffe can proceed out of filthy lips, so the noysome blasts of such euill seasoned breath annoyeth greatly the honest eares of

of the godly: and who will looke for swéete wine out of the same vessell from whence Vineger is daily drawne out?

The fayre water is defiled that passeth through miery springs.

Whatsoeuer thou wilt speake, before thou vtter it, shew it secretly to thy selfe.

Beware of lyes and tale-bearers.

The flying tales of light folkes are commonly the grounds of bad rumors.

Speake not to him that will not heare, for so thou shalt but vexe him.

Thinke not such things honest to be spoken, that are filthy to be done.

A man is by nothing better knowne, then by his communication.

If thou speakest what thou wilt, thou shalt heare that thou wouldest not. Diogenes.

Faire speech in presence,
with good report in absence,
And manners in fellowship
obtaineth good friendship.

He that speaketh truth, cannot be ashamed of that he speaketh. Aristotle.

Faire and smooth communication onely framed to please the hearer, is properly to be called a trap or snare of hony.

Tell not abroad what thou intendest to doe, for if thou spéed not thou shalt be mocked. Pittacus.

Be secret in counsell, and take héede what thou speakest before thine enemies. Isocrates.

He that is beautifull, and speaketh vnséemely things, draweth a sword of Lead out of an Iuory scabberd. Aristippus.

Let not the authority of the speaker perswade

thée, nor regard thou his person that speaketh, but marke well what is spoke.

Heare that which vnto thée belongeth.

Heare much, speake little, be farre spoken, answere aptly: thinke first, then speake, and last of all fulfill.

Pithagor. By silence the discretion of any man is knowne: and a foole kéeping silence séemeth wise.

Silence in a Woman is a great and godly vertue.

Plato. As empty Vessels make the lowdest sound, so they that haue the least wit are greatest bablers.

Plutarch. They that are ready to take a tale out of another mans mouth, are like vnto them who seeing one proffered to be kissed, would hold forth their lips to take it from him.

Seneca. As the vessell cannot be full, which alwayes sheddeth out, and taketh nothing in; so that man cannot be wise that euermore talketh, and neuer hearkeneth.

Aristotle. Like as cleare glasse can hide nothing, so there be many that can kéepe secret and dissemble nothing.

Aug. Cæs. The rewards of faithfull silence are without danger.

The summe of all.

Both speech and silence are excellent vertues,
Vsed in time and place conuenient,
Of which the best and easiest to abuse
Is speech, for which men oftentimes repent:
So doe they not where ere they be silent.
Yet be not dumbe, nor giue thy tongue to lease,
But speake thou well, or heare and hold thy peace.

Of

Of Fortune. Cap, III.

This tearme of Fortune or chance, vsed of men, proceeded first of ignorance and want of true knowledge, not considering what God is, and by whose onely fore-sight and prouidence, all things in this world are séene of him before they come to passe.

Fortune is such a Mistresse, that shée ruleth Realmes, ouer-commeth Armies, beateth downe Kings, exalteth Tyrants, to the dead shée giueth life, to some renowne, and to some shame.

Fortune giueth these euils, and we sée it not: with her hands she toucheth vs, and wée féele it not: shée treadeth vs vnder féete, and we know it not: she speaketh in our eares, and we heare it not; she cryeth aloud vnto vs, and we vnderstand her not: and this is because wée will not know her. And finally, when wée thinke we are most sure, then are we most in perill. Mar. Aur.

If the Fortune of this world make thée reioyce ouer thine enemies, it may make them reioyce ouer thée. Plato.

Be not proud in prosperity, nor despayre in aduersitie. Plato.

In prosperitie beware, and in aduersitie hope for better fortune.

The nature of Fortune is to be alwayes mutable and inconstant: neyther is she a giuer of any thing to any man for any continuance, but onely a lender for a very short time. And those whom Fortune seemeth longest to support and flatter with abundance of all things, them (many times) God least fauoureth.

Euill

Euill men by their bodily strength resist their misfortunes: but good men by vertue of the soule abide them patiently.

Mar.Aur. As in all prosperity alway there falleth some sinister fortune, eyther soone or late: so therewith Fortune doth arme and apparell vs, where shee seeth wee shall fall to our great hurt. Fortune comming with some present delight or pleasure, is a token that by flattering vs shee hath made ready her snares to catch vs. It is an infallible rule of enuious Fortune, that this present felicity is giuen with a pricke of a sodaine fall of mischance.

Such as Fortune lifteth vp with great Riches, shee full cruelly giueth them profound bitings.

Fortune is alwayes slippery, and cannot be holden of any against her will.

Anaxag. Through idlenesse, negligence, and too much trust in Fortune, not onely men, but Cities and kingdomes are vtterly lost and destroyed.

Mar.Aur. What number hath beene seene, that the chances of Fortune could not abate, and yet within a short while after, vnawares, with great ignominious shame haue ouerthrowne themselues?

Fortune with her tyranny chasteneth them that serue her, shee beguileth euery person, and no person beguileth her: shee promiseth much, and fulfilleth nothing: her song is weeping, and her weeping is song to them that be dead among wormes, and to them that liue in prosperity. At them that be present she spurneth with her feete, and threatneth them that be absent. All wise men shrinke from her, but a foole sheweth her his face.

Socrates. To haue beene fortunate is the most misfortune,

There

There cannot be a more intollerable thing, then a fortunate foole.

The adventures of men are so divers, and fickle Fortune giveth so many overtwart turnes, that after that shee hath a great space given great pleasures, incontinent we are cited to the subtile trailes of repentance. Mar. Aur.

The greatest hap of all, and the greatest desire of men is to live long: for divers chances that fall in short time, may be suffered and remedied by long space. Mar. Aur.

Right fortunate is that man that looseth his life, and leaveth behind him perpetuall memory.

Infortunate and unhappy are they that be in prosperity, for surely they that be set in high estate, cannot flye from the perill of Scilla, without falling into Charibdis.

Fortune is to great men deceitfull, to good men unstable, and all that is high is unsure. Tullius.

Mocke not another man for his misfortune, but take heed by him how to avoide the like misery.

Our lives are so doubtfull, and fortune so wayward, that shee doth not alwayes threat in striking, nor striketh in threatning: for oft times false Fortune shaketh her weapon, and striketh not: and another time striketh without shaking.

As Fortune beckeneth, so favour inclineth.

Fortune advanceth and lifteth up, but all men by nature are equall in dignity. Iustinus.

By Nature all men be equall in dignity,
By Fortune more one then another advanced:
This who so considers in his supremacy,
Ought looke to himselfe, and well be advised.
By fortunes good fortune who commeth in favour,
By fortunes misfortune may catch a displeasure.

The

Hermes. The wicked sometime séeme fortunate.

Aristotle. No man is happy indéede whiles he liueth.

Thales. If any man be happy, it is hée that hath bodily health, riches, a learned, and not a vaine minde.

This is a thing most happy, that Fortune in her cruelty, hath no weapon so sharpe and cruel, as can once pierce or wound the soule.

Wisedome and discretion are most to be vsed in time of missfortune.

Kéepe close thy missfortune, lest thine enemies reioyce at it.

Tullius. There is also moderation in the toleration of Fortune of euery sort, which of Tully is called equability, that is, there séemeth alwayes one visage and countenance, not changed either in prosperity or aduersity. Moreouer, a man should not bowe for any fortune or trouble of minde.

Nothing vnto a man is miserable, except he so thinke it: for all fortune is good to him that constantly with patience suffereth it.

Seneca. As a cunning workeman can fashion the Image of any matter: so a wise man should take in good worth all kindes of fortune.

The summe of all.

Fortune is a variable and strange Mistresse,
And vncertaine to trust to in all her doings:
For Fortunes crooked euils her name doth expresse,
Which daily are felt with her hasty short turnings:
She quencheth & destroyeth with her sharpe profound biting:
And for this intent chiefly missfortune should be suffered,
Because true friends are best thereby declared.

Of

Of Riches, and rich Men. Cap. IIII.

Riches are in the number of things that may be eyther good or euill, which is in the arbitrement of the giuer. Xenoph.

To delight in riches is a dangerous vice. Socrates.

He is rich that contenteth himselfe with his pouerty.

The richest thing to a man is his Soule and reason, by which he keepeth iustice and escheweth sinne. Hermes.

He is most rich that hath most wisedome. Polion.

There is no greater riches then the agréement of good mens mindes.

He that is contented and satisfied with himselfe, is borne with great riches.

Abstinence from couetousnesse is great riches.

Riches for the most part are hurtfull to them that possesse them. Plutarch.

Those that be rich, are not onely vexed with desire to encrease greatly their wealth, but also are sore troubled with feare, lest they should lose that which they haue already attained vnto. Cicero.

He hath most that coueteth least.

Not to desire riches, is the greatest riches.

None are in more surety then they that lacke most riches.

If thou séeke to be rich, thou shalt find therewith sorrow, carefull trauell, misery, vexation of minde, and much mischiefe. But if thou séeke to be godly, thou shalt finde comfort, wealth, prosperity, peace of conscience, and all felicity.

As sicknesse and health can neuer agree,
So gold without rest is but misery.

Vertues

Aristotle. Vertue is greater riches then either siluer or gold.

Pithagor. Hee is not rich that enioyeth not his owne goods.

Suffisance is better in riches then aboundance.

Plato. Labour for the riches that after death profiteth the soule.

Hermes. A couetous man cannot be rich.

Care not what riches thou loosest for the winning of true friends.

Purchase thy riches truely, and spend them liberally.

Aristotle. Seeke not the riches of this world, and shame in the other: seeing this world is no more but onely a bayting place to goe to the other world.

Mar. Aur. It is a great wonder to heare and see, how Fathers climbe to haue riches, and their children descend to haue viciousnesse, to see Fathers honour their children, and children to infame their fathers: to see fathers giue rest vnto their children, and little children to giue trouble to their old fathers: yea, sometime the fathers dye for sorrow, that their children dye so soone, and the children weepe because the fathers liue so long. Also the honour and riches that the fathers haue procured with great thoughts, the children loose with little care. And this is certaine, that the fathers may gather riches, with deceit and craft, to sustaine their children, but God will not haue durable that is begun with euill intention, and is founded on the preiudice of others, though possessed by an heyre, and though the heauy destinies of the Fathers permit that their riches be left to their children, to serue them in all their vices for their pastime,

pastime, at the last, according to their merits, GOD will that their Heyre and Heritage shall both perish. Finally, all that with great thought hath béene gathered for their children, whom they loue well, and with whom they much content themselues, sometime another heyre, of whom they thinke least inioyeth it.

God doth permit that the couetous fathers in gathering with great trauaile, should dye with the same, to leaue their riches to their vicious children to spend badly. Max. Aur.

Great abundance and plenty of riches cannot of any man be both gathered and kept without sinne. Hierome.

Riches and the substance of the world robbeth and spoyleth a man of much better Riches, that is to say, the loue of vertue, and of all godly exercise.

Gold is a corruptible matter or substance, and shall therefore once be consumed: but that treasure for the which Mans soule ought to labour, shall neuer be wasted, neyther in quality, nor in quantity impayred or diminished, that is, shall alway be like good, and like much. Wherefore whatsoeuer payne be taken about the getting of such Treasure, it ought not to be imputed grieuous: weighing well the vertue of the gayne, and the most happy reward in the end. Plato.

Great possessions or substance maketh Vertue suspected, because they be ministers of pleasant affections, and also nurses of wanton appetites. Alex. Seu.

Those riches are to be despised, which with liberality are wasted, and with sparing doe rot. Pithagor.

Be not carefull for worldly riches, for GOD hath prouided for each man sufficient. Socrates.

Prepare

Prepare thee such riches, as when the Ship is broken, may swim and escape with their master.

Plato. Trauell not to get that which will lightly perish.

Esteeme him as much that teacheth thee one word of wisdome, as if he gaue thee gold and precious stones.

Such things as thou hast, vse as thine owne, and keepe them not as though they were another bodies.

Boast not thy selfe of that which is another mans.

Homer. When prosperitie promiseth securitie and rest in the goods of this world, it is an hard thing and a rare to thinke God onely to be the giuer thereof, and can sodainely take the things away that haue beene gathered with great paynes and trauels.

Learning is great Riches to the poore, and it garnisheth the rich.

Where Riches are honoured, good men are despised.

Immortall honour is better then transitory Riches.

Plato. Hee that keepeth a Man from shame, is better then the Riches gotten thereby.

Desire of Riches waxeth infinite.

Hermes. It is a miserable thing, a rich man to be decayed and falne into pouerty.

Hee is not happy that hath Riches, but hee that rightly vseth them.

The Riches of this World abused, ingendreth pride and forgetfulnesse of God.

Solon. There be three causes noted, that chiefly moue mens mindes to desire these worldy goods: one is the

the loue of wealth, ease, mirth, and pleasure: the second is, the loue of worship, honour, and glory: the third is, the doubtfulnesse and mistrust of wicked and faithlesse men, that are carefull of liuing here in this life.

They be worse that be lately made rich, then they which haue béene rich a great while.

It is a foolish madnesse to thinke that rich men be happy.

He hath Riches sufficient that needeth neyther to flatter nor borrow.

The more that a man hath of abundance, Pithagor.
So much the lesse he hath of assurance.

Suffisance is the castle which kéepeth wise men from euill workes.

He is neyther rich, happy, nor wise, Solon.
That is a bond-man to his owne auarice.

Great businesse the heart hath to search for the goods of this world, and great trauaile to come to them: but the greatest dolor without comparison, is at the houre of death to depart and leaue them. Mar. Aur.

Rich men through excesse and delicious pleasures, are more foolish & corrupt then any others. Aristotle.

Rich men had néed of many lessons to doe well.

Rich men (their affection respected) had néede of many precepts and counsailes, both touching their kéeping of hospitality, and to the exercising also of their bodies with labour, lest they should most corruptly fal with consent into the filthy motions of the body, & other inconueniences, wherof the poore néede no such admonitions. Diogenes.

Treasure by falsehood seeming to augment, Hermes.
Are euill gotten, but worse spent:
Wherefore to be rich, who so doth intend,
Ought truely to winne, and duely to spend.

Anaxag. Men would liue exceeding quietly, if these two words (mine and thine) were taken away.

Pithagoras Couet not to waxe rich through deceit.

The time and riches are best bestowed, that are employed about the seruice of God.

Tullius. In thy prosperity, and when things flow towards thee, (euen at thy will and pleasure,) thou must the more earnestly flye pride, disdainfulnesse, arrogancy, immoderation of backe or belly, incontinency and loosenesse of life.

Spend not too outragiously, nor be too niggardish: so shalt thou neither be needy, nor in bondage to thy riches.

Upon a couetous man riches are lost, and are very pouerty to him: for he is neither the warmer, the better fed, nor the richer for them.

Diogenes. Rich men without learning, are called Sheepe with golden fleeces.

Charge not thy selfe with taking of vain goods, sith thou hast so small assurance of thy life.

Plutarch. The miserable rich person, the more that hee encreaseth in riches, the more hee diminisheth in friends, and groweth in enemies, to his damage.

Friendship is better then riches.

As the townes wherein men labour, waxe alwayes richer and richer, and such as are bent to idlenesse and pleasure decay daily, and come to utter desolation: so the goods that be gotten by trauaile, study, and diligence, and so kept, shall continue and increase, but that which is euill gotten, or sodainely wonne, shall euen as sodainely vanish away againe.

Socrates. Like as an arrow that lighteth vpon a stone glanceth away, because the stone wanting softnesse yeeldeth not to receyue it: so the riches that

Fortune

Fortune giueth, not guided with diligence and circumſpection, vaniſheth away without profit.

The hauing of riches is not ſo commodious, Ariſtotle.
As the departing from them is grieuous.

A mans riches are no where ſo well laid vp and ſafely kept, as in the hands of his friends.

Small expences often vſed, conſume great ſub- Seneca.
ſtance.

Hée which giueth riches or glory to a wicked Ariſtotle.
man, giueth wine to him that hath a feuer.

As a golden bridle, although it garniſh an horſe, Plato.
yet maketh him neuer the better: ſo although riches garniſh a man, yet can they not make him good.

Death deſpiſeth all riches and glory, and roleth Boëtius.
both the rich and poore folke together.

Such as truſt in their owne ſtrength or riches, abuſe and blaſpheme the name of God, which hath not béene vnpuniſhed, nor neuer ſhall be in this world, nor in the world to come.

The ſumme of all.

Sith the perfect riches is ſuffiſance,
He is more rich that's content with pouerty,
Then he that hath of treaſures abundance,
Which no man may poſſeſſe well with ſurety.
Rich is he that can himſelfe ſatisfie
With feweſt things which be both ſafe and ſure,
There Fortunes gifts are double to endure.

Of Blessednesse, and Misery. Cap. IIII.

Cicero. That man cannot be truely blessed, in whom vertue hath no place.

Those men be truely blessed, whom no feare troubleth, no pensiuenesse consumeth, no carnall concupiscence tormenteth, and those also that are not soone stirred to foolishnesse and gladnesse.

All things truely belonging to blessednesse, doe chiefly consist in the noble vertue of wisedome.

A man that is wise, although hee fall into extreame necessity and pouerty, yet is he very rich, and greatly blessed.

That man which hath strength, beauty, comely personage, nimblenesse of body, and thereunto likewise being added riches, honour, rule, and great glory of this world: yet if hée with all these be an vniust, intemperate, and fearefull man, and of no capacity, hée is not truely blessed, but most miserable.

That man is worthily counted blessed, to whom nothing can séeme so introllerable, as to discourage him: nor nothing so pleasant as proudly to puffe him vp, and make him vain-glorious.

A blessed life consisteth in the knowledge of things, which we doe attaine vnto by searching out the natures of them, and being once obtained, wée doe contemne all worldly things, and liue in security, which is the quietnesse of the minde, or to be void of vngodly care.

Plato. Finally, that man is truely blessed, to whom it shall chance, that once comming to old age, he then doe attaine vnto true wisedome, and fasten himselfe in true opinions.

Of

Of Beginning, and Ending. Cap. V.

GOD lacketh beginning and ending.

The most gracious and mighty beginner is God, which in the beginning created the World. Thales. Hermes.

Good counsaile is the beginning and end of good workes. Zeno.

Begin nothing before thou first call for the helpe of God: for God (whose power is in all things) giueth most prosperous furtherance and finishing to such good acts as we doe begin in his name.

Take good aduisement before thou begin any thing, but when thou hast begun it, dispatch it quickly. Aristotle.

Begin nothing before thou knowest how to finish it.

Take good héed at the beginning to what thou grantest, for after one inconuenience another followeth.

Before any fact be by man committed, the end is first in cogitation, and last of all the fact.

Of small faults not hindered at the beginning, oftentimes spring mighty mischiefes.

Not the beginning of things, but the last end, must declare whether the same be well attempted or not. Photion.

Many things at the beginning are counted good, which at the end are knowne to be euill. Pithagor.

The end of casuall things in the world, no man doth or may know.

To haue made a good beginning, is no small portion of the worke done. Socrates.

In all workes the beginning is the chiefest, and the end hardest to attaine.

Plutarch. Like as a spot ought to be wiped out at first, lest with long tarrying it staine through, and bee worse to be gotten out: so should dissention be remedyed at the first, that it grow not vnto hatred.

Aristotle. Like as the stroke which a man seeth, may be the better receiued and defended: so the mischiefe which is knowne of before, can one the lesse harme.

Horace. Stop the beginning, so shalt thou be sure,
All doubtfull diseases to swage and to cure:
But if thou be carelesse and suffer them brast,
Too late commeth plaister, when all cure is past.

Mar. Aur. Like as after the night commeth the dewie morning, and after that commeth the bright Sunne, and after the Sunne commeth a darke cloud, and after raine commeth faire weather, and after that commeth lightning and thunder, and then againe commeth faire weather: euen so after infancy commeth child-hood, and after child-hood commeth old age, and after old age commeth death, and last of all after death, commeth a fearefull hope of a sure life.

Euery man hath a beginning, a middle, and an end.

Plato. Good respect and consideration to the end of things, preserueth both body and soule.

Pacuuius. When the godly shall haue their full entrance and beginning to euerlasting glory: and make their happy change from mortality to immortalitie: and leaue the corruptible drosse of this life, for treasures incorruptible: for gold, glory: for siluer, solace without end: for vaine apparell, roabs royall: for earthly houses, eternall pallaces: mirth

mirth without measure, pleasure without payne, and felicity endlesse: then also shall the end of the wicked be most lamentable: then shall hastily come vnto them their iust reward of vengeance: then shall they with the end of this worlds vayne felicity enter into eternall damnation and misery, then shall they cry, woe, woe, with endlesse horrour, for their carelesse life, and worldly security.

The summe of all.

God, that is most glorious, was th'almighty beginner
Of all that in heauen or in earth haue their being:
Which was without beginning, he is th'onely helper,
And furtherer of good workes to come to good ending.
Without counsell and aduisement begin not any thing:
But consider well the end, and waigh discreetly,
What happily preserueth both soule and body.

THE ELEVENTH BOOKE;

Cap. I.

Of the Precepts of the Wise.

I Haue in this Booke (which I diuided into two parts) put together the precepts & Prouerbs of morall philosophy, and those both of the pitthiest and briefest that I thought méete. Because I would haue them better waighed and remembred, but specially put in practise: for the following of one good saying, is better then the learning of a thousand.

Solon. WOrship God.
Reuerence thy father and mother.
Helpe thy friend.
Hate no man. Maintaine truth.
Sweare not. Obay the lawes.
Thinke that which is good.
Moderate thine anger. Prayse Vertue.
Persecute the euill with extreame hatred.
Thales. Honour thy King. Try thy friends.
Be the selfe-same that thou pretendest.
Abstaine from vice. Loue peace.
Desire honour and glory for vertue.
Take héed to thy selfe, and be circumspect.

Deserue

Deserue praise of euery body.
Cast whisperers and tale-bearers out of thy company.
Take in good worth whatsoeuer chanceth.
Be not high-minded. Iudge iustly.
Be carefull for thy houshold.
Reade ouer good Bookes. Cleo.
Doe good to good people.
Refraine from foule Language.
Bring vp in learning thy children that thou louest best.
Be not suspitious nor iealous.
Vanquish thy parents with sufferance.
Remember them which haue done thee good, and forget not their benefits.
Despise not thine vnderlings.
Desire not other mens goods.
Runne not head-long into doubtfull matters.
Keepe thy friends goods as safe as thou wouldest thine owne.
Doe not that to another, which thou thy selfe hatest.
Threaten no body, for that is woman-like.
Be readier to goe to thy friend in time of his misery, then of his prosperity.
Beare no malice.
Vse temperance. Fly filthy things. Chilon.
Get thy goods iustly. Loose no time.
Vse Wisedome. Please the most.
Be well mannered. Suspect nothing.
Hate slander. Be not importunate.
Let not thy tongue runne before thy wit.
Proue not that which thou mayest not atchieue.
Loue as if thou wouldest hate, and hate as thou wouldest loue shortly after.

Please

Please euery body. Hate violence.

Periander. Be alwayes one to thy friend, as well in aduersitie, as in prosperity.

Performe whatsoeuer thou promise.

Kéepe close thy misfortune, lest thine enemy reioyce at it.

Sticke to the truth. Abstaine from vice.

Doe that which is rightfull and iust.

Giue place to thy betters, and to thine elders.

Abstaine from swearing. Follow vertue.

Moderate thy lusts and affections.

Prayse honest things. Hate debate.

Be mercifull to the penitent.

Instruct thy children. Requite benefits.

Enhaunt wise mens company.

Estéeme greatly good men. Fly rebuke.

Heare that which vnto thée belongeth.

Be enuious to no man. Answere aptly.

Doe nothing that may repent thée.

Honour them that haue deserued honour.

Be fayre spoken. Feare the officers.

Maintaine concord. Flatter not.

When thou dost amisse, take better counsaile.

Trust not to the time. Hope well.

Be seruiceable to euery body.

Take good héed to thy selfe.

Reuerence thine elders with obedience.

Fight and dye for thy country.

Mourne not for euery thing, for that will shorten thy life.

Get a witty woman to thy wife, and she shal bring thée forth wise children.

Liue and hope, as if thou shouldest dye immediately.

Spare as though thou wert immortall.

Hate

Hate pride and vaine-glory.
Swell not in wealth. Seale vp secrets.
Tarry alwayes for a conuenient time.
Giue liberally for thy profit.
Doe no man wrong. Auoide griefe.
Mocke not the dead. Use thy friends.
Giue blamelesse counsayle, and comfort thy friends. Bias.
Behold thy selfe in a looking-glasse, and if thou appeare beautifull, doe such things as become thy beauty: but if thou seeme foule, then performe with good manners the beauty that thy face lacketh.
Talke no euill of God, but search diligently to know what he is.
Heare much, but speake little.
First vnderstand, then speake.
Prayse not the vnworthy because of his riches.
Get by perswasion, and not by violence.
Get thee sobernesse in thy youth, and wisedome in thine age.
Tell not abroad what thou intendest to doe: for if thou speed not, thou shalt be mocked. Plutarch.
Pay thy debts. Reuile not thy friend.
Rule thy wife. Be not sloathfull.
If thy fellow hurt thee in small things, suffer it, and be as bold with him.
Take not thine enemy for thy friend, nor thy friend for thine enemy.
Be not iudge betweene thy friends.
Striue not with thy Father and mother, though thou saist the truth.
Reioyce not at any mans misfortune. Hermes.
Let thy minde rule thy tongue.
Be obedient to the Law. Heare gladly.

Attempt

Attempt nothing aboue thy strength.
Be not hasty to speake, nor slow to heare.
Wish not the things which thou maist not obtaine.
Aboue and before all things worship God.
Reuerence thine elders.
Refraine thy lusts. Breake vp hatred.
Be obedient vnto thy King, and worship those that be in authoritie vnder him.
Loue God and truth, and so shalt thou saue thy soule.
Enuie not though an euill man prosper, for surely his end shall not be good.
Be satisfied with little, and it will increase and multiply.
Trust not to the time, for it deceiueth sodainely them that trust therein.
Vpbraid no man with misery.
Marry thy match.
Take good aduisement or thou begin any thing, but when thou hast begun, dispatch it quickly.

Plutarch. Before thou goe from home, deuise with thy selfe what thou wilt doe abroad: and when thou art come home againe, remember what thou hast done abroad.

Philotas. Neither flatter nor hide thy wisedome before strangers.

Be not proud in prosperitie, neither despaire in aduersitie.
In prosperity beware, and in aduersity hope for better fortune.
Learne by other mens vices, how filthy thine owne are.
Doe not that thy selfe, which thou dispraysest in another.

Couet

Couet not to waxe rich through deceit. Aristotle.
Looke what thankes thou rendrest to thy Parents, and looke for the like againe of thy children.
Rule not except thou hast first learned to obay.
Yéeld vnto reason. Flye euill company.
Slander not them that be dead.
Prepare thee such Riches, as when the ship is broken, may swim and escape with their maister.
Learne such things while thou art a childe, as Plato. may profit thée when thou art a man.
Endeauour thy selfe to doe so well, that others may enuy thée therefore.
Spend not too outragiously, nor be too niggardish: so shalt thou neyther be néedy, nor in bondage to thy riches.
Be patient in tribulation, & giue no man cause Hermes. to speake euill of thée.
Looke wel to the safe-guard of thine owne body.
Know thy selfe, so shall no flatterer beguile thée. Seneca.
Be vertuous and liberall, so shalt thou eyther stop the slanderers mouth, or else the eares of them that heare them.
Meddle not with that wherewith thou hast Xenoph. nought to doe.
If thou hast well done, thanke God: if otherwise, repent, and aske him forgiuenesse.
Desire God at the beginning of thy workes, that thou mayest by his helpe bring them to good conclusion.
Walke not in the way of hatred.
Doe not what thou wouldest, but what thou Aristotle. shouldest.
Prayse not a man, except he be prayse-worthy.
If thou wilt correct any man, doe it rather with gentlenesse, then with violent extremities.

Use

Socrates. Vse measure in all things.

When thou talkest with a stranger, be not too full of communication, till thou knowest whether he be better learned then thou, and if hee be not, speake thou the boldlier, else be quiet and learne of him.

Socrates. Giue thy wife no power ouer thee, for if thou suffer her to day to tread vpon thy foot, shee will to morrow tread vpon thy head.

Fixe thy will to doe iustly, and see thou sweare not.

Haunt not too much thy friends house, for that engendreth no great loue: nor be too long from thence, for that engendreth hate, but vse a meane in all things.

Aristotle. Trouble not thy selfe with worldly carefulnes, but resemble the Birds of the ayre, which in the morning seeke their foode but onely for that day.

Doubt them whom thou knowest, and trust not them whom thou knowest not.

Wander not by night, nor by darke.

Labour not to enforme him, that is without reason, for so shalt thou make him thine enemy.

Vse no womans company, except necessity compell thee.

Esteeme him as much that teacheth thee one word of wisedome, as if he gaue thee gold.

Sweare not for any matter of aduantage.

Seneca. Affirme nothing before thou knowest how to finish it.

Plato. Be not hasty, angry, nor wrathfull, for they be the conditions of a foole.

Refraine from vice, for vertue is a precious garment.

Measure

Meaſure thy pathes, and goe the right way, ſo ſhalt thou goe ſafely.

Refraine from Couetouſneſſe, and thine eſtate ſhall proſper.

Uſe Juſtice, and thou ſhalt be both beloued and feared.

If thou wilt diſprayſe him whom thou hateſt, ſhew not that thou art his enemy.

Take héede to the meate that a iealous woman giueth thée. Hermes.

Let neyther thy beauty, thy youth, nor thy health deceyue thée.

Breake not the Lawes that are made for the wealth of thy country.

Apply thy minde to vertue, and thou ſhalt be ſaued.

Prayſe nothing that is not commendable: nor diſprayſe any thing that is prayſe-worthy.

Trauaile not much for that which will lightly periſh. Plato.

Enſue the vertues of thy good anceſtours.

Array thy ſelfe with iuſtice, and cloth thée with chaſtity: ſo ſhalt thou be happy, and thy workes proſper. Seneca.

Enforce thy ſelfe to get wiſedome and ſcience, by which thou mayeſt direct both thy Soule and body.

Endeauour thy ſelfe to kéepe the law, that God may be pleaſed with thée. Pithagor.

Couet not thy friends riches, leſt thou be deſpiſed therefore.

Reproue not any man in his wrath, for then thou maiſt not rule him. Hermes.

Reioyce not at another mans misfortune, but take héed by him that the like chance not to thée.

Stabliſh

Stabliſh thy wit both on thy right hand, and on thy left, and thou ſhalt be free.

Socrates. Giue to the good, and he will requite it, but giue to the euill diſpoſed, and hee will aske more.

Be not ſlack to recompence them that haue done for thee.

Thinke firſt, then ſpeake, and laſt fulfill.

Accuſtome not thy ſelfe to be ſodaynely moued, for it will turne to thy diſpleaſure.

Pithagor. If thou intendeſt to doe any good, tarry not till to morrow, for thou knowſt not what may chance thee this night.

Ariſtotle. If thou feeleſt thy ſelfe more true to thy King then many other, and haſt alſo leſſe wages of him then they, yet complain not, for thine will continue and ſo will not theirs.

Diogenes. If any man enuy thee, or ſay euill of thee ſet not thereby, and thou ſhalt diſappoint him of his purpoſe.

Forget not to giue thanks to them that inſtruct thee in Learning, nor challenge to thy ſelfe the prayſe of other mens inuentions.

Socrates. Loue all men, and be ſubiect to all Lawes, but obay God more then men.

Plato. If thou wilt be counted valiant, let neyther chance nor griefe ouercome thee.

Giue good eare to the aged, for he can teach thee of thy life to come.

Flye lecherous luſts as thou wouldeſt a furious Lord.

Attempt not two things at once, for the one will hinder the other.

Ariſtotle. Let no couetous man haue any rule ouer thee, nor yeeld thy ſelfe ſubiect to couetouſneſſe: for the couetous man will defraud thee of thy goods, and

couetouſneſſe

couetousnesse will defraud thee of thy soule.

Receiue not the gifts that an euill disposed man doth proffer.

Be sober and chast among yong folks, that they Plato. may learne of thee, and among old that thou mayst learne of them.

Order thy wife as thou wouldest thy kinsfolke. Seneca.

Apply thy selfe so now in vertue, that in the Plato. time to come thou mayest therefore be prayscd.

Thinke that the weakest of thine enemies is stronger then thou.

Be not ashamed to doe iustice, for all that is done without it is tyranny.

Fortifie thy soule with good workes, and flye from couetousnesse.

If thou intendest not to doe good, yet at least refrayne from doing euill.

Giue not thy selfe much to pleasure and ease, for Aristotle. if thou vsest thy selfe thereto, thou shalt not be able to sustayne the aduersity that may afterwards chance to thee.

Endeauour thy selfe in thy youth to learne, though it be painefull: for it is lesse payne for a man to learne in his youth, then in his age to be vnlearned.

When thou art weary of study, sport thy selfe with reading of good stories.

Couet not to haue thy businesse hastily done, but rather desire that it may be well done.

Reioyce without great laughter.

Desire not to be wise in words, but in workes: for wisedome of words wasteth with the World, but works wrought by wisdome, increase into the world to come.

If thou doubtest of any thing, aske counsaile

of wise men: and be not angry although they reproue thee.

Worship good men, so shalt thou obtayne the peoples fauour.

Diogenes. Keepe no company with him that knoweth not himselfe.

Be not like the Boulter that casteth out the flower, and keepeth in the bran.

Commit the gouernance of people neyther to a Childe, nor a foole, nor a couetous, nor vnto any hasty person, that is desirous of reuengement.

Plato. If thou desirest to be good, endeauour thy selfe to learne to know, and to follow truth: for he that is ignorant therein, and will not learne, cannot be good.

Aristotle. Keepe a measure in thy communication: for if thou be too briefe, thou shalt not be well vnderstood: and if thou be too long, thou shalt not be well borne in minde.

To him that is full of questions, giue no answere at all.

Pithagor. Use examples, that such as thou teachest may vnderstand thee the better.

Aristotle. Reason not with him that will deny the principall truth.

Take good heede at the beginning to what thou grantest: for after one inconuenience another followeth.

Seneca. If thou desirest to haue delight without sorrow, apply thy minde to study wisedome.

Marry a young Maide, that thou mayest teach her good manners.

Keepe company with them that may make thee better.

We

Be bound vnto wisedome, that thou mayest obtaine thy true liberty.

Loue if thou wilt be loued.

So talke with men, as if God saw thee.

So talke with God, as if men heard thee.

Feare followeth hope, wherefore if thou wilt not feare, hope not.

Desire not to dwell nigh a rich man, for that will make thee couetous.

Eschew anger, though not for wisedomes sake, yet for bodily health.

If thou desirest to be quiet minded, thou must either be a poore man indeede, or else like a poore man.

Take no thought to liue long, but to liue well.

Forasmuch as thou art not certaine in what place death abideth thee, be thou ready prepared in each place to meete him.

Prayse a man for that which may neither be giuen him, nor taken away from him: which is not his faire house, his goodly garments, nor his great houshold, but his wit and perfect reason.

Labour not for a great number of Bookes, but for the goodnesse of them.

Use thine eares more then thy tongue.

Desire nothing, that thou wouldest denye if it were asked thee.

Whatsoeuer thou wilt speake, before thou shew it to another, shew it secretly to thy selfe. Seneca.

Whatsoeuer thou wilt haue kept secret, shew it it vnto no body.

Search forth the cause of euery deed.

Let not thy thoughts depart from the truth.

Promise with consideration, and performe faithfully.

Prayse little, but disprayse lesse.

Let not the authority of the speaker perswade thee, nor regard thou his person that speaketh, but marke well what it is that is spoken.

Performe more fully then thou hast promised.

Such things as thou hast, vse as thine owne, and keepe them not as if they were another bodies.

Be gentle and louing to euery body, flatter none, be familiar with few, be indifferent and equall towards euery man, be slow to wrath, swift to mercy and pitty, be constant and patient in aduersity, and in prosperity wary and lowly.

Worship gentlenesse, hate all cruelty.

Fly and eschew thine owne vices, and be not curious to search out other mens.

Be not busie to vpbraid men with their faults, for so shalt thou be hated of euery body.

Sometime among earnest things, vse merry conceits, but measurably.

Liue with thy vnderlings, as thou wouldest thy betters should liue with thee, and doe to all men, as thou wouldest be done by.

Thinke not thy selfe to be that which thou art not, nor seeme greater then thou art indeede.

Thinke all things may be suffered saue filthinesse and vice.

Eate rather for hunger, then for pleasure or delight.

Be apt to learne wisedome, and diligent to teach it.

Be merry without laughter.

Charme thy tongue, thy belly, and thy priuities.

Anacharsis Thou shalt be loued of God, if thou doe good to all men, and hurt no body.

Beleeue

Beleeue not him that saith he loueth truth, and followeth it not.

Sée that thy gifts be according to thine ability: for if they be too big, thou shalt be thought a waster: and again, if they be too small, thou shalt be thought a niggard. Solon.

Let thy gifts be such as hée to whom thou giuest them doth delight in.

Giue no vaine and vnméet gifts, as armour to women, bookes to plow-men, or nets to a student. Seneca.

Giue to the néedy, yet so that thou néede not thy selfe.

Succour them that perish, yet so that thou thy selfe perish not thereby.

If thou bestowest a benefit, kéepe it secret: but if thou receiuest any, publish it abroad.

Speake not to him that will not heare, for so thou shalt but vexe him.

Giue at the first asking, for it is not fréely giuen that is often craued.

Boast not thy selfe of that which is another mans.

Blame not nature, for shée doth for euery man alike.

If thou wilt prayse any man because hée is a gentleman: prayse his Parents also: if thou prayse him for his riches, that appertaineth to Fortune: if for his strength, remember that sicknesse will make him weake: if for swiftnesse of foot, remember that age will take it away: if for his beauty, it will soone vanish. But if thou wilt prayse him for manners and learning, then prayse thou him as much as appertaineth to man, for that is his owne, which neither commeth by heritage, nor altereth with fortune or age, but is alwayes one.

Socrates. Flye the company of a lyar, but if thou must néedes kéepe company with him, beware that in any case thou beléeue him not.

Giue part of thy goods to the néedy, so shall God increase them.

Sow good workes, and thou shalt reape the flowers of ioy and gladnesse.

Boast not of thy good déedes, lest thine euill be also laid to thy charge.

Company not with him that knoweth not himselfe.

Be not ashamed to heare the truth, of whomsoeuer it be: for truth is so noble of it selfe, that it maketh them honourable that pronounce it.

If thou hast not so much power as to refraine thine ire, yet dissemble it, and kéepe it secret, and so by little and little forget it.

Pithagor. Honour wisedome, and deny it not to them that would learne it, but shew it not to them that disprayse it.

Sow not the Sea-fields.

Isocrates. Giue not too light credence to a mans words, nor laugh thou them to scorne: for the one is the property of a foole, and the other the condition of a mad-man.

Thinke not such things honest to be spoken, that are filthy to be done.

Accustome not thy selfe to be heauy and sad, for if thou doest, thou shalt be thought fierce: yet be thoughtfull, for that is a token of a prudent man.

So doe all things, as if euery man should know them, yet kéepe them close a while, and at length discouer them.

Learne diligently the goodnesse that is taught thée:

thee: it is as great a shame for a man not to learne the good doctrine that is taught him, as to refuse a gift proffered him of a friend.

Let it not grieue thee to take paynes to goe to learne of a cunning man: for it were great shame for young men not to trauell a little by Land to increase their knowledge, since Merchants saile so farre by sea to augment their riches.

Be gentle in thy behauiour, and familiar in communication: for it belongeth to gentlenesse to salute gladly them that wee meete, and in familiarity to talke gently and friendly with them.

Behaue thy selfe gently to euery body, so shalt thou make the good thy friends, and keepe the bad from being thine enemies.

Use thy selfe to labour by thine owne accord, that if it chance thee to be compelled thereto, thou mayest the better away with it.

Performe thy promise as iustly as thou wouldest pay thy debts: for a man ought to be more faithfull then his oath.

For two causes if thou be constrayned, thou mayest sweare, as to discharge thy selfe from any great offence, or to saue chiefe friends from great danger: But for money thou shalt not sweare any oath, for if thou doest, thou shalt of some be thought forsworne, and of others, to be desirous of money.

Thinke it a great shame to be ouercome with thy friends benefits, and with the iniury of thine enemies.

Allow them for thy friends, that be as glad for thy prosperitie, as they seeme sorrowfull for thy misfortune: for there be many that lament a mans misery, that would enuy to see him prosper.

If thou doost good to the euill, it shall happen to thee as it doth to them that feed other mens dogs, which bark as well at their feeder as at any other stranger.

Pithagor. Doe not such things thy selfe, as thou wouldest dispraise in another.

Enforce thy selfe to refrayne thine euill Lusts, and follow the good: for the good mortifieth and destroyeth the euill.

Socrates. Speake alwaies of God, and God will alwayes put good words in thy mouth.

Set thine owne workes alwayes before thine eyes, and cast other mens behinde thy backe.

Fixe not thy minde vpon worldly pleasure, nor trust to the World, for it deceyueth all that put their trust therein.

Be content with little, and couet not another mans goods,

Be sober in thy liuing, and replenish thine hart with wisedome.

Dread God, and keep thy selfe from vain-glory.

Mocke not another man for his misery, but take heed by him how to auoid the like misfortune.

Let no man perswade thee by flattery to doe any euill, nor to beleeue otherwise of thy selfe then thou art indeede.

Receiue patiently the words of correction, although they seeme grieuous.

Hermes. Feare the vengeance of God as much as thou maist, and consider the greatnesse of his puissance and might.

Beware of spies and tale-bearers.

Socrates. Tell nothing to him that will not beleeue thee, nor demand not any thing which thou knowest will not be granted.

Feare

Feare GOD aboue all things, for that is rightfull and profitable: and so order thy selfe, that thy thoughts and words be alwayes of him: for speaking & thinking of God surmounts so much all other wordes and thoughts, as God himselfe surmounteth all other creatures, and therefore men ought to obey him, though they should be constrayned to the contrary.

Make thy prayers perfect in the sight of God, for prayer is like a Ship in the Sea, which if it be good, saueth all therein, but if it be nought, suffereth them to perish.

Pray not to God to giue thee sufficient, for that hee will giue to each man vnasked: but pray that thou mayest be contented and satisfied with that which hee giueth thee. Plutarch.

Beleeue not him that telleth thee a lye by another body, for hee will in like manner make a lye of thee to another man.

If thou desire to be beloued of euery body, salute each man gladly, be liberall in giuing, and thankfull in receyuing. Forget thine anger lightly, and desire not to be reuenged.

If thou desirest to continue long with another man, striue to instruct him well in good manners.

Looke well to thy selfe, that the reyne of thy youth, and liberty of thine high estate, cause thee not to commit vice. Mar.Aur.

It is a poynt of great folly, well to know other men, and not to know himselfe.

Be not proud in wisedome, in strength, nor in riches: it is one God that is wise, puissant, and full of felicity.

Trust rather in wisedome and prowesse, then Alex.Scu.

in vnstable fortune. And desire victory for renowne and honour, rather then for mony and corrupt treasure.

Tholon. Neuer open the gates to flatterers and dissemblers, nor listen with thine eares to murtherers.

Arsasides. Neuer choose a rich tyrant, nor abhorre the poore iust man. Neuer deny iustice to a poore man for his pouerty, nor pardon a rich man for his great riches. Neuer giue for reward, nor doe good for affection, nor giue correction only for punishment. Neuer leaue wickednes vnchastised, nor goodnes without reward. Neuer deny iustice to them that demand it, nor mercy to them that desire it. Neuer correct for anger, nor promise rewards in thy mirth. Neuer commit euill for malice, nor villany for auarice. Labour alwaies to be beloued of them that be good, and to be dreaded and feared of them that be euill. Finally, be thou fauourable vnto the poore, who can doe but little, and thou shalt be fauoured of GOD, who is able to doe much.

When thou arisest in the morning, determine so to passe the day following, as though at night a graue should be thy bed.

Let the feeding and apparrelling of thy body, be altogether referred to health and strength, and not to voluptuousnesse.

If we well consider what an excellency and dignity there is in our nature, wee shall quickly perceyue how foule a thing it is to ouerflow in Riot, and to liue deliciously and wantonly: and on the contrary, how honest a thing it is to lead our liues warily, chastly, and soberly.

Riot to euery age is reproachfull, but for an old man most shamefull.

At thy downe-lying and vprising, at thy sporting, eating, and banketting, be mindefull of God. be thankefull vnto him, and remember his benefits not onely towards thy selfe, but also towards all mankinde, euen throughout all the world. Mar.Aur.

And whatsoeuer thou takest in hand, thinke with thy selfe that before thou end it, death may suppresse thee. Seneca.

He that will haue glory in this life, and after death be beloued of many, and feared of all, let him be vertuous in doing good workes, and deceiue no man with vaine words. Plato.

Prouerbs and ſayings of the wiſe. Cap. II.

The euils to come, may with wisdome and knowledge be vanquished and eschewed. Pontanus.

That City is safe whose dignities are well bestowed.

Bribery vsed in a City, engendreth euill manners, by meanes whereof both faith and friendship are little set by.

A good City should care more for vertue then for people.

The weale publike in the estimation thereof, ought to be preferred before the materiall City, as much as the life of men, and the renowne of vertue be of more value then the stones and timber, wherewith the wals and houses are builded. Alex.Seu.

A City is not a place builded with houses, and enuironed with wals, but it is a company which haue sufficient liuing, and is gathered together to liue well, to the example of others: And therefore the assembly of vertuous people, and the wealth of the City maketh the City. *What a City is.*

The

Mar.Aur. The great cities full of good inhabitants ought to be praysed, and not the great buildings.

He is not to be accounted strong, that cannot away with labour.

Rest must needes be pleasant, for it is the medicine of all the diseases that are in labour.

Ouid. That creature cannot long endure, that wanteth his natural kinde of rest.

As the body being alwayes oppressed with labour, looseth his strength and so perisheth: so doth the minde of man, oppressed with cares and pleasures of this world, looseth the force, lust, and desire which shee had to the rest of eternall life to come.

It is a signe of a mighty and noble courage, to set little by great and waighty things.

Mar.Aur. Though euery new chance causeth presently new thoughts, yet thereby commeth more cause of stedfastnesse in the time to come.

Seneca. He is very valiant, who neuer reioyceth much, nor sorroweth out of measure.

That which a man hath accustomed long time, seemeth pleasant, although indeed it be painefull.

Plato. It is as difficult to breake custome long vsed, as to change or alter nature.

Custome is as it were another nature:

Manners are more requisite in a Childe, then playing vpon instruments, or any other kinde of vaine pleasures.

Aristotle. Man is the measure of all things.

Exercise eyther hurteth or profiteth nothing.

Musicke is good to refresh the minde, to passe the time, and to helpe pronunciation, and therefore of children ought to be learned.

When

When a man doubteth of doubtfull things, and is assured of them that be euident, it is a signe of good vnderstanding.

Much running maketh great wearinesse. Plato.

He findeth fetters that findeth benefits. Mar. Aur.

Our custome is to receiue forth-with and merilly, and to giue slowly, with euill-will and repentance.

He is as much a thiefe that robbeth priuilly, as he that stealeth openly.

Such as be borne deafe and blinde, haue their inward parts the more perfect.

There is no greater victory then for a man to vanquish himselfe.

He that neglecteth wife and children, depriueth himselfe of immortality.

Men should rather be drawne by the eares, then by the cloakes, that is, by perswasion, and not by violence. Chilon.

Where sensuality raigneth, reason taketh no place.

Peace and concord cannot long time endure among those who know not to whom honour and reuerence is due: for whereas all men be like, there is neither wealth nor vertue, but contention and hatred, the ground of all miseries there raigneth. Iustinus.

Of all things in this life pertaining to mans commodity, of what nature or condition soeuer they be, none is more excellent and worthy to be had in estimation and honour, then the vertue of peace, which of all men ought to be commended and sought for. Alex. Seu.

The great signe and strong pillar of peace, is to put away the perturbers of peace.

That City cannot prosper, where an Oxe is sold for lesse then a Fish.

Much babling is a signe of small knowledge.

He that helpeth the euill, hurteth the good.

Hope of reward maketh paine seeme pleasant.

Experience is a good chastisement.

Demosth. It is better to seeke and not to finde, then to finde and not to profit.

He hath helpes in aduersity, that lendeth in prosperity.

Little things by concord encreaseth, and great things by discord decreaseth.

Alex. Seu. Without harmony nothing is seemely or pleasant, and by concord or discord publike weales doe stand or fall.

A mans life doth neuer returne thither againe, from whence it departeth.

No life once lost neuer turneth: so if a man loose once his fidelity and credit, he shall neuer get it againe.

Beare hard things, that thou mayest beare easie things the lighter.

Beare incommodity, to the intent thou mayest carry away commodity.

Hermes. A graue minde hath no wauering sentence.

He is happy whom other mens perils maketh wary.

A foole knoweth the thing done: but a wise man considereth things before they come to passe.

Tullius. A discommodity well couched, ought not to be stirred.

In deeds done three things are to be noted, first in acknowledging things well done, not onely to reioyce in them, but also to follow them: the second is in sad things and heauy, to be sad and

sorry

sorry for them: the third is, in peruerse acts to beware and eschew them.

Dissemble with dissemblers, if singlenesse will not take place. Xenoph.

There is an alteration of all things.

There is nothing among men perpetuall, nor nothing stable, but all things passe and repasse, euen like vnto the ebbing and flowing of the sea. Salust.

The law which commandeth to be borne and to dye, is generall.

Counterfaited things will soone returne to their owne nature.

Diuers conditions can neuer ioyne hearts in a feruent affection. Alex. Seu.

Riotous liuing and praise cannot be coupled together.

The end of a riotous liuer and prodigall spender is commonly beggery.

He that looketh for profit, must not flye from labour.

Continuance of time begetteth prudence. Aristotle.

Leasure keepeth vs that we doe nothing rashly.

When that thing cannot be done which thou wouldest, seeke and compasse that thou knowest may be brought to passe.

Dig not fire with a sword, labour not in vaine, nor goe about the thing which in no wise can be brought to passe. Pithagor.

Cleane keeping of the body (delicate nicenesse of meates and drinks laid apart) doth greatly both maintaine the health of the body, and much comfort he wit.

The fairest body is nothing else but a dung-hill couered with white and purple. Tullius.

Refuse the familiarity and acquaintance of him

him whose company thou séest honest men eschew.

Periander. Nothing is profitable that is not honest.

Time is the most precious and costly thing that can be spent.

Time is glorious to him that gloriously spendeth it, but that time is accursed that is wickedly spent and passed ouer in sluggish ignorance, without any profit.

It auaileth much to all estates, and specially to Princes, and such as be in authority, to reade Histories, wherein they may learne to beware, fore-see, and auoyde all such inconueniences as they shall there reade, and vnderstand oftentimes to chance in such Common-wealths as are viciously and corruptly gouerned: for the same chances will happen in their common-wealths, if they be in like manner corruptly gouerned, albeit the persons be changed.

Thucidi. Histories are treasures which ought neuer to be out of our hands, that being thereby ayded, we may the more commodiously and with spéede handle the like businesses and chances in the Common-wealth, forasmuch as the like chances oftentimes happen.

Examples are to be found in Histories conuenient for euery man priuately in his degree: as the obedience of subiects due vnto Magistrates, and such as be in authority: and that they neuer escaped vnpunished, who disobeyed and rebelled against them.

Alex. Seu. As in euery Art patternes are giuen to be followed: euen so in Histories are paynted before our eyes the examples of all kindes of Vertues.

Whiles power with pleasures getteth great acquaintance

acquaintance, vertue is unknowne, and in the Court friendlesse.

Contempt is a thing intollerable, forasmuch as no man can thinke himselfe so vile that he ought to be despised.

Many labour to deliuer themselues from contempt, but there be moe that study to be reuenged thereof.

The rusticall and rude people (as experience teacheth) are commonly prompt to iniuries, murmuring at Iustice, grudging at labours, desirous of pleasures, and ingratefull for benefits. If a man be familiar and homely with them, hee shall alwayes finde them churlish and sturdy. If hee doe change his coppy, and become towards them more strange of countenance, more rare in speaking, more slow in pardoning, or more quicke in reuenging, they without weighing their due desert, or confessing their beastly folly, swell vp in pride, kindle disdaine, stirre vp strifes, awake mischiefes, and in such wise worke their intent, that in the end (by due Iustice) they themselues sustayne the griefe of that by which most maliciously and beastlily they sought for to disquiet others.

Where there is suspition, there the life is unpleasant. Seneca.

With great perill is that kept that is desired of many.

Their liues be nought, who thinke they shall liue euer.

There is but one way to goe surely, that is, for a man to set little by worldly things, and to hold himselfe onely sufficiently contented with honesty.

There is no griefe in lacking, but where there is inordinate desire of hauing.

Tullius. Ambition and striuing for worldly honour and promotion, is a very miserable thing, short of continuance, and hasteneth an euill end.

The eye could offend, if the minde could rule the eye.

Mar. Aur. Euery lightnes done in youth, breaketh downe a loope of the defence of our life.

When the vicious man is laid in his graue, his wickednesse is ended, and hee cannot be corrected.

Hee deserueth great chastisement, that with rash hardinesse (as doth a foole) putteth himselfe into high and difficult things, without good and deliberate counsell.

Hee seldome perisheth by falling, that before feareth to fall.

A good Captaine ordereth his men better by keeping them from doing euill, then by grieuous and sore chastisement.

Tullius. In a Captaine or Leader of an Army, there ought to be these foure things, that is, knowledge in warre, valiantnesse, authority, and worldly wealth.

Fame cannot profit the wicked, nor infamy hurt the good.

Ptholom. A good fame euen in darkenesse looseth not her beauty and renowne.

Infamy alwayes insueth arrogancy.

Danger commeth soonest, when it is the least thought vpon.

Val. Max. There is no end appoynted vnto the study of wisedome in this world, for life and it must end together.

There

There are two things that alwayes ought to Qui. Cur.
be in a mans remembrance during his life: that is to say, how he may thinke well, and how he may doe well.

They that trust much to their friends, know not how shortly riuers be dryed vp.

Good debters oftentimes spared, become euill Alex. Seu.
payers, and small iniuries oftentimes pardoned, maketh of neighbours pernicious enemies.

The deepenesse of good wils ought to be won Thales.
with the deepenesse of the heart, some with gifts, some with words, some with promises, and some with fauours.

Vaine men with vaine words shew and declare their vaine pleasures.

The nature of man is such, that it most lusteth after the thing which is most forbidden.

Man can better suffer to be denyed, then to be Seneca.
deceiued.

Doctrine is of such puissance, that in good men Galatius.
it is an armour to vertue: but to vicious and corrupt persons a spur to doe mischiefe.

Contention, emulation, back-biting, and vaine desire of glory must be eschewed.

That man ought to be reputed good, that is alway well occupyed, and the idle man without further delay ought to be condemned as nought.

It is an infallible rule, that he that is giuen to exercise, is a vertuous man, and he that is giuen to loytering and idlenesse, is a vicious person.

No man of what condition soeuer he be, except hee haue some one thing or other in ordinary exercise, shall haue his body lusty and his spirit quicke, but shall be cloyed in all things, and wander from streete to streete like a vagabond.

Tullius. As a corne-field be it neuer so fertile, will not be fruitfull except it be tilled, no more will a wit be ready be it neuer so prompt, except it be exercised.

A good minde neuer assenteth or lendeth his seruice to him that erreth from the path-way of good manners.

Hée that hath good hands, must néeds haue good customes.

All things that are desired of men are attained by trauaile, sustained with thought, and parted from with much griefe and great disquietnesse of minde.

Tullius. We are not so brought vp by nature that wée should séeme to be made for mirth and solace, but rather for grauity, or some serious or waighty studies.

Alex. Seu. Where a man in a common-wealth hath many matters of sundry effects to order, it fareth with him as it doth with a mans stomacke: for the stomacke receiueth meates diuers in qualities and effects, which altogether cannot be by one mans nature duely concocted and digested.

He that is perfectly wise, sporteth in this world with trauailes, and in trauailing in bookes is his rest.

The more thou transportest thy selfe for things corporall and earthly, vnto things celestiall and heauenly, the more perfect and godly life shalt thou leade.

Bodily workes be vnsauoury, except they haue sauce from the heart.

Hée is a double offender, which taketh the name of GOD in vaine, and deceiueth his Neighbour.

The

The punishment of periury, by Gods Law is death, by mans Law perpetuall infamy. Tullius.

The practise of vsury is vtterly repugnant against all humanity, charity, and naturall beneuolence, which ought to be among people that doe liue in mutuall concord, but most specially among them which liue vnder one obedience, and vnder one law or policy.

Gaine with an euill name is damage and losse.

There is no greater paine, then when the heart is kept backe from that which it longeth sore to haue.

Preferre damage before filthy lucre.

After the vnlawfull getting by Fathers, there followeth a iust losse by their children.

A false and vpbraiding reproch, is a malicious lye. Mar. Aur.

The heyres mourning is vnder a visour a laughing, for he bewaileth the death of his ancestour in outward resemblance, but inwardly hée laugheth.

The outward things which the eye of man onely beholdeth, are but weake and vncertaine tokens of the inward secrets.

Such as procure and pretully séeke the death of man, the Law punisheth cruelly. Iustinus.

Nothing auayleth the malice of tyrants against innocents and good men, where the almighty God will not haue them perish. Alex. Seu.

It is oftentimes proued that they who desire the destruction of others, procure their owne death.

Tyranny in Princes ought euer to be had in extreame detestation.

If thou mayest not cléerely escape out of perill,

chose rather to dye honestly, then liue shamefully.

It is honourable to dye for thy Countrey.

Great Cities full of good inhabitants, ought to be praysed, and not the great and gorgeous buildings.

Plinius. Selfe-loue sometime so blindeth the senses of many, that they not well weighing what they be of themselues, but rather vainely flattering themselues, doe conceiue such opinions of themselues, that they thinke all men should worthily glory in them: Whereof innumerable offences doe spring and flow forth, when men puft vp with opinions be shamefully scorned, and wrapped in foolish errours.

Mar.Aur. It is a great shame to say, and no lesse infamy to goe about to make the trauailes of ancients in times past, now in these dayes to be turned into follyes.

Socrates. Perfect felicity is the vse of vertue.

It is better to dye a wise and vertuous man among godly and wise men, then to liue viciously in ignorance among the common sort of men.

It is a thing consonant to reason, that they that be good among so many euill as be in this life, should be greatly honoured with God after their death.

Tullius. One day deemeth another, but the last day giueth iust iudgement of all that is past.

Mar.Aur. As we are set in diuers pleasures by our vice, so we fall hourely into diuers miseries, and are noted to our great infamy and shame.

We see God diuers times to diuers persons forbeare diuers sinnes a great while, but at last vnawares we haue seene them all chastised with one onely punishment.

Men

Men among whom wee be borne, be of so euill disposition, the World with whom wee liue, so fierce and cruell, and the gliding Serpent Fortune, so full of poyson, that they hurt vs with their féet, bite vs with their téeth, scratch vs with their nailes, and so swell vs with their poyson, that the passing of this life is nothing but the suffering of death.

Helpe from God is not onely gotten with prayers, but also by vigilant study, diligent executing, and by wise counselling, all things otherwhiles come well to passe.

The Twelfth Booke.

Diuers manners of pithy Meeters, Prouerbs, and Semblables: wherein chiefely consisteth mans happie life in this World.

My friend the things that doe attaine
the happy life, be these I finde:
The riches left, not got with paine,
the fruitfull ground, the quiet mind:
The equall friend, no grudge & strife,
no charge of rule nor gouernance:
Without disease the healthy life,
the houshold of continuance:
The dyet meane, no dainty fare,
wisedome ioyn'd with simplenesse:
The night discharged of all care,
where wine the wit doth not oppresse.
The faithfull wife without debate,
such sleepes as may beguile the night:
Content thy selfe with thine estate,
neyther wish death, nor feare his might.

Pithagoras.

When a reasonable soule from vertue flyeth,
it waxeth beast-like, and naturally dyeth:
For as the soule giueth life to the corse,
so iustice in the soule is cause of liuely force.

Plato.

To such as custome diuine meditation,
this life is a thing of small reputation.

Hermes.

Hermes.

Lust, pleasure, and worldly vanities
doe cause the soule all vertues to despise.

Aristotle.

Blessed is the soule which doth not transgresse
her Makers Law through filthinesse:
But alwayes is mindefull of his blessed estate,
contemnes the world, & sinfull lusts doth hate.

Pithagoras.

He is not wise, who knowing he must hence,
in worldly buildings maketh great expence:
But he that buildeth for the World to come,
is wise, expend he nere so great a summe.

Thales.

He that most dreadeth to breake Gods behest,
is he that loueth and serueth him best.

Aristotle.

He that loueth the world hath trauell and care,
but he that hateth hath quiet and wel-fare:
Who so then desireth to liue most at rest,
must most flye the world, & meddle with it least.

Pithagoras.

This worldly wealth that men so much desire
may well be likened to a burning fire:
Whereof a little can doe little harme,
but profiteth much our bodies to warme:
But take too much and surely thou shalt burne,
so too much wealth to too much woe doth turne.

Socrates.

This worlds fond loue doth make a man
so deafe, so blinde, so dumbe:
That heare, nor see, nor aske he can
where wisedome is become.
To enuy eke he makes him thrall,
to trouble, care, and dread:

With-

With-drawing his hand, his heart, and all
from euery vertuous déede.

Seneca.

Sith we are vncertaine where Death will vs méete,
and certaine that alwayes he followeth our féete:
Let vs in our doings be so wise and steady,
that where euer he méete vs hée may finde vs ready.

Seneca.

Death is the ender of all tribulation,
and therefore to wise men a great consolation.

Socrates.

For doing wrong and mischieuous déedes,
the soule after death must be punished néedes:
For God is not God except he be iust,
and Iustice to all things their due render must.

Socrates.

Talke euer of God, and he will procure
to fill thée with wisedome and words that be pure.

Aristotle.

To worldlinesse who so doth giue his minde,
these griefes he shall full sure be to finde:
The lacke of things which he shall neuer haue,
or losse of that which he gladliest would saue.

Hermes.

The world was of God created indéede
a place of pleasure, reward of méede:
Wherefore such as in it for truth suffer trouble,
with ioy no doubt are recompenced double.

Aristotle.

Better it is to dye, the soules life to saue,
then to lose the soule, the bodies life to haue.

Socrates.

The soules of the righteous shall after the course
of this life haue better, but the wicked worse:

For

For right it is, that what we here imbrace,
be giuen vs double in another place.
Hermes.
Of bodily imprisonments sicknesse is the chiefe,
but the galle of the soule is sorrow and griefe.
Seneca.
It is better to haue the soule garnished with vertue,
then the body decked with purple, gold, or blew.
Plutarch.
As excesse of wine oppresseth the minde,
so worldly pleasure maketh the soule blinde.
Seneca.
Wisedome, knowledge, and vnderstanding,
are the soules most gorgeous clothing.
Plato.
Woe to the soule which wanteth grace,
to returne home to her state and place:
Whom filthy workes, and bodily offence
excludes and kéeps downe from Gods holy presence.
Socrates.
Prayer to God is the onely meane,
to kéepe a man from a wicked queane.
Xenophon.
In place where men of God commune euer,
fooles become wise, and the wise proue wiser.
Plato.
When naughty Rulers, and wicked people die,
then are all good men safe and in surety.
Socrates.
It is wisedome, yea, wisedome that maketh the wise
all troubles, all torments, yea, and death to despise:
Therefore ought wisedome of all to be imbraced,
a meane whereby death, and all feare is defaced.
Cicero.

Cicero.

Of all worldly comforts true friendship is chiefe,
because it is alwayes our speciall reliefe:
In wealth and woe a stay strong and stable,
and also to man-kinde a good most agréable.

Isocrates.

To himselfe and his friend a friend must be one,
for a friend is ones selfe in another person.

Pithagoras.

These troublesome words, mine, thine, and our owne,
(the cause of all strife) with friends are unknowne:
The title of ours, none counteth ought his,
for all things are each mans where true friendship is.

Socrates.

Such things as are hurtfull, uncomely, and nought,
are easily attained, yea, or they be sought:
But wisedome and honour, with other such like
are hard to be gotten howsoeuer we séeke.

Plato.

Who so for friends, and true friendship watches,
must séeke of such as may be his matches:
For he that of another any friends procureth,
may chance finde friendship, but not that endureth.

Aristotle.

Although many wicked in one may agrée,
yet cause they no friendship, but conspiracy:
For friendship is a vertue by nature so cleane,
as can with the vicious be mixt by no meane.

Plato.

Betwéene Lord and seruant no friendship may fall,
because their estates are too far unequall:
Yet sith they be men, good friends they may be,
because that in manhood they both doe agrée.

Seneca.

Who so denies his friend his aide,

the

the while he is well taken:
Shall at his most neede be denaid
their helpe, and quite forsaken.

Tullius.

In trouble, sorrow, aduersity and griefe,
friends are a comfort, a refuge, and reliefe:
Likewise in wealth right ioyfull treasure,
to be partakers of any kinde of pleasure.

Plato.

By bearing good will first fauour doth grow,
through vse whereof sweete friendship doth follow.

Aristotle.

The friendship that is betweene good men engendred,
can be by no meanes broken or ended:
Wherefore he that doth from friendship disseuer,
is nought by nature, as was a friend neuer.

Ennius.

Whom men doe feare they hate, and whom they hate
they wish to dye, or perish from his state:
Who therefore longs long time chiefe rule to beare,
must get mens loue with fauour, not with feare.

Socrates.

Glory of good deeds by the Father done,
is the best inheritance that he leaues his sonne:
Which who so doth by his vicious life appayre,
bewrayes him a bastard and vnworthy heyre.

Tullius.

He cannot be counted a liberall giuer,
which hath not beene also a liberall getter:
For true liberality is to helpe many,
and in getting thereof not to hurt any.

Seneca.

Who so desireth to liue without care,
ought slowly to spend, and swiftly to spare.

For

For at the bottome to leaue is but vaine,
where both the least part, and worst doth remaine.

Isocrates.

By wine beauty fadeth, and age is hasted,
drinke maketh forgotten that late was imbraced.

Socrates.

He that to wrath and anger is thrall,
ouer his wit hath no power at all.

Hermes.

Be merry and glad, honest and vertuous,
for that sufficeth to anger the enuious.

Pithagoras.

The more that a man hath of abundance,
so much the lesse hath he of assurance.

Socrates.

The friends whom profit or lucre increase,
when substance faileth, therewithall will cease,
But friends that are coupled with hart and with loue,
neither feare, nor fortune, nor force may remoue.

Musonins.

If that in vertue thou take any paynes,
the paine departeth, but vertue remaines:
But if thou hast pleasure to doe that is ill,
the pleasure abateth, but ill tarryeth still.

Solon.

If that by destiny things be decréed,
to labour to shun them, is paine lost indéed.
But if that the chance of things be vnset,
it is folly to feare that we know we may let.

Plato.

It is the part of him that is wise,
things to foresée with diligent aduise:
But when as things vnluckily doe frame,
it becommeth the valiant to suffer the same.

Hermes

Hermes.

If not to spéede thou thinke it a paine,
 will not the thing thou maist not attaine:
For thou and none other art cause of thy let,
 if that which thou maist not thou trauell to get.

Plato.

To faine, to flatter, to glose, and to lye
 require colours and wordes faire and slye:
But the vtterance of truth is so simple and plaine,
 that it néedeth no study to forge or to faine.

Horace.

To the auaricious there is no suffisance,
 for couetise increaseth as fast as the substance.

Solon.

He is neyther rich, happy, nor wise
 that is bond-man to his owne auarice.

Pithagoras.

To strike another if thou dost pretend,
 thinke if he stroke thée thou wouldst thée defend.

Solon.

To beasts much hurt hapneth because they be dumbe,
 but much more to men by meanes of spéech come.

Thales.

All enuious hearts with the dead men depart,
 but after death dureth the slanderous dart.

Hermes.

He that at one instant another will defame,
 will also at another by thée doe the same.
For none are so dangerous and doubtfull to trust,
 as those that are readiest to obey euery lust.

Plato.

Sith making of manners in company doth lye,
 enhant the good, and the bad sée thou flye:
But if to the euill thou néedes wilt resort,
 returne betimes, for feare thou come short.

Isocrates.

Isocrates.

Loue betwéene wise men by effect may fall
but not betwéene fooles, though folly be equall:
For wit goeth by order, and may agrée in one,
but folly lacketh order, so that concord is none.

Socrates.

He that of all men will be a correctour,
shall for the most part win hate for his labour.

Pithagoras.

They that to talke of wisedome are bent,
not following the same are like an instrument,
Whose pleasant sound the hearers doth delight,
but it selfe not hearing, hath thereby no profit.

Pithagoras.

Beware of thine enemy when he doth menace,
and trust thou him not, if fayre séeme his face:
For Serpents neuer so deadly doe sting,
as when they bite without any hissing.

Plutarch.

Sith the world vnstedy doth oft ebbe and flow,
it behoueth a wise man all tides to know,
And so for to saile while he hath faire weather,
that th'hauen may kéep him when hold may no anker.

Diogenes.

Of a churlish nature procéedeth foule language,
but fayre spéech is a token of noble courage.

Anarcharsis.

A friend is not knowne but in aduersity,
for in time of wealth each man séemeth friendly.

Socrates.

Wisedome and science which are pure by kinde,
should not be written in bookes but in minde:
For wisedome in bookes with the bookes will rot,
but writ in the minde will nere be forgot.

Seneca.

For couetous people to dye is the best,
for the longer they liue the lesse is their rest:
For life them leadeth their substance to double,
where death them dischargeth of endlesse trouble.

Antisthenes.

Men ought not to wéep for him that guiltles is slain,
but for the slayer that quicke doth remaine:
For to die guiltlesse is death but of body,
but body and soule both are lost of the guilty.

Xenocrates.

Of workes begun when goodnesse may bréede,
we ought with all swiftnesse therein to procéede:
But if by our workes may grow any ill,
we should be as swift to conquer our will.

Socrates.

What euer it chance thée of any to heare,
thine eye not consenting, beléeue not thine eare:
For the eare is a subiect full oft led awry,
but the eye is a iudge that in nothing will lye.

Seneca.

Wisedome and honour most commonly be found
in them that in vertue and goodnesse abound:
And therefore are better then siluer and gold,
which the euill commonly haue in hold.

Xenophon.

If that it chance thée in warre for to fight,
more then to thy wit, trust not to thy might:
For wit without strength much more doth preuaile,
then strength without wit to conquer in battaile.

Aristotle.

Both hatred, loue, and their owne profit
cause Iudges oft times the truth to forget:
Purge all these vices therefore from thy minde,
so shall right rule thée, and thou the truth finde.

Plato.

Although for a while thy vice thou maist hide,
yet canst thou not alwayes keepe it vnspide:
For truth, the true daughter of God and Time,
hath vow'd to detect all sinne, vice, and crime.

Plato.

Happy is that Realme that hath a King.
endued with wisedome, vertue, and learning:
And much vnhappy is that Realme and Prouince,
where these poynts doe lacke in their Prince.

Plutarch.

To whatsoeuer a King doth him frame,
his men for the most part delight in the same:
Wherefore a good King should vertue ensue,
to giue his subiects example of vertue.

Socrates.

Almes distributed vnto the indigent
is like a medicine giuen to the impotent:
But to the vnneedy a man to make his dole,
is like ministring of playsters vnto the whole.

Pithagoras.

Better it is for a man to be mute,
then with the ignorant much to dispute:
And better it is to liue solitary,
then to enhant much ill company.

Plato.

That thing in a Realme is worthy renowne.
which rayseth vp right, and wrong beateth downe.

Seneca.

Goodnesse it selfe doth men declare,
for which many moe the better doe fare.

Socrates.

Vnhappy is he wheresoeuer he become,
that hath a wit and will not learne wisedome.

Parables.

Parables and Semblables: by *Hermes*, *Socrates*, and *Plato*.

LIke as a Surgeon payneth for his patients body, with lancing, cutting, and searching putrified members: euen so doth the soule of man striue with his vnruly affections to driue them from voluptuousnesse.

Hee that being reproued, departeth immediately hating his counsaylor, doth as a sicke man, who as soone as his Surgeon hath cut his vlcer, goeth his way, not tarrying till his wound be dressed, and his griefe asswaged.

As Plants measurably watred, grow the better, but watred too much, are drowned and dye: so the minde with moderate labour is refreshed, but with ouer-much is vtterly dulled.

Like as a ship that hath a sure anker, may lye safe in any place: so the minde that is ruled by perfect reason, is quiet euery where.

As fire smoaketh not much that flameth at the first blowing, so the glory that shineth at the first is not greatly enuied, but that which is long in getting, enuy alwayes preuenteth.

Like as a good musition hauing any key or string of his Instrument out of tune, doth not immediatly cut it off and cast it away, but eyther with strayning it higher, or slacking it downe lower, by little and little causeth it to agree: so should Rulers reforme the transgressors, and not cast them away for euery trespasse.

As they that taste poyson destroy themselues therewith: so he that admitteth a friend before hee know

know him, may hurt himselfe whiles that hee proueth him.

Like as the bitternesse of the Allowe Tree taketh away the sweetnesse of the sweetest hony: so euill workes destroy and take away the merit of the good.

Like as a vessell is knowne by the sound whether it be whole or broken: so are men proued by their speech, whether they be wise or foolish.

Like as a crazed ship by drinking in of water, not onely drowneth it selfe, but all others that are in her: so a Ruler by vsing viciousnesse, destroyeth not himselfe alone, but all others that are vnder his gouernment.

As it becommeth the people to be obedient and subiect vnto their Lord and King, so it behoueth the King diligently to intend the weale and good gouernement of his people, and rather procure their profit then his owne pleasure: for as the soule is ioyned with the body, so is a King united with his people.

As no Phisitian is reputed good, that healeth another, and cannot heale himselfe: so he is no good Gouernour that commandeth others to auoid vice, and will not leaue it himselfe.

Like as a gouernour of a ship is not chosen for his riches, but for his knowledge, so ought Rulers of Cities to be chosen for their wisedome and learning, rather then for their dignity and riches.

As a man in a darke caue cannot see his owne proper figure: so the soule that is not cleane and pure, cannot perceiue the true and perfect goodnesse of almighty God.

As the goodnesse of wise men continually amendeth, so the malice of fooles euermore increaseth.

As

As liberty maketh friends of enemies, so pride maketh enemies of friends.

As they who cannot suffer the light of a candle, can much worse abide the brightnesse of the Sun: so they that are troubled with small trifles, would be more amazed in weighty matters.

Like as the sauour of carraine is noysome to them that smell it: so is the talke of fooles to wise men that heare it.

Prouerbs and Semblables: by *Anaxagoras*, *Aristippus*, *Alexander*, Solon, and *Marcus Aurelius*.

As God is naturally most louing, pittifull, and alwayes hath the name of mercy and pitty: so are wee alwayes most vnkinde, euill and wicked, and our wicked and shamefull words deserue alwayes to haue most bitter and grieuous chastisements.

As hee that giueth a blow to another, the higher hee lifteth his hand the greater is the stroke: so God in like manner, the more yeeres he forbeareth our sinnes, the more grieuously afterwards he punisheth vs.

Like as when a great and sumptuous building will fall, first there falleth some stone: in like manner there was neuer City or Countrey, that had any great plague or vengeance from God falne vpon them at any time, but first they were threatned and admonished with some signe or prodige from heauen.

As the Ideot or foolish man keepeth his dyet from Bookes, and resteth vpon the onely pleasure of

of meat; so the wise man (in comparison) abhorreth meat, and draweth to his Bookes.

As the sloathfull man is made lesse then a man by his negligence: so certainely blessed is he that is not contented to be a man, but procureth to be more then a man by his vertue and diligence.

The simple Oxe or Sheepe are more worthy their liues, then the idle and foolish Ideot, for the beast liueth to the vtility of diuers, without doing damage to any other, but the idle and foolish Ideot liueth to the damage of all others, and without profit to any person.

Like as riches with thought nourisheth couetousnesse: euen so by riches the enuious nourisheth enuy.

Like as the wicked and malicious person is most hardy to commit greatest crimes: so is hee most cruell, and ready, wickedly to giue sentence against another for the same offence.

Wee behold our owne crimes as through small nets, which causeth things to seeme the lesser: but we behold the faults of others in the water, which causeth things to seeme greater then indeede they be.

As the greene leaues outward, shew that the tree is not dry inward, so good workes done openly, shew the inward heart.

As we see the trees when the fruites are gathered, the leaues fall, and when flowers dye, that then more greene and perfect are the rootes: euen so, when the first season of youth is passed (which is the Summer time) then commeth age (called Winter) and putrifieth the fruit of the flesh, and the leaues of fauour fall, and the flowers of delight are withered, and the veynes of hope dryed

out-

outward, then it is plaine that the rootes of good workes be much better.

As much as the shame of sinne ought to be fled of them that be good, euen so much it ought to be kept for the euill.

As wee eate diuers things by morsels, which if wee should eate whole would choake vs: so by diuers dayes wee suffer trauailes, which all together would make an end of vs in one day.

As in all Arts a man is contented at the first, so at the last, be they neuer so sweet, they turne to wearinesse.

In all naturall things Nature is contended with very little, but the spirit and vnderstanding is not content with many things.

As it is necessary first to purge the opilations and lets of the stomacke, to the intent the medicines may profit them that be sicke: so likewise none can conueniently giue his friend good counsell, except he first shew him his griefe.

As sinne is naturall, and the chastisement voluntary, so ought the rigour of Iustice to be temperate, and the ministers thereof should rather shew compassion then vengeance, whereby the trespassers should haue occasion to amend their sinnes past, and not to reuenge the iniury present.

Though the wood be taken from the fire, and the imbers quenched, yet the stones oftentimes remayne hot and burning: so though the flesh be chastised with hot and dry maladies, or consumed by many years trauaile, yet concupiscence abideth still in the bones.

Oftentimes some wholesome flesh (for meate) corrupteth in an vnwholesome pot, and good wine

sometime sauoureth of the foyst: euen so, though the workes of our liues be vertuous, yet shall we féele the stinch of the weake flesh.

As arrogancy, pride, and presumption, are notably hated of GOD, and had in derision euery where among men: So contrariwise, lowlinesse, méekenesse, and an humble spirit, purchaseth both the fauor of God, and knitteth vnto man the beneuolence of man.

As the knowledge of God ought not to be vnperfect or doubtfull, so prayer should not be faint or slacke, without courage and quicknesse.

As the body is néere to health, which (though it be wasted) is yet frée and out of the danger of noysome humours: euen so is the minde more receiueable of the blessing of God which is not defiled with grieuous offences, though shée yet lacke true and perfect vertues.

It is naturall for the body to die, which if no man kill, yet néedes must it die, but the soule to die is extreame misery. Our hearts grudge at the remembrance of the death of the body, as a terrible thing, because it is séene with bodily eyes: but very few feare the death of the soule, because no man séeth, and few beléeue it: and yet is this death so much more terrible then the other, as the soule excelleth the body, or as God excelleth the soule.

As the body is visible, mortall, lumpish, and heauy, delighting in things visible and temporall, so the soule being mindefull of her celestiall nature, inforceth vpward with great violence, and with a terrible haste striueth and wrastleth with the heauy burthen of the earthly body, despising things mortall, and séeking permanent and immortall things.

Parables.

Parables and Semblables; by *Aristotle, Plutarch,* and *Seneca.*

LIke as it is a shame for a man that would hit the Marke to misse the whole But, euen so it is a shame for him that desireth honour, to faile of honesty.

As a scarre giueth vs warning to beware of wounds: so the remembrance of euils that are past, may cause vs to take the better héed.

As the complaints of children may be soone appeased, so small affections vanish lightly.

Hée that bringeth an infirme body unto voluptuousnesse, is like him that bringeth a broken ship into the raging Seas.

They who goe to banquet onely for the meates sake, are like them who goe onely to fill a vessell.

Seruants when they sléepe feare not their masters, and they that be bound forget their fetters: in sléepe vlcers and sores leaue smarting, but superstition alone vexeth a man when he sléepeth.

Like as they iudge worse of a man, who say that he is wrathfull and vngracious, then if they denyed him to be aliue: so they thinke not so euill of God, who say there is no God at all, as the superstitious, who say God is froward and full of wrath and reuenge.

As a vessell cannot be knowne whether it be whole or broken, except it haue liquor in it: so no man can be throughly knowne what he is, before he be in authority.

As Darnell springeth vp among good wheate, and nettles among Roses, euen so enuy groweth vp among vertues.

They

Like as the Hare both deliuereth, nourisheth, and is with young all at once: so an Usurer before hee hath beguiled one, deuiseth how to deceiue another by making a false bargaine.

Like as an Horse after he hath once taken the bridle, must euer after beare one or other: so hee that is once falne in debt, can lightly neuer after be throughly quit there-from.

Like as Physitians with their bitter drugs doe mingle sweet spices, that they may be the better receyued: so ought checkes to be mingled with gentle admonitions.

Like as the Bookes which are seldome times occupyed will cleaue fast together, so the memory wareth hard if it be not oftentimes renued.

The poyson which serpents continually keepe without any harme, they spit it out to others destruction, but the malicious contrariwise hurt no man so much as themselues.

As it is great foolishnesse to leaue the cleare fountaines, and to fetch water in puddles, so it is likewise to leaue the written truth, and to study the dreames of mens imaginations.

As the Adamant by little and little draweth the heauy yron, untill at the last it be ioyned with it, so vertue and wisedome ioyne men unto them.

As he which in a game-place runneth swiftest, and continuing still his pace obtaineth the crown of his labour, so hee that diligently learneth, and earnestly followeth wisdome and vertue, shall be crowned with euerlasting glory.

FINIS.

THE

THE TABLE.

The Contents of the firſt Booke.

Of the liues and anſweres of Philoſophers, Princes, and Wiſe men, whoſe worthy and notable Counſailes, Precepts, Parables, and Semblables, are ſet downe in this Booke, and theſe be their names:

Epimenides.

The Contents of the second Booke.

The

The Contents of the third Booke.

The Contents of the fourth Booke.

The Contents of the fift Booke.

The Contents of the sixt Booke.

The Contents of the seauenth Booke.

The Contents of the eight Booke.

The

The Contents of the ninth Booke.

The Contents of the tenth Booke.

The Contents of the eleuenth Booke.

The Contents of the twelfth Booke.

FINIS.

A TREATISE OF MORALL PHILOSOPHIE